Guerrilla
Financing

Also by Jay Conrad Levinson

The Most Important $1.00 Book Ever Written

Secrets of Successful Free-Lancing

San Francisco: An Unusual Guide to Unusual Shopping
  (with Pat Levinson and John Bear)

Earning Money Without a Job

555 Ways to Earn Extra Money

150 Secrets of Successful Weight Loss
  (with Michael Lavin and Michael Rokeach, M.D.)

Guerrilla Marketing

Guerrilla Marketing Attack

Guerrilla Marketing Weapons

An Earthling's Guide to Satellite TV

Small Business Savvy

Quit Your Job!

The 90-Minute Hour

Also by Bruce Jan Blechman

The Secret to Getting Money in Northern California

GUERRILLA FINANCING

Alternative Techniques to Finance Any Small Business

Bruce Jan Blechman *and*
Jay Conrad Levinson

Houghton Mifflin Company
Boston   1991

For information about permission to reproduce selections from
this book, write to Permissions, Houghton Mifflin Company,
2 Park Street, Boston, Massachusetts 02108.

Library of Congress Cataloging-in-Publication Data

Blechman, Bruce Jan.
Guerrilla financing : alternative techniques to finance any small
business / by Bruce Jan Blechman and Jay Conrad Levinson.
p.   cm.
Includes index.
ISBN 0-395-52263-3
1. Small business — United States — Finance.   I. Levinson, Jay
Conrad.   II. Title.
HG4027.7.B55   1991   90-24203
658.15'224—dc20   CIP

Printed in the United States of America

DOH 10 9 8 7 6 5 4 3 2 1

This publication is designed to provide accurate and authoritative
information in regard to the subject matter covered. It is sold with
the understanding that the publisher is not engaged in rendering
legal, accounting, or other professional service.

If legal advice or other expert assistance is required, the services
of a competent professional person should be sought.

Guerrilla Financing is dedicated to helping America's entrepreneurs get the financing they deserve. The money is there if you know where to look.

Acknowledgments

I want to thank my wife, Sylvia, and my children, Rachel, Noah, Amy, and Jonah, for putting up with me through eighteen months of research and writing. Without their patience and support, this book could never have been written.

I want to thank my associate and good friend Rajiv Gujral for helping me state my ideas more succinctly.

Many thanks to the following experts for their assistance with specific chapters: Michael Daoud, Money Management Administrators, Inc. (Receivable Financing); Dan Emerson, Emerson & Associates (Real Estate Financing); Kris Morris, Perry Morris Corporation (Equipment Financing); and Reid Rutherford, Concord Growth Corporation (Receivable Financing).

Most of all, I want to thank the hundreds of Capital Institute clients for their patience and persistence in trying the guerrilla financing techniques developed for them. Their pioneering spirit has paved the way for future entrepreneurs to achieve their financing goals.

— Bruce Jan Blechman

First and foremost, I want to publicly thank my co-author, Bruce, for his dazzling knowledge about money matters. Next, I express deep gratitude to Michael Larsen and Elizabeth Pomada, literary agents extraordinaire, and to Henry Ferris of Houghton Mifflin, who nurtured and believed in this project from day one. Lisa Loritz McDonald bravely served as the pioneer editor. Myrette MacPherson, she of the flying fingers, transformed a messy manuscript into a true work of editorial art. And Pat, my patient, understanding, and loving wife, was on hand all along, offering advice, inspiration, and love. Finally, I want to convey my appreciation to each and every reader of my *Guerrilla Marketing* books for showing the world that guerrilla techniques can replace textbook techniques in today's and tomorrow's business world.

— Jay Conrad Levinson

Contents

1 What Alternative Means   1
2 The Five Steps to Finance Any Business   6
3 Understanding the Value of Your Business   12
4 How to Find the Appropriate Source of Funds   36
5 All About Receivable Financing   64
6 All About Equipment Financing   78
7 All About Real Estate Financing   90
8 All About Government Financing   110
9 All About Agricultural Financing   135
10 All About Aggressive Bank Financing   139
11 All About Traditional Venture Capital   149
12 All About Informal Venture Capital   171
13 101 Guerrilla Financing Techniques   211
14 How to Write an Effective Business Plan   248
15 How to Get an Appointment to Present Your Plan   287
16 How to Negotiate the Best Terms   309
17 Parting Advice to Guerrillas   326
    Index   336

1
What Alternative Means

Guerrilla financing is a step-by-step method to finance any type of business anywhere in this country, no matter what the circumstances. Even if you have been turned down by your bank, run out of collateral, established poor credit, or are plumb out of cash, the techniques in this book can help you solve any financing problem.

For the past fifty years, small businesses have discovered, on Main Street and Wall Street, nontraditional, guerrilla methods of achieving their financing goals. Creative, street-smart financing techniques have come through when conventional sources fell flat.

Thousands of people have solved their financial problems with guerrilla financing, so why reinvent the wheel? Just tap into the techniques most appropriate to your business and take the steps to get that cash you need.

The challenge of succeeding as an entrepreneur

In a recent college survey, students listed "entrepreneur" as their top choice of a career. It won out over doctor, lawyer, even president of the United States. Today's frontier of freedom is running your own business. Today's pioneers are small business owners. And the country is teeming with them: 97% of America's 18 million businesses are small businesses — defined by the Small Business Administration as having 500 or fewer employees, defined by the authors as firms seeking less than $1 million.

One out of three working Americans want to be their own boss.

What's stopping them? *Lack of capital.* Capital is the fuel that energizes the business.

You frequently read about the billions of dollars that large and medium-size companies raise when they need to. You hear how foreign countries get billions more from our financial institutions. You also hear that finding money for a small business is tougher than impossible. When you hear that, you're hearing *a big lie.*

Money is not difficult to find. Available cash always exists in great abundance. But *you've got to know where to look for it and the proper way to get it.*

It is true that many small business owners get their start-up capital from wealthy friends or relatives. Guerrilla financing enables you to get it from *strangers.*

You've undoubtedly heard that many businesses fail because of undercapitalization. That's because many business owners operate under the mistaken belief that money comes from banks.

Understand now, if you haven't learned it already, that the banking community doesn't exist to finance small businesses. Banks can't afford to take the risk, so most are squeamish about small business loans. Anyhow, the economy of volume borrowing just isn't there. Banks are attracted to mature, proven businesses with consistent records of profitability, not to mention substantial collateral.

That's why banks tend to think negatively. You can't really blame them. But you're going to think positively, knowing there are alternative sources of capital. It's just a matter of finding the right one for you. When you can select the right one and say the right words so that you're handed the check you need, you will have become a financing guerrilla.

The process of raising money

Just as marketing is not an event but a process, raising capital is also a process, a continual process. That means, as with marketing, the financing doesn't happen instantly. Time is required to locate your right source, then prepare your oral and written presentation to that source. Guerrillas don't take shortcuts.

Instead, they explore new terrain, avoiding the handful of formal venture capitalists and scouting out the tens of thousands of informal venture capitalists. Some people call these investors "entrepreneurial angels." They are everywhere in America, ready and waiting at this very moment to invest in your company.

As a financing guerrilla, you're going to have to embrace the financing word of the future: partnerism. It refers to an alliance with others to improve your business. Entrepreneurs of the future may still dominate their ventures, but they'll be in partnership with employees, customers, suppliers, financiers, and even with competitors. Surprisingly, even though business owners will have many partners, fewer of them will have to give up control — a delightful side benefit of guerrilla financing.

This unique form of financing suggests no pie-in-the-sky methods, only solid, proven solutions — the kinds you can take to the bank. If you've been intimidated by financing, realize that guerrillas actually find it enjoyable, not to mention enlightening and exciting.

You may as well forget all you know about old-fashioned financing. The abundance of new small businesses has created new financing technology — not high-tech, but fi-tech. Most of it is unknown to small business America.

If you can't get the money

If you can't raise all the money you need by applying guerrilla financing, take it as a clear message that *you shouldn't get the money in the first place*. Guerrillas make investment opportunities available to large numbers of people who want like crazy to make the investment. If they don't make it, there's an excellent reason. It probably means there is something critically wrong with your plan.

Guerrilla financing sources come in all sizes and forms. Some fund receivables you will generate. Some fund equipment you might obtain. Others fund real estate. Still others are to be found in government programs. And many are those informal venture capitalists that are so plentiful.

These sources take a risk if they can earn a profit. Many are really and truly *waiting for you to contact them* because their primary business is financing small businesses.

Most likely, you won't have to leave the friendly confines of your own state to find a source to invest in your company. There's a decent chance the source is right in your own neighborhood. Guerrillas know where to look.

Where the action is

The bad news is that the bigger financing requests are the most easily funded because the traditional financial community still caters to the big guys. The good news is that there are *far more financing sources* for the smaller requests, those in the $50,000–$250,000 range.

Guerrilla financing techniques are specifically recommended for companies looking for anywhere from $25,000 to $1 million. These techniques offer so many options that if one doesn't work, another is waiting in the wings.

To succeed, you don't really have to know financing as much as you have to know your own business. Lenders are looking for certain hot buttons, and guerrilla financing techniques offer a treasury of these buttons.

The keys to the treasury are *information, patience,* and *commitment.* Although some have used these keys and raised their capital in a matter of weeks, it's more realistic to think in terms of several months. (Sorry, but most dreams don't seem to come true in a hurry.)

Four ways to spend the money you'll raise

When your financing dream does come true, you'll be able to spend the money you've raised in any of four ways: to buy an existing business, to start a new business, to operate a business, or to expand a business. Know exactly which your way is before you even begin to raise money.

Recognize that there is a source of funds for *every small business.* It's probably not a bank. And it's going to make funds available to you regardless of your other business circumstances.

This isn't opinion. This is hard, cold, delicious guerrilla fact.

Bruce Jan Blechman brings a high level of enthusiasm and thirty years of financing experience to these pages. He has turned down loan requests totaling billions of dollars. Investigating the borrowers through the years, he discovered many funding alternatives later found by the most savvy of those people, and he set up a firm that identifies them for entrepreneurs. Today, his company, the Capital Institute, in San Mateo, California, is the largest small business financing firm in America.

Jay Conrad Levinson brings an innovative mind and thirty years of successfully applying unorthodox methods of earning profits for small businesses. His *Guerrilla Marketing, Guerrilla Marketing Attack,* and *Guerrilla Marketing Weapons* have been translated into nine languages and are the best-selling marketing books in the world. There is little question that he is a guru to many a small business.

The combination of Bruce's financing experience and Jay's rich, yet offbeat years as a guerrilla makes us an ideal team to present the *real secret* to getting money in America. That secret is guerrilla financing. Go for it!

2
The Five Steps
to Finance Any Business

Each financing for a business is unique. Unlike real estate financing, where there are known and limited variables (financing a home is so straightforward that the government has created forms for borrowers to fill out so that the lender can easily determine if they qualify), business financing involves many factors, such as the age of the business, type, industry, methods of payment, collateral, management, credit, and even national economic factors. The variables are limitless. Not only are there many methods to finance a business, there are also many different sources for each method. Consequently, the marketplace for getting money for businesses is widely dispersed. And each source of financing has different qualifications. Where raising money to finance real estate is fairly standard, raising money for a business is anything but.

Virtually all the people who finance businesses seem to have a very narrow view of the process. *They understand and concern themselves only with their own areas of financing.* The bankers know short-term financing; the receivable lenders know factoring and receivable financing; the equipment lenders know equipment financing; the real estate lenders know real estate financing; and the venture community knows equity financing. But each group knows very little about the other areas of finance.

The bankers know very little about equity or venture financing, and the venture capitalists know little about banking.

In medicine today, if you have a cold you go to the ear, nose, and throat doctor. If you have a stomach problem you go to a gastroenterologist. You seek out a specialist. We are now learning that this approach is not always the most effective way to treat patients. For a fuller picture of the patient, we are turning to holistic medicine.

The same situation occurs in finance. Since business financing is so complicated, everyone has become a specialist and knows only their area of expertise. No one has an overall view of the subject.

A holistic view of business financing

To develop an effective method of financing a business, you must take *a general view of all the possible choices available.* This is the guerrilla's view.

Who gets financing and why they get it

Why do some businesses get financing and others don't? Everyone says you need a three-year track record of earnings or lots of strong collateral. Many businesses have neither, *yet they still get financing when they need it.*

The more you know about your business, the more options become evident. Both lenders and investors look for the same thing in a business — *value.* That value is the assets of the business minus its liabilities. An interesting irony is where one financing source considers an asset as having value for financing and another source considers it to have no value at all! Projected earnings and management skills are considered assets by some sources and not by others. A guerrilla financing method of analyzing any company enables the *analysis itself* to uncover which assets have value, the worth of each asset, and to whom it might be valuable.

To unlock the secret of obtaining money for any business is to first understand the *exact credit potential of each asset* in the business to be acquired and each asset of the owners. Since different sources are interested in financing different assets, the trick is to match the appropriate sources to the appropriate assets. This method is the beginning of the guerrilla financing of a small business by studying its assets.

When you evaluate your business, study the assets your accountant puts on the balance sheets as well as the value of other "intangible assets" that might have a particular value. Accountants might call these assets "goodwill." That is but one of a list of overlooked assets.

A list of assets starts with the earning power or success formula of a business: whatever makes it different and profitable. The list ends with the management of a business, not only its personal assets but, more important, its experience in operating that business. *Management is a key ingredient of a growing business; this ingredient has value and can be considered an asset.*

After all, if you owned a plumbing business for 20 years, your experience should have some value. To certain financing sources it does. *It is merely a matter of finding the right sources.*

Many sources finance assets most people think cannot be financed, such as leasehold improvements, contracts, and future invoices. You will learn about them all as you read on.

True net asset value

A guerrilla's balance sheet for a business shows all its assets, all the owner's assets, and all the assets it intends to buy with the money it is trying to get. Subtract any liens from these assets and you'll have a "true net asset value" of a company. Discovering this value is what makes the difference between getting financing and not getting financing. Most businesses have *more* true net asset value than they realize! And it is this factor that attracts capital. This value is the borrowing, investment, or financing power of your business — the amount of capital it can attract at any given time.

Step one. Evaluating your assets

There are five steps you must take to raise capital for your business. Subsequent chapters will go into detail on how to use these steps in your quest for capital. Each step is so important that it merits an entire chapter, and each one is just as important as the other and must be used in the order explained in this book for them to work correctly and effectively.

To start, determine each asset in your business by its value in the eyes of an appropriate source of funding.

Step two. Matching the appropriate sources with each asset

Once you understand the true net asset value, you must put the different assets into appropriate financing categories. Then you can concentrate on finding the best sources of funding for each category. *Matching the appropriate sources of funding to each asset is the second step in guerrilla financing.*

Financing sources can be divided into secured and unsecured sources. Secured sources like to finance tangible assets, which you can see and touch. Unsecured sources like to finance assets that produce extraordinary profits, usually intangible assets such as patents, trademarks, and formulas.

For example, you may find that your business builds up quite a bit of receivables and that receivables are your main guerrilla asset category. Then find the appropriate guerrilla financing source. Your search can lead you from factors, a name for lenders who buy receivables, to receivable lenders to special banks that lend on receivables. You may also discover receivable financing sources that specialize in your particular industry.

On the other hand, you may find that your only real asset is your connections for buying cheap goods in a foreign country. Such an intangible asset might be financed by a private venture source who sees the potential of your connections for an import business.

Whatever your assets, find the appropriate sources of funding for them. Most of this book will be devoted to the subject of *how to match the correct assets of your business to the appropriate financing sources.* You will learn how to identify your potential sources of capital. By the end of the book, you will develop a guerrilla's insight into financing your business, regardless of what kind it is.

Step three. Guerrilla financing techniques

Even though you have identified all the assets, this may still not be enough to raise the necessary capital. What you need then is *guerrilla financing techniques* to raise the rest of the capital or, if necessary, to get the things you need for your business without raising capital.

There are at least 101 guerrilla financing techniques to help you attain your financing objectives; one chapter contains all 101. Mastering these techniques is the third step in your quest for money.

A good percentage of these techniques involves noncash solutions to financing problems: you get what you want without actually raising any money. There is probably a noncash solution to just about every financing problem.

Step four. Making the proper presentation to a source

When financing sources have been identified, find a way to contact them and get them interested in lending money or investing in your business. *Making the proper presentation to a source* is the fourth step in guerrilla financing.

The proper presentation, both written and oral, is extremely important in raising any type of financing. Learn how to communicate to get money. Lenders and investors depend on the written word to make decisions. Most of the time they are making decisions based solely on the information you have given them. That information must be clear, accurate, neat, and persuasive. When you raise money, you are really *marketing your entire business*, not just your product or service, and both the written and oral presentations should be made from a *marketing standpoint*. Many venture capital books say that entrepreneurs should write their own business plan. This sounds good, but in the real world of raising money most entrepreneurs, though they are good at many things, are not particularly good at written communications. Most business plans or requests for money are written from the entrepreneur's point of view and are ineffective. To be effective, they should be written from *the lender's or investor's point of view*.

Later, we will devote two chapters to the subject of presentation.

Step five. Negotiating the best possible financing terms

The final step in guerrilla financing is *negotiating the best possible financing terms for your business*. After all, even though you have found a way to finance your business and have a source who is interested, you must still negotiate a good deal so that the cost of getting the money does not make it impossible to repay the loan or show a good return on the investment.

A good deal or the best possible terms should represent a win/win situation. You get the money you need for your business; the investor gets a good return with the least amount of risk.

Most entrepreneurs do not understand the significance of many of the terms in a financial contract. An improper presentation already has the terms in it. To a guerrilla, this is a big no-no. You never know what the source wants in return for financing. The terms you put into your presentation may either kill the deal or influence the source to ask for tougher or more costly terms.

The five steps of guerrilla financing

1. First, value all the assets of your business, including the assets you are going to buy with the financing and your personal assets, less your liabilities. This will give you the true net asset value or financing capability of your business.
2. Look for the specific sources of financing for each of your categories of assets. This book shows you how to match the appropriate funding sources to each asset.
3. Use the many innovative techniques of guerrilla financing to reach your financing goals, many of them finding noncash solutions to getting the things you want.
4. Once you have identified the most likely sources, you convince them to invest in or lend to your company. To do this, you make effective oral and written presentations to each source.
5. After you have contacted your sources, negotiate the terms that will be best for both you and your source.

Once you accomplish these five steps, you can raise all the money you need to start, buy, operate, or expand your business.

3
Understanding the Value of Your Business

This chapter does three things. First, it gives you an idea of how to value each of your assets. Second, it gives you insight into how to value your entire company from a financing point of view. Third, it imparts an understanding of how financing resources think when they look at each asset and liability in a company. By the end of this chapter, you will be prepared to absorb the financing technology you can apply to your own business.

Everyone thinks of technology as high-tech, but in reality technology is simply new ideas to solve old problems. When guerrillas think of financing technology, they are attracted to the innovative methods of guerrilla financing.

The first step in guerrilla financing deals with the *asset valuation* of your business to determine which category of financing is appropriate.

Every business financing source makes its decision to either lend or invest in your company based on how your business is *valued*. The value of your business is the total value of its assets less any liabilities. A liability is just something that decreases the value of assets, so look at the net value of each asset — asset worth minus any specific liens.

The value of a business is usually more or less than the value of all its net assets because there are two ways to value a business. First you value each asset; then you value the business as a whole. When you do the latter, you will find that there are certain intangible qualities that can increase or decrease the true net worth or financing capability of a company. For example, your business can have a large number of tangible assets such as inventory and equipment, but its net value is decreased because your credit is bad.

Once you have identified the value of your business assets and know how each financing source interprets those values, you will then know which source to locate.

Why it is imperative *not to skip this chapter*

This chapter is extremely important because you can't start looking for sources before you have identified which assets in your business have value to which particular source. In other words, you have to understand the uniqueness of your own particular assets before you can find out which source will most likely be attracted to your business. It is like the old saying that the first step to understanding the world is to know yourself.

The definition of assets in this book is quite different from that of your accountant.

What is so different about the guerrilla definition of an asset?

Accountants say that assets are something a business owns and liabilities are something a business owes.

Guerrilla financing says that assets are things that give a business value and liabilities are things that take away that value.

Employees and management are not listed by your accountant in your balance sheet. But their experience and know-how is definitely an asset.

Another example is years in business. Accountants ignore that figure, but for financing purposes, years in business is definitely an asset.

Poor credit does not appear as a liability on a balance sheet, but it is certainly a liability when it comes to raising capital.

Purchase orders, contracts, work-in-progress, and back orders all have some value and for our purposes are considered assets. You will learn ways to finance purchase orders, contracts, work-in-progress, and more.

You might be leasing a very expensive printing press, but because you lease it, it does not appear on your balance sheet as an asset. Guerrillas know it is an asset even if it is leased. Of course, its value is decreased somewhat when you add the lease obligation or liability against it. But it is still doing something of value for your business.

How can you determine your assets?

Analyze *every* asset in your business, every asset about to be acquired from the proposed financing, and every asset belonging to the owners of the business.

Analyze every liability or lien against each asset in order to determine the real net value of the asset. After all, if an asset has a 100% liability or lien against it, then it has no real value.

Assets in business are anything that add value to it. If you spend money hiring people, they become an asset. If you buy equipment, it becomes an asset. If you spend time developing a trademark, it becomes an asset. If you spend time and money developing a new way to do something and you patent that idea, that patent becomes an asset.

If a company has been in business for ten years and has made very little money but now says that the ten years was spent developing a formula to make money, then its real asset is that formula. It is up to the company to convince some third party that this new asset (the formula) is valuable.

As a guerrilla financier, what you have to do is to find a third party who will believe you and take a chance on what you have developed. This book shows how to find sources that invest in formulas for success.

Don't think that anything you spend money for is an asset. For anything to be considered an asset by a financing source, it must add value to your business and you must *prove* it adds value. You will do it in writing in your business plan and orally when you talk to each source. *You must always back up your assumptions with some form of evidence.*

Later on you will learn how to present your financing proposal to a financing source. At that time, how you arrived at all your figures will become very important. So make notes explaining your decisions as you value your own business in this chapter.

Value of the asset in the eyes of a third party

Each asset must not only have value to you. It must have a value to someone else, too. You might think that being a plumber for 20 years is an asset. But if you lost money each year and learned nothing, then the time has little, if any, value.

It is not how you value an asset subjectively. It is how a financing source will value that asset.

What constitutes the marketing value of an asset?

The accounting profession and the IRS have to stick to certain guidelines and rules in regard to what constitutes an asset. But the financial community usually doesn't go by those rules. For example, accountants depreciate certain assets, sometimes to zero. The financial community values an asset not at its book value but by its marketability and liquidity. The most highly liquid and marketable asset would be certificates of deposit or Treasury bills. These assets are not only highly liquid (they can be sold in a very short period of time), they are also extremely marketable (they can be sold at a price that can be fairly determined). In other words, their value does not decrease with time.

An asset may be marketable but not liquid if it takes a long time to sell it. You might have a very valuable piece of special machinery that is almost irreplaceable; its value might actually increase each year. But if only three companies in the world can use this piece of equipment and none of them wants to buy it, in reality, it has no liquidity.

The financial community is usually interested in the present and future value of an asset. The more marketable and more liquid an asset, the more value it has. When deciding the credit value of an asset, the future value is the most important because that is when the financing obligation will occur. The future value depends on many factors, such as obsolescence and salability. A computer may have value now, but if you're looking for a 5-year loan to finance it, the decision will be based on its value in 5 years.

Auction or gavel value

Most financing sources can't wait 6 months to sell an asset if the borrower can't meet its obligations. So the value they place on an asset is determined by how quickly it can be sold. Most lenders place an auction or gavel value — also known as a quick sale value — on all assets that are to be considered as collateral for a loan. Quick sale value usually means the value of the asset if it is sold within 30 to 60 days of being repossessed by the lender. A general-purpose piece of equipment would be easier to sell at auction than a very special single-purpose piece of equipment. If the single-purpose machinery had to be sold, the auction company would have to look for a specific user of that equipment, which might take six months or more. So from the lender's point of view, the quick sale value is the only real value for lending purposes. It is also the credit value, since some lending institutions will give credit up to that value.

Most real estate is highly liquid and easily transferable to another owner, and it usually holds or increases in value. That is why sources like to lend on real estate and will lend from 70% to 95% of its value. Stocks and bonds on a listed exchange are much more marketable and liquid than privately held stocks. While a source might lend up to 80% of the value of a listed stock, it might not lend anything on a privately held stock.

Value of tangible assets

The value of a tangible asset, from a guerrilla financing point of view, is what a source will lend on it or buy it for. Factors buy receivables outright. The price is determined by the creditworthiness of the company that *owes* the receivable, not the creditworthiness of the company that owns it. You could be a new business with no assets or history and still sell your accounts receivable from AT&T, because everyone knows that AT&T pays its bills.

How do you value inventory?

Use the rule of thumb of its marketability: raw material usually keeps its value. Once other things are added or subtracted, that inventory has little value until it is turned into a finished product. A jewelry store has a better chance to get an asset-based loan than an apparel store. Why? Because the former's inventory usually keeps its value and is highly marketable, while the apparel store's inventory is based on fashion, which could lose all its value almost overnight.

Just because your business has a lot of assets, it does not mean that those assets are liquid, marketable, or have any value to a lender.

The guerrilla financing balance sheet

In this and every subsequent chapter are explicit instructions on how to adapt guerrilla financing information to your particular business project. Following these instructions will take the guesswork out of raising capital. So get out a sheet of paper and create a guerrilla financing balance sheet that shows the real value of your company!

As you complete this step, list all the assets in the business you own, or want to own, and all the personal assets of the owners, plus any other asset you can use to support your financing request. As you identify each asset, place a financing value on it.

There are third-party assets that could be significant. For example, if your parents are going to put their home on the line for you to get a loan, then that home should be studied, just as you study the business assets and the owners' assets. Any asset being used to support financing should be studied in detail.

An asset is tangible if you can see it, touch it, or smell it. It is intangible if it is an idea, opinion, or attitude of a third party. For example, back orders are tangible assets. They can be seen, touched, counted, and analyzed. Intangible assets such as patents and credit ratings usually can't be touched.

What asset do I list first?

First list any asset being used for business purposes or to be purchased with the proceeds of the financing. Then, look into your personal assets.

Tangible assets

Cash or the cash equivalent: CDs and the rest
This category is self-evident but should be listed in your guerrilla financing balance sheet at its market value.

Pre-receivables: purchase orders, contracts, work-in-progress

If you know anything about accounting, you will see that you are starting with the asset side of a balance sheet. But your first asset is not listed on any accountant's balance sheet. (In the eyes of the accounting profession, it has no value.) The first asset is *sales that will happen in the future*: potential sales based on firm commitments in the form of contracts, purchase orders, back orders that will be filled, or even work-in-progress.

These assets are agreements for future sales. They have not yet turned into receivables, but are still considered assets from a financing point of view. Let's say you have a contract to haul dirt for the military; it hasn't started yet, but it is to haul $1 million worth of dirt. Isn't that an asset? Believe it or not, the accounting profession and most of the traditional financing sources say that contract has *no value*! But guerrilla financing sources know that it does have value and should be listed on your guerrilla financing balance sheet.

What about a backlog? If you wondered, you are getting the hang of it. A backlog means there are orders in-house that have not been filled. These are guerrilla assets and should be put into your balance sheet.

Go ahead and list these pre-receivable arrangements, and value them by listing the receivable or gross revenue that will occur when they are fulfilled.

Have you ever walked into a bank to get a loan and never thought of listing your contracts or back orders as assets? Not anymore.

Remember, the assets in this category are not accounts receivable because they represent orders that have not been filled. When the orders are filled and actually billed, then they become receivables, the next category of guerrilla assets.

Accounts and notes receivable

If you sell for cash, you can probably go on to the next category, but those of you who sell on terms have created an accounts or notes receivable.

You might wonder if you should list a receivable that you know has little if any chance of being collected. The answer is no. Be realistic when looking for money. List only those receivables that you have a high probability of collecting.

Notes receivable are usually from some transaction in which an individual or company has a specific agreement (note) to pay you an amount of money for any reason. Again, be realistic: *if you don't have any hope of collecting this note, don't list it as an asset.*

For financing purposes, notes or loans from yourself, or from any owner who has more than a 20% interest in the business, should not be included as a note receivable. The reason is that you can easily create an asset by writing a note to your own company that you have no intention of paying. Guerrillas are innovative but ethical. If some owner other than the majority owner, partner, or stockholder has committed to paying this note receivable, and specific payments are being made, then it is okay to leave it on your balance sheet.

Inventory

You are not showing this balance sheet to your accountant or the IRS, so be realistic and write down the actual cost or manufacturing cost of the raw materials of your inventory. If the inventory has gone up in price and would cost more, value it at today's cost. Accountants call this the first-in, first-out method of inventory valuation, or FIFO. Whatever method you use, don't kid yourself or the financing source. The source wants to know the actual value of your inventory, as if you went out and bought all of it today. Honesty is paramount.

If your inventory has deteriorated, then you will have to mark it down to its present salable value, even if that happens to be below cost. Ouch!

Obviously, if your inventory cannot be sold, then it has no value whatsoever.

The same is true for raw materials that have risen or dropped in price. Put down the replacement cost of the raw material as if you bought it right now.

Equipment

Include everything from telephones to desks and chairs, everything except material that will be used up, such as office supplies and stationery. Do not include permanent leasehold improvements because they fall into a separate category. If you are leasing equipment, include its value here.

Even used equipment should be on this list, as long as you feel it has some value. If you have old tools that have no value, do not include them. Desks and chairs can be resold and do have value.

Unattached leasehold improvements that you can pull out of the wall and take with you — shelves, fans, and the like — should be included in equipment. And don't forget to include rolling stock like vans and trucks.

Value

Equipment should not be valued at cost but at market or auction value. What would it bring on the open market if you had to sell it within a reasonable period of time, say 30 to 60 days?

Leasehold improvements

This depends on the terms of your lease. Assume you have a 5-year lease that is renewable for two more 5-year terms, and assume you have just put $100,000 worth of leasehold improvements into your facility. Won't those improvements have value? Of course!

On the other hand, if you only have a few years left on your lease and you know you will need a different space, the leasehold improvements that you cannot take with you have little if any value.

How do you value leasehold improvements? Usually by how much they cost to install.

Your landlord's lease

A long-term lease on valuable property has value. It can even be appraised. A man was buying a fast-food franchise. Besides his equipment, his only real assets were the leases, which after appraisal turned out to be *twice* the value of the franchise. So don't forget lease values.

Leases

Leases can be appraised, but to save the cost of an appraiser, ask a Realtor for an estimated value. If the Realtor says your lease has significant value, then before you go for financing you might get an official appraisal to impress the financing source.

Real estate

This category covers any real estate you use for business purposes, for example, a warehouse you own or a yard for your equipment. All commercial and residential real estate that is used for and owned by your business should be listed here. Don't list real estate that you own personally or use for investment purposes. That will be listed separately.

Real estate is the easiest property to value because the market is always willing to bid for it. Its value is what you could sell it for today or within a short period of time.

Intangible assets

Here is another place where guerrilla financing balance sheets differ from normal accounting statements. These are assets that are definitely unique to each business.

Keep in mind that whatever figure you put on your balance sheet must be justified to your financing sources. Don't be too optimistic or pessimistic. Pick a value that someone else could get for this asset in the marketplace. Obviously, the patent to produce floppy disks would be worth millions while the copyright on your logo is probably worth very little, at least at this stage of your development.

How do you place a value on the intangible assets? The answer is another question. If *you* can't, how can you expect anyone else, especially a financing source, to put a value on it? You must try to put a dollar value on all your intangible assets and liabilities.

Goodwill

Don't be too keen on *goodwill* as it is presently being used by the accounting profession. For tax purposes, goodwill is being put on balance sheets where no real goodwill exists.

If you bought a business for $100,000 and the only asset was one piece of machinery worth $20,000, then you paid $80,000 for goodwill. Assume this company was making an annual profit for the old owner of $25,000 per year. Paying four times earnings is not unusual, so $80,000 of goodwill simply means that if you just do what the old owner did, you should be able to pull down $25,000 each year operating this business.

On the other hand, if you bought the same business and had it for a year and the company was actually losing $25,000 each year, that company has no goodwill, or the goodwill has no value.

Instead of *goodwill*, use the phrase *success formula*. Learn how to value your business's *success formula*. Hold your estimate of goodwill until you get to *success formula*, even if it means dropping what your accountant says is goodwill.

Patents, trademarks, and copyrights

What was Edison's patent for the light bulb worth? Items such as patents and trademarks can be judged to have value only if they produce value for the company. An example of a valuable trademark is Colonel Sanders. Kentucky Fried Chicken has spent a fortune on building up the Colonel. Wouldn't you give some value to this trademark?

Now think about your situation. What has value and how will you place a dollar amount on it? The only answer is to consider what the market would pay to own this trademark, patent, or copyright. After all, some of these assets never lose their value, such as the trademark Kleenex or the word Coke. Speaking of Coke, what do you think the formula for Coca-Cola is worth? The answer is, you couldn't possibly spend it in a lifetime.

Research and development costs

These have value if your research produces something of value. For example, Genentech used its research to develop the largest biotech firm in the country. List what you have spent on R&D or what you think these costs have added to the value of your business.

List the assets you have so far

1. Cash or cash equivalent
2. Purchase orders, contracts, work-in-progress
3. Receivables
4. Inventory
5. Leasehold improvements
6. Leases
7. Equipment
8. Real estate
9. Trademarks, patents, copyrights
10. Research and development

There are still more intangible assets.

Your most important asset: your success formula

Have you left any asset out? You surely have, one of the most important assets any business has, the asset that can bring the most money to the bargaining table, and it doesn't appear on any balance sheet!

You must know that the asset of greatest importance is your *success formula*. Don't mistake it for the goodwill figure your accountant has put on your balance sheet. This figure has no meaning in guerrilla financing.

On the other hand, every business has some sort of *success formula*, that is, some different way of doing business so that the sales from its customers more than support its owners. Some businesses do that very well, and there is lots of money left over after the owners have covered their expenses. This is called *profits*. *The success formula of a business is its unique ability to consistently produce a profit.* And the real value of a business *depends* on the profit it produces for its owners. This ability to consistently produce a profit is a business's most important asset. The more profit produced, the more valuable the *success formula* of a business. Commit that to memory.

McDonald's and Walt Disney's cleanliness and consistency are good examples of *success formulas*. Nordstrom department store's and IBM's service policy are other examples. It's true these are examples of very large companies' *success formulas*. But every successful business, large or small, has some sort of *success formula*.

What makes your business unique and consistently profitable?

This is hard to answer yourself, but until you can express it, you are not going to raise any capital.

Demonstrate your uniqueness by identifying why anybody would buy your product or service as opposed to someone else's. In discussing profits, either historically or projected, you must convince investors specifically why they should invest money in your business. If you can't discuss these issues, you shouldn't be looking for capital.

If you are losing money or only making enough to support yourself, don't despair. All you have to show is how you are going to operate differently, and then explain how that new mode will become your *success formula*. Here, projected cash flow and profits would be involved in calculating your *success formula*.

The success formula asset is sometimes so valuable that even if it is your only asset, it is enough to attract capital. Ask any guerrilla financier.

When you prove the validity of your *success formula*, the job of raising all the money you want is easier.

How do you value your *success formula*? There is no one way, but guerrillas have a formula that works very well. Take your annual true net profit after all draws and taxes and average it for the last 3 years. Then multiply that figure by three. Subtract the tangible assets from this figure and you have a thumbnail valuation of your success formula.

You may believe this is too conservative, and you may be right. But this is what financing sources want to see. If you think the multiplier should be higher, be prepared to show why your business is worth more than three times its earning power.

Here is another way to look at it. Suppose someone bought your business for three times its earnings. It would take him three years to get his money back if there were no changes in profits. You might think that 33% is a very high rate of return, but this is not so, considering the risk of lending to or investing in a small business.

As this book goes to press, you can get a 10% return on money market funds. A dramatic shift in the cost of money might change the above formula. If money market funds were earning 20%, you would lower the formula to *two* times average earnings. If money market funds were earning 5%, then you would raise the formula to four times earnings. The more you earn on your money with little or no risk, the less value your business is with lots of risks. On the other hand, the less you earn on your money with little or no risk, then the more valuable your business becomes.

People are assets

Finally, include the management of your business as an asset. Capability and experience are definitely worth something to the financial community. That is why a new business can sometimes raise money solely on the strength of its management. That is also why most professional investors of money, whether it be for debt or equity, always start their investigations of a business by looking at its management.

How do you value management?

It is tough to put a dollar sign on management and experience, so guerrillas use another approach. They have created an objective scale by which you rate your company, 1–10, with 10 being the highest and 1 being the lowest. View yourself and your managers as if you were a consultant to your company and had to judge its management.

Recognize that a team of fairly talented people is much more valuable than one highly talented person. Clearly, one person can get sick or have an accident, and the whole place would fall apart. The larger your management base, the less the chances of that happening. This scale gives you an example of how the financial community values your management.

Scale   Characteristic of Management
1   Owner-manager does everything
2   One part-time assistant

3   One full-time assistant
4   One full-time highly qualified assistant who could replace you
        if you left for a short period of time.
5   One full-time highly qualified assistant who could replace you
        if you left for a long period of time.
6   Management team of at least two key people besides owner.
7   Management team of at least three key people besides owner.
8   Management team of at least four key people besides owner.
9   Management team of at least five or more key people besides
        owner.
10   Absentee owner. Management runs business without the
        owner being there full-time.

Each key person must be in a different position. You can't have
two key people in marketing, administration, or manufacturing. They
must have expertise in different areas that affect your business, such
as marketing, management, accounting and finance, production, or
computers.

The following values should be added to your multiplier of net earning to determine the value of your *success formula*.

Management Scale	Additional Multiplier to Net Profit
1	1
2	1.1
3	1.2
4	1.3
5	1.4
6	1.5
7	1.6
8	1.7
9	1.8
10	1.9

If the normal success formula multiplier is three, and if your scale
of management is eight, then your real multiplier is

$3 + 1.7 = 4.7 \times$ net earnings = *success formula*.

Go ahead and calculate your own *success formula*. Don't make the
mistake of including your own wages in your net earnings. Net earnings means earnings after all expenses, and if you are working in the
company, you are an expense.

If you don't show a profit, you can use projected net earnings aver-
aged over the next 3 years, but you must start with a multiplier of two,
not three. If you have been in business for less than 1 year or are just
starting out, you should use the multiplier of two times net projections
and be prepared to justify your projections!

Owner's personal assets or third-party assets that can be pledged or used for financing purposes

Personal real property

This includes the market value of any real property or real estate that
can be pledged for the financing.

Securities

You can list the market value of any stocks or bonds or any type of
receivable you own. Unlisted stocks, limited partnerships, pension
funds, and Keogh plans have no real value and should *not* be listed on
your guerrilla financing balance sheet. These personal assets cannot be
pledged or sold to any third party; therefore they have no value to a
third party.

Stock in your own company

It's true that your company is worth something to the financial community, but it is only worth something *if someone wants to buy it or
buy part of it*. So stock or ownership in your own business should *not*
be listed as a personal asset in your balance sheet.

Collectibles

Here list personal property that does have resale value, such as classic cars, paintings, Oriental rugs, silverware, rare stamps, and similar
items. These items must be valued at forced sale or liquidation sale
value. In other words, what could you get for the collectible within
30 days?

Personal assets

Watch out for personal assets valued for insurance, such as jewelry,
which is usually worth ten times its liquid or quick sale value. The
value that an insurance company puts on an item of personal property

has no relation to its forced sale value. List your personal assets at their quick sale value. You might own some assets that have more value than you think. All personal property has value to someone somewhere. After all, if you held a garage sale, you would get some money out of your personal assets.

Some unusual personal assets have been used to support a business loan: jewelry, paintings, ceramics, just about any collectible, coin collections, rare musical instruments, and antiques. Even a country club membership has been used as collateral.

Why study personal assets if this is a book about business?

If you are going to ask a third party to support your business, you must commit your own personal assets to the cause. These assets may or may not be used to help with the financing, but your attitude toward their use is a major factor in obtaining the trust of the lender or investor. If you won't commit your own assets to your business, why should another person or institution commit theirs?

In short, your personal assets should be listed on a guerrilla financing balance sheet if they have any salable or marketable value. As a rule of thumb, personal items or collectibles worth less than $500 should not be listed.

Remember, list them at their auction or quick sale value, not at any insurance appraiser's value.

List of guerrilla assets

1. Cash
2. Purchase orders, contracts, work-in-progress
3. Receivables
4. Inventory
5. Leasehold improvements
6. Leases
7. Equipment
8. Real estate
9. Trademarks, patents, copyrights
10. Research and development

11. Success formula
12. Management
13. Stocks, bonds, and securities
14. Collectibles
15. Other personal property

Lendable value

Before considering any obligations or liens against these assets, first
reduce them to their *lendable value*: the point up to which any lending
institution will lend. It is the credit value of an asset. For example, if
you own a commercial building and its market value is $100,000, its
lendable value is usually 70% of that, or $70,000.

The following is the lendable value of your guerrilla assets:

Guerrilla Financing Asset	*Lendable Value Percentage*	
	Low	*High*
Contracts and purchase orders	70%	80%
Receivables (within 60 days)	70%	90%
Inventory	30%	50%
Equipment	50%	80%
Leasehold improvements	50%	70%
Commercial real estate	70%	90%
Raw land	40%	50%
Residential real estate	80%	95%
Stocks, bonds, and securities	70%	80%
Collectibles	80%	90%
Other intangible assets	50%	80%

Notice how much the percentage varies. In the following chapters
you will learn about each financing source and how it arrives at the
appropriate percentage for each asset.

On your balance sheet, list the lendable value of each asset next to
the market value of that asset. Each will be used for different purposes
later in this book. Financing sources that will share in your profits are
more interested in *market* value. Financing sources that will only lend
to your business for a fixed return are more interested in the *lendable*
value.

Liabilities

Now it is time to understand liabilities. They must be listed, too. When you study the assets of a business, you must study all the liens against those assets. It is fine to have lots of receivables, inventory, and equipment. But if there are liens up to their maximum lendable value, you must look for another category of asset on which to raise capital.

Current liabilities are due to be paid within 12 months. If they are unsecured, do not subtract them from the value of any asset. If they are secured, subtract them from the appropriate asset. Include the 12 months of lease obligations on equipment.

Long-term liabilities are due to be paid over a period of time greater than 12 months. Again, they are to be deducted from an asset only if the liability is collateralized or secured by that particular asset. Include the total long-term payments on all leased equipment.

Intangible liabilities reduce the value of a company, not any particular asset. They are poor credit, former bankruptcy, criminal record, inexperience in that particular field, poor moral character, and more.

You really can't put a dollar value on intangible liabilities, but they must be listed anyway since they will determine where you look for financing. Later, we will assign a percentage value to each intangible liability which will reduce your *true net worth*.

A company may have many tangible assets and very few tangible liabilities but be unable to raise capital because of many intangible liabilities. The solution in this case is to find the particular source that is not influenced by a strong intangible liability.

On your guerrilla financing balance sheet, list all your liabilities, including your intangible liabilities. They have an impact on the *true net worth or financing power* of your business.

Net value of an asset

Liabilities determine the net value of an asset. *The net value of an asset is the lendable value of an asset minus any liens against it.*

Sometimes the liability completely wipes out the value of an asset. What would be the value of a home if you borrowed 100% of its value and your mortgage equaled the market price of the house? Who really would own that house, you or the mortgage holder? You might have title, but the mortgagor would really hold all the strings. You couldn't sell it without having to pay off the owner of the mortgage. So from a financing point of view, that home has no real value. What if you borrowed 80% of its value? Even then, your home would have little value as defined for guerrilla financing purposes. Since the lendable value of a home is approximately 80% of its market value, 80% of $100,000 equals your mortgage; theoretically your home still has no *lendable value*. But to some financing sources there is still 20% equity in that home. To banks and savings and loan institutions your home would have no value. But if you are willing to give an investor a second mortgage on your home, then that 20% has value. Value depends on who is looking at it.

Overall liabilities reduce the value of assets. They also reduce the potential of the business to meet its obligations. If you owe $100,000 in current liabilities and have only $150,000 in current assets, that means you have a margin of $50,000 to pay your debts.

Net worth

If you total all the assets of a business and subtract the liabilities, you have its value. This is called its net worth.

Don't place much credence in the term *net worth* as used by the accounting profession because it doesn't take into effect all the assets or liabilities that have value to a business.

Instead, take the broader guerrilla definition of assets and subtract the liabilities. That's the *true net worth* of a business. This then represents the strength of a business's ability to get financing. The larger the *true net worth*, the easier it will be to obtain financing. The smaller the *true net worth*, the more difficult it will be to obtain financing. Pure and simple.

How to arrive at secured and unsecured net worth, or true net worth

In order to arrive at *true net worth*, first subtract each guerrilla liability from its corresponding guerrilla asset.

Net worth can now be divided for financing purposes into two parts: *secured net worth* and *true net worth*.

Take all your tangible lendable assets and subtract your corresponding tangible liabilities. This gives you your *secured net worth*. Take your tangible and intangible assets, minus your corresponding tangible and intangible liabilities. Simply subtract the correct percentage for each intangible liability from *true net worth* as listed below. This gives you your *true net worth*.

Intangible Liability	Deduct from True Net Worth
Poor credit	20%
Bankruptcy	30%
Inexperience in your particular business	20%
Criminal record	30%

If your *secured net worth* is $100,000 and you have a criminal record, you must deduct 30%, or $30,000, giving you a *true net worth* of $70,000.

In the next chapter we will discuss how to use your *secured* and *true net worth* to determine what category of financing sources to go after. Basically, *secured net worth* is approximately how much you should be able to borrow, and *true net worth* should give you an approximation of how much investment capital you can attract.

What if your true net worth turns out to be very low or even a minus figure?

Your calculations can result in a ridiculously low figure, even a minus figure. If you have no profits or predict very low profits in the future or have few if any assets, the above formula will not be effective in predicting your financing capability, but it will indicate the degree of difficulty you will have in raising capital. Don't panic! *It does not mean you can't get financing.* There is a way to finance any company, and guerrillas know it. Chapter 13 alone lists 101 ways to finance a business with little or no net worth. So hang in there. Guerrilla financing provides many ways to solve your financing problems.

Determining your net worth shows you how financial sources keep score on who to invest in. Being aware of this mathematical system to value a business forces you to consider all the factors that sources review before funding a business. If you know what they think is important, then you are halfway to understanding your chances of success and learning what to emphasize when you make your presentation.

In the next chapter you will learn how to determine what assets appeal to what sources. If most of your *secured net worth* is made up of receivables, you will look for a secured financing source such as receivable financing. On the other hand, if your *success formula* makes up most of your *true net worth*, you will begin with unsecured financing sources, such as the venture capital community.

What does a guerrilla financing balance sheet look like?

The XYZ Company has been in business for one year, has a management rating of 5, has poor credit, and has no intangible liabilities.

Here is an example of its guerrilla financing balance sheet:

GUERRILLA BALANCE SHEET OF THE XYZ COMPANY
As of August 1, 1990

Tangible Assets	*Market Value*	*Value %*	=	*Net Value*	*Liability*	=	*Lendable Assets*
Cash	500	100	=	500	0	=	500
Back order	1,000	80	=	800	0	=	800
Accounts receivable	50,000	80	=	40,000	0	=	40,000
Inventory	10,000	50	=	5,000	0	=	5,000
Equipment	25,000	75	=	18,750	13,000	=	5,750
Leasehold improvements	5,000	70	=	3,500	0	=	3,500
Lease	0	0		0	0		0
Real estate	0	0		0	0		0
TOTAL TANGIBLE ASSETS	$91,500			$68,550	$13,000		$55,550

GUERRILLA BALANCE SHEET OF THE XYZ COMPANY
As of August 1, 1990

Intangible Assets	*Market Value*	*Value %*	=	*Net Value*	*Liability*	=	*Lendable Assets*
Patents	18,000	100	=	18,000	0	=	18,000
Copyright	1,000	100	=	1,000	0	=	1,000
Success formula *	16,450	100	=	16,450	0	=	16,450
Management	5						
TOTAL INTANGIBLE ASSETS	$35,450			$35,450	0		$35,450
TOTAL GUERRILLA ASSETS	$126,950			$104,000	$13,000		$91,000

* Success formula is 2 × $30,000 {first year net} = $60,000; management is 5, so add 20% to $60,000 = $72,000 less tangible assets of $55,550 = $16,450 as the success formula.

Tangible Liabilities							
Current unsecured	29,000	0	=	29,000	0	=	29,000
Long-term secured	0	0	=	0	0	=	0
TOTAL TANGIBLE LIABILITIES	$29,000			$29,000			$29,000

Intangible Liabilities

Poor credit: minus 20%

GUERRILLA BALANCE SHEET OF THE XYZ COMPANY
As of August 1, 1990

TOTAL GUERRILLA LIABILITIES	$29,000	$29,000	$29,000
SECURED NET WORTH ASSETS	$62,500	$39,550	$26,550

*TRUE NET WORTH (Total lendable guerrilla assets minus total guerrilla liabilities) = $49,600

* Take $62,000 less intangible liability − poor credit of − 20% ($62,000 × .20 = $12,400) = $49,600.

Applying guerrilla financing to the XYZ Company

The *true net worth* of the XYZ Company is $49,600 and the *secured net worth* is $26,550. For financing purposes, most secured financing sources will finance the XYZ Company up to the *secured net worth* of $26,550. Many unsecured financing sources might finance the XYZ Company up to the *true net worth* of $49,600. *To put it another way, using secured sources, you should be able to raise approximately $26,550, and using unsecured financing sources, you should be able to raise $49,600.* These figures are general guidelines and may not be accurate under certain circumstances.

Unsecured sources can usually get you more money. But remember, most unsecured sources will want equity in your company as a reward for the financing, whereas secured sources will usually accept debt financing that you pay back over a period of time.

In this example, the tangible assets that had value are mostly in receivables and some inventory, which means that receivable financing would be most appropriate. But since the bulk of the guerrilla assets are in intangibles, venture financing would probably produce the most capital for the business.

You now understand the guerrilla value of your business but are unclear about how to use that information to actually raise capital. The next chapters will make everything clear.

4
How to Find the Appropriate Source of Funds

There are many different types of sources of funds just as there are many different types of assets. Just as you labeled your different assets and liabilities guerrilla assets and guerrilla liabilities, it makes sense to label the different financing sources guerrilla financing sources.

Since each source values each asset differently, you must learn each source's qualifications to determine the source that is most appropriate to finance each asset. Once you have determined the proper category, you can refer to a chart that outlines what percentage of each asset can be financed. Using the formula from the preceding chapter, you can then get a rough idea of the amount of financing you should be eligible to raise.

This phase of guerrilla financing is understanding the characteristics of each guerrilla financing source and how to match it with the appropriate guerrilla asset.

Guerrilla financing knows that every financing source wants some type of asset to support its financing. Now you will see why you spent time identifying every conceivable asset, tangible and intangible, that can support a financing source. You will also see why you used all the guerrilla liabilities to come up with a true net worth that determines the approximate limits of the amount of capital you can raise.

You have listed many assets that are not traditional, especially the intangible ones. *Guerrilla financing is based on the belief that there is an appropriate source that is interested in financing each and every guerrilla asset, including intangible assets.* These guerrilla financing sources can be divided into the following categories:

Secured sources
    Aggressive banks
    Factors

Accounts receivable finance companies
Leasing companies
Real estate lenders
Government funding programs
Unsecured sources
Venture sources
Corporate strategic alliances

Before you study each source in detail, you must understand how they relate to the list of assets you created in the last chapter. This chapter will give you a general description of every financing source, and the following eight chapters will describe each major source in detail.

Secured and unsecured financing sources

Just about every financing source can be divided into secured and unsecured sources. Both types make their decision to lend to or invest in your business based on two important considerations. The first is your ability to pay them back in the form of principal and interest and/or return on their investment; the second is the strength or value of the asset backing up their loan or investment. Backing up is another word for collateral, something of value pledged to secure the loan or investment in case of loss.

Collateral

Collateral is commonly referred to as a secondary source of repayment in case the first source dries up. The first source, of course, is the cash flow of the business. The cash flow from your business should be sufficient to meet any principal and interest payments and earn investors a sufficient return on their money. If it is not enough and you default on any payment, the secured financing source wants something else of value from you, something that they can sell to reimburse themselves for any losses incurred by your not meeting your payments. *That something of value is called collateral.*

All secured financing sources base their funding decisions on two main qualifications: one, there must be enough cash flow at the time of the loan to cover all monthly payments. Two, there must be enough value in the collateral to cover any losses if the borrower can't pay back the loan.

On the other side of the picture, the unsecured financing source looks at the assets as justification for making the investment. Unsecured sources analyze the value of both the tangible and intangible assets. If they see enough value to support an investment, they will usually invest. If they don't see enough value, they will not invest. The unsecured source rarely takes a legal lien on an asset to secure an investment, as does the secured financing source. Therefore, to an unsecured financing source, collateral is not security in the sense of something to foreclose on but security in the sense that its value (such as good management) will protect and enhance the investment.

Most of the time the secured financing sources use the tangible assets to secure their loans, while the unsecured financing sources use the intangible assets to support their investment. Both see all the assets as some form of collateral.

Unorthodox tangible assets

As you're discovering, guerrilla financing encourages you to recognize unorthodox tangible assets, such as contracts, invoices, back orders, leasehold improvements, and even leases. These assets can be used to secure a loan from some secured sources.

Intangible assets

The intangible assets, such as patents, copyrights, trademarks, research and development costs, success formula, and even management, actually become the collateral to support an unsecured financing source. These assets are used as justification for the investment.

Traditional sources: debt and equity financing

Traditional financing says your financing choices are limited to debt or equity.

Debt financing means you are incurring some form of obligation to pay back money that has been lent to your company. Debt financing sources use assets as collateral for their loans. Most debt financing sources are secured sources.

Unsecured financing sources, because they are taking more of a risk, want to benefit from the result of the financing and usually take an equity position or an option for an equity position in most companies they finance.

Therefore, equity financing means you are giving up some percentage of your ownership in return for an investment in your company.

Nontraditional guerrilla sources

Guerrilla financing goes beyond the traditional debt and equity financing. It includes guerrilla assets not commonly used to support loans or investments. It also includes techniques in which no money changes hands, such as strategic alliances, in which two companies get something from each other that each wants but doesn't have independently.

Guerrilla financing techniques include many innovative and creative nonfinancial ways to get the goods, services, and equipment you need without any exchange of money. All these techniques are covered in detail in Chapter 13.

Secured lending sources and the importance of cash flow

Secured financing sources are usually called lenders. Their main financing criteria are based on the company's ability to pay its obligations on time. The next criterion is the value of the collateral to secure the loan or the strength of the asset being used as the support or collateral for the financing. The words *asset-based financing* usually mean secured sources looking at the collateral as the main security for the loan. But even asset-based lenders will not finance a business that does not show the cash flow to service the debt. Almost all types of financial institutions do not want to incur the added cost of foreclosing on collateral. So the first test for secured financing is the ability of the company to service the debt out of historical or projected cash flow.

Traditional asset-based lending

The traditional concept of asset-based lending started when financial institutions made loans based *solely* on the value of the asset. A leasing company would lend a certain amount of money on a piece of equipment knowing that if the company failed, it could sell the equipment and get its money back. Today there are few, if any, traditional asset-based lenders. Most want to know about the asset *and* the business before they lend their money. This is because it is hard to separate the business from an asset, and some assets keep their value only to a going business but lose their value when the business fails. This change in value of an asset has made most traditional asset-based lenders more cash flow–oriented. That is, they will not lend on a strong asset alone without the creditworthiness of the supporting business.

Matching the appropriate financing source to the appropriate asset

A unique characteristic of guerrilla financing is that it allows you to match the appropriate sources to appropriate assets. All you have to do is to identify your assets, then determine the financial sources that agree with the value you have placed on those assets.

Most people waste valuable time looking for the wrong financing sources, not knowing that a formula is available.

This formula is spelled out in the following chart. Please understand that the percentages listed represent an approximate percentage of the asset a source will finance.

Financing Asset Category	Financing Source Categories	Percentage That Can Be Financed
Working capital	All sources	100%
Back orders, contracts, purchase orders, work-in-progress	Finance companies	80%–100%
Receivables	Banks, factors, receivable lenders	70%–95%
Inventory	Banks, finance companies	40%–50%
Equipment	Banks, leasing companies	70%–100%
Leasehold improvements	Leasing companies	70%–80%
Leases	Banks, finance companies, real estate lenders	50%–80%
Real estate, commercial	Real estate lenders	70%–90%
Real estate, residential	Real estate lenders	70%–100%
Raw land	Real estate lenders	40%–50%
Patents, trademarks, copyrights	Venture capital, strategic alliances, government programs	100%
Research and development	Venture capital, government programs, strategic alliances	100%
Success formula	Venture capital, strategic alliances, government programs	100%
Management	Venture capital	100%
Stocks, bonds, securities	All secured debt sources	60%–80%
Collectibles	Government programs, venture capital, pawnbrokers	50%–80%
Personal property	Pawnbrokers, garage sales	40%–75%

Guerrilla source qualifications

As you study each guerrilla asset category and the appropriate guerrilla financing sources, focus on three considerations. The first is the risk as seen by the financing source. If you can understand how each source defines a risk, you will have a better understanding of how to communicate with that source. The second is the qualifications the sources look for in financing each particular asset. Here is a chance for you to match up your own qualifications with that of each source to see if there is a match that would make you a likely candidate for financing. The third is the sources themselves and how to contact them.

For purposes of guerrilla financing, the difference between major and minor sources is a matter of availability. Major sources are more prevalent and easy to locate in your area. Minor sources are rare and hard to find.

Working capital

Working capital is a new asset category that really isn't an asset at all.

Working capital is the short-term use of money, such as office and warehouse supplies, payroll, and items that don't fit into any one of your asset categories and are expensed, not capitalized. For example, working capital usually represents expenses that do not have any lasting value but will be used up or expensed in a short period of time.

Usually, working capital is a requested use of funds when you just can't put your finger on what you are going to use them for. It is not a tangible or intangible asset as defined in the last chapter. Maybe you need the money to pay off payables or other debt. Whatever your use, all sources of financing can be used for working capital purposes.

So the book will discuss how to finance working capital needs last, since it is such a catchall category.

Pre-receivables: back orders, contracts, purchase orders, work-in-progress

Believe it or not, you can finance a receivable before it becomes one. Once you have sold your product or service on terms, you already have, or very soon will, invoice your customer or client. When you invoice, you create a receivable.

But what about that back order you couldn't ship because you were out of inventory? It is not a receivable until you ship it. What if you are holding a contract to either deliver a product or perform some services, but it will take time and resources to fulfill that contract? That certainly is not a receivable until you can bill or invoice your customer. What about work-in-progress that you cannot bill until it is complete?

All of the above come under the category of pre-receivables. Under some circumstances, it is possible to finance these pre-receivables.

Risk

The risk for the financing source is that something terrible will happen and the contract or back order will never be billed. That is a big risk, and most accounts receivable finance companies will not finance this category. Can you blame them? They do not have the same legal protection that they would if they took your receivable as collateral. A receivable creates an obligation to pay because a product or service was delivered to the customer or client. A contract creates no obligation to pay until it is fulfilled. That contract must be valid and the company must be in a position to fulfill it. All those things must happen before a purchase order can become a legal receivable. To finance a contract or purchase order before it has been fulfilled is quite a risk, and only certain companies will qualify.

Qualifications

First of all, start-up situations very rarely qualify. There are just too many variables. So the first qualification is an existing business with a success record of making money and paying its bills. Second, the contract, purchase order, or work-in-progress must be valid and deliverable. Third, collateral is sometimes required, though not always, depending on the strength of the customer or client. For instance, a firm contract from the U.S. government or a Fortune 500 firm will probably not require backup or secondary collateral. On the other hand, a contract from an unknown firm might require some other collateral besides the value of the contract.

Sources

The sources for this type of financing are special finance companies or *factors*, and receivable lenders who will do this kind of financing. An especially good source would be a finance company or factor you are already dealing with. Usually, this is a one-transaction situation, not a continually recurring program. The source will finance some contracts but not every contract you offer.

Use the information in Chapter 5 to find the factors and receivable lenders who will perform this kind of financing. Just remember that not all factors and receivable lenders will do it. You will have to hunt and peck to find ones that will. If you don't find one in your area, the Capital Institute knows of special companies that will consider financing pre-receivables. Their names can be obtained by contacting the Capital Institute, listed at the end of this book.

Receivables

If most of the time you will be selling on credit as opposed to cash, then factoring or receivable financing is a good choice for funding some, or maybe even all, of your needs.

Just about any type of receivable can be financed, even construction receivables. So if you sell anything on credit, you always can either sell your receivable to a factor or use the receivable as collateral for a loan from a bank or accounts receivable lending institution.   ·

Risk

Of course, the risk to the source is the danger of not collecting on that receivable. The factor and receivable lender has to look not only at the creditworthiness of your company but also at the company owing the receivable. A receivable from a strong company is more easily financed than a receivable from a weak company, and usually at a lower cost.

The stronger the company owing the money, the easier it is to finance. Receivables due in less than 60 days are usually acceptable to both factors and receivable lenders. Once you get past 60 days, it becomes unlikely that you can ever finance that account.

Sources

Banks, factors, and receivable lenders make this type of financing. Every major metropolitan area in the United States has these kinds of lenders. How to find the correct one for you will be discussed in Chapter 5, which focuses specifically on factors and receivable lenders.

Inventory

Inventory financing is getting tougher and tougher to finance independently of receivables. Most receivable lenders will finance 50% of the value of your inventory if it is part of an accounts receivable loan.

If you sell very durable products, like cars, appliances, electronic equipment, computers, or furniture, you may be able to finance this type of inventory. The method used is called *flooring*. Flooring is when the financing source legally owns the inventory until it is sold. In effect, it "places it on the floor of your showroom" but keeps legal title until you sell it, at which time it transfers it over to you to make the sale.

Financing raw materials is by itself very difficult, but it can be done by a financing institution, such as a bank, that knows you and understands the value of the raw material.

Sometimes the inventory is locked up in a warehouse, a receipt is given, and only the financing source has access to the warehouse.

Risks

The risk to the source is that the value of the inventory is very elusive and could be worthless under some circumstances. For instance, if you are a manufacturer, your work-in-progress has no real value to anybody, especially a financing source. What happens if you go broke? What is the financing source going to do with an unfinished product? Most likely, the source will have to pay someone or some firm to finish the product before it can be sold, thus incurring extra expense before it can sell the inventory and get any money out of it.

Even some finished products lose their value quickly. For example, an apparel store's inventory has little value to support a loan unless it is part of a line of credit secured by other assets.

Durable products are excellent types of inventory to finance, versus perishable products or products with a short life span, such as fashionable clothing.

The risk to the financing source will therefore depend on the durability or marketability of the inventory. The source has to determine the risk involved if it has to foreclose and take possession to get its money back.

Your greatest chance of success for financing your inventory will come if you can combine it with receivable financing. Today, when a company is not satisfied with borrowing only 80% but needs to finance 100% of its receivables, it is a common procedure to add the inventory as collateral. That way, a receivable loan can be increased to 100%, with the inventory acting as extra collateral. Remember, most lending institutions value inventory at 50% of its marketable value.

Sources

Your best sources are a receivable lender or bank that is already financing your receivables and will accept some of your inventory to "increase your receivable line." Next would be durable goods financing, which can be arranged from finance companies and banks. How to find the appropriate finance companies will be discussed in Chapter 5. How to find an appropriate bank to finance inventory will be discussed in Chapter 10.

Equipment

Any piece of new or used equipment can be financed today through leasing companies. There are four types of leasing companies: (1) the generalists, who lease all types of equipment; (2) the specialists, who lease only certain types of equipment; (3) the vendor leasing companies, who in effect become private sources of funding for manufacturers of particular equipment; and (4) venture leasing companies, which will lend in more risky situations, but which usually want some type of option for equity in your business to compensate for the increased risk. That's only fair.

Risks

The risks to the leasing companies are the credit of the lessee and the work of the equipment at the end of the lease. Most leasing companies today are charging their customers as though the equipment has little, if any, value at the end of the lease. With the rapid advance in technology, most equipment is becoming obsolete so quickly that it is impossible to predict what its value will be in the future. So the leasing companies are making a calculated guess at the future value of the equipment they lease or rent, charging as if the equipment had no value at the end of the lease.

Just about any company, new or old, can qualify for leasing. The only things that would disqualify some businesses are poor credit and cash flow. This will be covered in detail in Chapter 6.

Sources
See Chapter 6, on leasing.

Leases on real property

A long-term lease that has a resalable value or can be subleased over a fairly long period of time can be financed by banks or some finance companies. Obviously, the lease must be appraised and the lessor must allow the lender to take possession in case of default.

Risks
The length of the lease and the terms of the lease are critical to the financing source. If you have a short-term lease with less than five years to go and no renewable option, most financing sources will not help you. But if you have ten or more years on a lease, the source may lend you money based on the value of that lease. With the appreciation of real estate today in most areas of the country, long-term leases are becoming more valuable. Recently, three restaurants on leased property had their leases appraised; it turned out that the leases had more value than the restaurants!

Most real estate appraisers can appraise a lease. If the lease shows value and the lessee shows the ability to continue making payments on it, there is a good chance it can be financed. But don't think every lease has value. Most leases have no financing value unless there is a unique set of circumstances that give the lessee a good low rental payment schedule for a long period of time. In effect, leases only have value if for some reason the landlord was not sharp enough to foresee the increasing value of the property and did not increase the rent sufficiently to take advantage of the current real estate rental prices.

Sources

Some aggressive banks and finance and leasing companies will lend money using the lease as collateral. Some mortgage companies will also finance leases. To find these sources, look in Chapter 6 for leasing companies, Chapter 7 for real estate sources, and Chapter 10 for aggressive banks.

Leasehold improvements

Equipment leasing companies are also starting to lease the improvements you make in your landlord's building. This is new, and only a few companies are doing it, but it is another source of funding.

Risks

This is risky for the funding source. The only collateral the leasing company takes is the value of the lease because it can't rip out the permanent improvements.

Usually, when you finance leasehold improvements, your source will require an appraisal to determine the value of the lease. Obviously, the value of the lease after the improvements and the credit strength of the borrower are the two major qualifications for a financing source. Start-ups usually do not qualify.

Sources

Leasing companies seem to be the only type of funding source that will take a chance on leasehold improvements.

Real estate

Real estate is the easiest asset to finance because it is easily appraised, hard to destroy, very marketable, and the laws of this country support easy foreclosure in case of default.

This is a business financing book, so it concentrates on financing commercial and industrial uses of real estate, not residential. However, increasing numbers of businesses are operating out of homes. Since residential real estate is the most secure form of collateral in this country, it should not be difficult to finance its purchase. Most of the principles of commercial real estate financing also apply to residential real estate financing. Read all about it in Chapter 7.

Risk

The risk to any financing source is that the borrower will not be able to meet the mortgage payments. Under those circumstances, the lender will lose income from the property and might have to undergo the cost of foreclosure, which could be equal to 10% of the value of the property.

Real estate financing usually depends on the value of the property and the ability of the borrower to meet mortgage payments. As you read the chapter on real estate financing, you will notice that many different types of buildings — single purpose, multi-use, and others — require different types of financing.

The reason real estate financing is covered in a business financing book is not only because many businesses are involved in real estate, but also because all guerrilla-minded small business owners should look into the possibility of owning their own industrial or office building. With the favorable financing terms available on real estate today, the mortgage payments will probably not be any higher than the rent you will have to pay on a lease. If you are looking for only a small amount of space, you can buy an office or small industrial condominium. That way, you pay rent to yourself. This is especially true if you are intending to make many leasehold improvements. Why should you use your money to improve the value of your landlord's property?

Even if you are starting a business, you should consider buying your own building. In ten years, your greatest asset will probably not be your business but the building that houses it!

Sources

Sources are varied, from banks, savings and loans, thrifts, and pension funds to insurance companies. In fact, just about any lending institution in this country will gladly finance or refinance real estate.

Where residential real estate financing is standard because of government funding requirements, commercial and industrial real estate is just the opposite. This means that each deal is unique and has to be structured differently.

A major source for commercial and industrial real estate financing is the commercial mortgage broker, who is usually in contact with quite a number of real estate lenders, depending on the type of real estate and its occupant. Most entrepreneurs should go through a commercial mortgage broker instead of contacting the direct source, because the broker is more skilled at knowing what the best deal is and where to find it. Always look for brokers close to the real estate you want to finance.

Raw land

Undeveloped or raw land is usually unproductive land with few or no buildings on it and no immediate cash flow for its owners. Financing raw land is a world unto itself and is covered in Chapter 7.

Risks

The financing source's risk is minimal, except for the fact that raw land produces no income, just appreciation. If the financing source had to foreclose, it would have to pay all the taxes and other expenses to maintain the land until it could be sold or developed.

Anyone with raw land can usually finance 50% of its market value.

Sources

Any source that would finance real estate will usually finance raw land.

Patents, trademarks, and copyrights

Patents, trademarks, and copyrights are considered intangible assets. How you value them is completely subjective, depending on who is making the valuation and for what purpose. You want to raise capital using these assets as a form of collateral. The more valuable they are in the eyes of the financing source, the more the source will lend or invest.

On one extreme is the patent on the recipe for Kentucky Fried Chicken and its trademark, which is obviously worth millions of dollars to the Colonel's people. On the other extreme is your patent or trademark. The real test of value comes from what it would be worth if you tried to sell it by itself, outside your business.

Though it is difficult, try to put some value on any intangible asset you own that will fit into this category.

Risks

The biggest risk is if the company goes out of business. What value will the patent, trademark, or copyright have by itself? And who could use it without the company? These assets must stand by themselves. For example, Coca-Cola could be used by another beverage or bottling company if the existing company went out of business.

Financing sources look for marketable values in order to lend or invest in this category of assets. So you must prove that your patent, trademark, or copyright has value even if your company ceases to exist. Remember, a lender always looks at the downside of a loan: what if it goes sour? The only time it forecloses on the collateral is when the business is at its weakest point or even out of business. Therefore some tangible or intangible assets are valued on their own, out of the context of the business because the business probably won't be there by the time the collateral is sold off.

Sources

A compatible business in the same industry would be an excellent source to see value in these types of assets. Thus, a strategic alliance or corporate partnership could use the patent, trademark, or copyright to improve its line of products or services.

Once in a while, a major patent, trademark, or copyright can be used as collateral for debt financing. This is the case only where the value of this type of intangible asset is easily marketable.

The other main source of funding for this asset is the venture capital community. It is willing to bet on the patent or trademark's producing future sales for the company.

Some government programs are built around new patents, so they can be a source for this category of guerrilla assets. You have to find the program that would be your most likely source by contacting the appropriate government agency. Find it in Chapter 8.

Research and development

Ask any biotech company about the value of research and development.

If the information you create from your research and development can be put to practical use, you have created value for your company.

Your time and effort have created something downright new. If that new technology can produce a lot of new things that are practical and affordable, you have an excellent chance of financing your project, and the research and development has finally paid off.

You must prove the contribution that the research and development makes to the bottom line of a business before any financing source will seriously consider using it as intangible collateral for financing.

Of course, this refers to pure research and development, not the end or finished product. Once you have the finished product or service, if that has value, then *it* becomes the collateral. Research and development has to be able to produce some sort of tangible bottom-line result to the company to be of value.

Spending a lot of money on research and development does not necessarily mean that the category will have value to any financing source. It usually comes down to some expert, representing the financing source, who determines if the research will add to the company's bottom line and what the value of that addition would be.

Risks

This guerrilla financing category uses the research and development that has not yet produced any tangible results but shows signs of doing so in the future. Once your research and development has produced some evidence of success, it would no longer be called research and development. The evidence would be a finished product, service, or patent. The risk is that no practical information will come "out of the labs," and therefore this intangible asset is worthless. That does happen. This is where expert opinion is necessary to understand the long-term value of the research and development.

How do you value this intangible asset? There is no easy answer except to expose the research to someone who can appraise its value. You must locate an appropriate expert who understands the technology. Obviously, you wouldn't use a tennis pro to evaluate developmental computer research.

What we do know is that some financing sources do indeed put a value on research and development as collateral for financing. They seem to think that research makes the world more efficient and that this efficiency can be turned into dollars when complete.

Sources

Unsecured sources — strategic alliances, venture capital, and some government programs of assistance — are ideal sources for these types of assets. All three are covered later, with a chapter on each.

Success formula

This is the essence of a company. Can you produce profits consistently over a period of time? If so, then you have developed some kind of *success formula*. *That formula is your business's most valuable asset.*

A *company's success formula is that system of doing things in such a manner that the company continually produces a profit above any owner's draw.* The formula is even more valuable if the ownership is made up of a team, not just one individual. A *success formula* based on projections doesn't hold as much value as a formula based on historical figures. Turnaround situations and new businesses must prove that their projections will come true. To prove this to a financing source requires many logical assumptions to back up the data.

Risks

For a going business, the only risk is that something will change, either internally or externally, that will reduce the profits of a company, which in turn will reduce the value of its *success formula*. For a new business or for a turnaround situation, a *success formula* based on projections has a much smaller value to any financing source.

Every lender and investor want some sort of *success formula*. Consistent profits represent stability. Increasing profits, along with a consistent growth rate, add to the value any financing source uses to make a commitment. The lender is looking for the company's ability to pay a loan back and uses cash flow and profits as a cushion to protect its payments. An investor is looking for a return on an investment.

Not every company will have a *success formula*. If your company is losing money, you must prove that the financing you are seeking will turn the company around and produce a *success formula*. If you have been in business for more than five years and are still not producing a decent profit, it will be hard to justify any evidence that you can turn the company around.

People believe historical data first and projections second. Projections for fairly new companies sometimes can be justified. But projections of good results versus a history of poor results are very hard to justify. For an existing company, raising capital based on the assumption that the company will now meet its projections when it hasn't before will require much convincing. Good luck.

Most companies are inconsistent when it comes to making a profit. So when they look for financing, they put together projections based on their ability to change their past and now to consistently produce profits. In order to justify this, they must prove all their assumptions in their projections.

Proving your assumptions is the goal of a good business plan and presentation.

Sources

All sources want a success formula, but secured sources will not lend on just that one asset. Secured sources demand some sort of success formula but will not lend if it is the only asset upon which to make a loan.

On the other hand, unsecured sources, like the venture community, can invest or lend based solely on the value of a company's success formula.

Strategic alliances with other companies can also be based solely on the value of a success formula. Some government programs in some states rely heavily on a company's success formula.

Management

Venture sources are really the only guerrilla source that will finance a company based solely on its management. The strength and depth of the experience of the management team are important to all financing sources. However, it is exceptionally important to the venture community, even to the extent that in certain situations, money can be raised simply by adding to the management in a way that appeases the venture sources.

Many budding entrepreneurs who were having a very difficult time getting capital achieved venture financing quickly when they added a stronger management team to the company.

Risks

Management can come and go, so the real risk is the motivation of the management to stick it out. Employment and incentive agreements for top managers become very important and should be discussed in any presentation to a financing source. Buy and sell agreements and key man insurance are also important, to protect the business from sudden changes in management.

Does any management team qualify a company for venture financing? Obviously not. The venture sources are looking for experience in the relevant industry and in the various positions within the business.

Good, experienced management by itself can attract venture capital if it has a proven track record of success in similar industries. With start-ups and turnaround situations, the management team itself might be enough to swing the deal to get venture capital.

Never underestimate the importance of quality management in attracting capital. Financing sources bet on *people*, not products or services. The old saying that "an excellent management team with a weak product or service has a much better chance of succeeding than a weak management team with an excellent product or service" is very appropriate when it comes to raising capital.

Although every source wants good, experienced management, the venture sources absolutely insist on it. Without a good management team, your chance of attracting any type of venture or private capital is practically nil. In a business where the founder is nominally experienced in that industry or in management, it is extremely important to attract a strong management team to assist the founder. Smart money doesn't put all its eggs in one basket, nor does it bet on just one person to run a business successfully. That person must be able to work with a team.

Partnerism

It is time to be introduced to the concept of *partnerism* and what it means to all future entrepreneurs. A strong management team is a good example of *partnerism* in action. Most successful businesses today will have to be partners with their employees, especially their key management team. Each person on that team must participate in the rewards that the business has to offer.

A successful business should compensate its employees based on quantifiable contributions to the total effort. Incentive based on this concept provides the best atmosphere in which to work.

Smart money, which most venture money is today, understands the value of motivating, compensating, and keeping top management.

If you can prove the value of your management team, you are a long way toward getting financing for your business.

Sources

Venture and private capital are the major sources that will finance a business based solely on its management. The venture capital community actually consists of many layers of sophistication. First is the traditional, formal venture community. Then there is the investment banking and advisory community. Finally there are the informal investors, or "angels," as they are often called, who are the least sophisticated, not only in their requirements for venture capital, but also in their "due diligence" process. Due diligence is the analysis that an investor or investment group performs before it decides to invest. One extreme is the formal venture capital firm, using its MBAs to research the investment; the other is the entrepreneurial angel, using gut feel and experience to decide whether to invest.

Personal assets of the owners

Now that you understand the tangible and intangible assets of a business and the secured and unsecured sources that are attracted to those assets, concentrate on the tangible assets of the *owners* that could be useful to support financing.

Stocks, bonds, and other securities

These personal assets can be used as collateral to attract any one of the secured sources.

Certificates of deposit (CDs) and other savings certificates are as close to cash as you can get. They can be used as collateral to secure a loan from just about any secured source.

Common or preferred stock is only valuable if it has a market. Stock in a privately held company is practically worthless because of the difficulty in selling it to a third party.

Risks

Stocks and bonds that are listed on the major exchanges are excellent sources of collateral for any secured source. Most secured sources will lend you 70%–80% of the listed market value of any stock or bond of a publicly traded company.

Stocks or bonds of privately or closely held companies are practically worthless for money-raising purposes. This does not refer to the stocks or bonds of the company raising the money. Sometimes a private investor will see some value in these private securities. But, on the whole, only publicly listed securities have value for financing purposes.

Limited partnership shares or units have no value except to other limited partners and maybe to the general partner of the partnership. So any limited partnerships you own will *not* help you raise any money from an outside source. The chapter on guerrilla financing techniques discusses selling limited partnerships in your own business to raise capital. This is quite different from using limited partnership ownerships as collateral for financing your own business.

In order for a stock or bond to be used as collateral for a loan from any secured source, it usually must be listed on a major stock exchange. Listing provides liquidity so that if anything goes wrong with the loan or investment, the stock or bond can be easily sold to fulfill any financing contract.

Sources

Most secured sources will use listed stocks and bonds as collateral for a loan. Brokerage firms will lend money on listed stocks. See "Stock and Bond Brokers" in the Yellow Pages of your phone book. Secured sources can easily sell the stocks or bonds if you can't meet the payments.

Collectibles

Most traditional banks will not even consider using personal property as collateral for a loan, but guerrilla sources will.

Most owners of a business don't realize that *some* of their personal possessions can be used as collateral for a loan from a secured financing source. In order for a personal asset to be used as collateral, it must have liquidity and marketability. It must be able to be sold within thirty to sixty days, at close to the market price.

Here is just a partial list of personal assets that have been used for collateral for a loan from secured financing sources: classic cars, jewelry, fur coats, silverware, fine china and porcelain, paintings, baseball cards, antiques, Oriental rugs, antique musical instruments, rare books, sculptures, ceramics, stamp and coin collections, and membership in a country club.

Many more items can be added to this list, but it gives you a good idea of what can be used to support a loan. Consider these assets collectibles because they have a market value to people other than the owner.

Risks

There are many risks for secured sources using this type of collateral. First, its market value may decrease during the term of the financing. Second, its marketability could decline, making it harder to sell upon foreclosure. Sometimes it is hard to find a buyer for some of these assets. Finally, there is the cost of keeping a record of where the collectible is and the risk of the condition and environment where the asset is being stored. Sometimes a valuable asset can be kept in a museum so that its owner and the public can at least admire it while it is being used as collateral.

In order for a personal asset to be used as collateral for a loan, it should have a liquid market value of at least $500. Personal property under $500 is not economical for the source because of the difficulty of recordkeeping.

These assets should be liquid and marketable. For instance, something of personal value to your family but not to the rest of the world would not be marketable.

When a financing source values a personal asset, it usually hires an appraiser who is knowledgeable about that particular asset. For one financing, the business owner had to find an expert on rare violins to estimate the market value of some restored violins. The business was a violin repair shop, which also restored rare old violins. Its only collateral was restored violins. One of the main problems in this instance was the arrangement of how and where to store the violins under the necessary climatic conditions.

Sometimes a collectible asset can be quite valuable and makes ideal collateral. Why keep it in a garage, closet, or vault when it can be used to support the acquisition of capital? The owner retains ownership, but usually not possession, until the loan has been paid off.

The insurance valuation trap

Don't fall into the insurance valuation trap. Most people insure their personal collectibles for much more than they would bring at a forced sale auction. *Forced sale auction value is the amount the collectible would bring at a quick, 30-day auction and the only value that any secured financing source would use for lending purposes.*

The forced sale value is the value to put down on your guerrilla financing balance sheet, not the insurance valuation.

Sources

Not every secured financing source will use personal assets as collateral for a loan. But just about every type of secured financing source will use some personal assets to support a financing. You will have to contact each one and find out its policy.

Some government guaranteed lending programs also allow this type of collateral to be considered.

Other personal property

Other personal property is property that one might not consider a collectible but that can be pawned at a pawnbroker's or sold at a garage sale.

This category is not really a guerrilla financing asset, but it demonstrates that pawnshops are a source of capital and can be used when necessary. Anything of value in your home that can be turned into money and used for business must be considered by a guerrilla.

Although some collectibles can be pawned, it is likely that a pawnshop would probably lend you less money than a guerrilla financing source. However, if you can't find a financing source, then your only other choice might be to pawn the collectible.

Working capital

Working capital is not an asset, not even a guerrilla asset. It is a catchall for uses of money in a business that are hard to define. Good examples of uses of working capital are payroll and other expenses that are constantly being used up in any business and will never be considered an asset.

For guerrilla financing purposes, working capital is money to be used for ongoing expenses that are not to be turned into an accountant's definition of an asset. Money for rent, labor, utilities, payment of debt — all would be considered working capital.

Here you will put all uses for financing that you cannot categorize elsewhere: reducing payables or paying off debt. Money being used for marketing programs is another good example of working capital.

Now that you have the picture, who finances working capital? The answer is *every source*, including all secured and unsecured sources.

If your company needs working capital and only working capital, and you cannot find another financing category for the use of the funds, then venture capitalists, corporate strategic alliances, and government programs are the only sources available to you other than using guerrilla financing techniques as a nonmonetary approach to getting the things you need.

Of course, you can use receivable and equipment financing for working capital, but if you have no receivables or equipment, or if your receivables and equipment are already liened up or used as collateral for existing financing, then strategic alliances and venture capital are the most likely guerrilla sources to consider.

Guerrilla sources

A brief review of the guerrilla sources reveals:

Secured sources
Aggressive banks
Factors
Accounts receivable finance companies
Leasing companies
Real estate lenders
Government funding programs

Unsecured sources
: Private or venture sources
Corporate strategic alliances

Match your major category first

By now you realize that your business will probably not fit neatly into a single category and that you will not always be able to match just one category of sources with only one category of assets. But, while most businesses will need different sources for different categories of assets, most businesses generally rely on one or two main categories. It is those categories that you should match up first to get the bulk of your financing.

Suppose your main guerrilla assets are in management and research and development. Then the appropriate categories to start with would be the venture sources, strategic alliances, and maybe some government programs.

If you are in the temporary help business, most of your assets are tied up in receivables from your clients. Consequently, receivable financing or factoring will be your main category. If you are a machine shop, most of your assets are tied up in equipment, so leasing and equipment financing will be your major category. If you are building a special single-purpose building for your business, a good percentage of your assets are obviously tied up in real estate, so real estate financing will be your major category. If you are in a service business with hardly any assets at all, then your categories will be noncollateralized, or unsecured financing, such as some government programs, venture financing, and strategic alliances.

Now, if your business is a machine shop, you know that the bulk of your assets will be tied up in machinery. But let's say you also need money for labor, rent, and insurance. Still, your biggest investment will be the machinery you use. Therefore, machinery or equipment financing is the key or main category asset to finance your business. To finance the rest of your assets, you might have to go to the venture community or perhaps create a strategic alliance with one of your suppliers or customers.

If you are a software programmer, your largest asset might be computers. Therefore, computer equipment financing is your main category. A software company will also tie up its capital in salaries. Only the venture community will finance payroll exclusively if it thinks that payroll will produce profits. If you are a distributor or retailer of electronic equipment, then inventory financing is your category. Obviously, if you are going to be a real estate developer, real estate financing is your main category of financing.

Value of the matching concept of guerrilla financing

Now you have a good idea of all the different categories of sources in the second step of guerrilla financing. The matching aspect of the second step helps you focus on approaching the right financing sources for your particular situation. If you follow the above steps, you won't waste time trying to convince an inappropriate source to lend to or invest in your company.

When do banks make unsecured loans?

The answer is, only when they have a very creditworthy account with a proven track record of making a profit and paying its bills on time.

How much can I expect to finance?

The charts in this book list the percentages of each category to give you an idea of what you can expect to raise. If you have taken the time to value each asset, as discussed in the preceding chapter, and multiplied by the appropriate percentages, you now have an idea of how much you can expect to raise from each asset in your business.

Why bother to determine net worth?

Secured net worth will usually tell you how much debt you can raise, and *true net worth* will tell you in general terms how much capital you can raise. These figures are only approximations and are intended to give you a guide to the limits of what you can expect to raise for your business.

Success formula is a key variable

Your *success formula* is where you can dramatically increase your true net worth, because your *success formula* depends on past or future earnings. You can use either one. It is a matter of what is believable.

Obviously, net worth can be increased dramatically using projections that predict great things in the future. If you can convince any source that you have a very good chance of meeting your projections, you may be able to raise the amount you are seeking.

If you are in business, you should use historical figures and a multiplier of three times your average net earnings. If you are a new business, you should use projections and a multiplier of two times your average projected net earnings.

Obviously, these multipliers are conservative and your particular multiplier might be more, depending on the company, the industry, and other related circumstances. The key is your ability to justify to any financing source how you value your own success formula.

By identifying all your guerrilla assets, then matching them to the appropriate guerrilla funding sources, you have taken the first two steps of guerrilla financing.

5
All About
Receivable Financing

A major category of guerrilla financing is using receivables as the asset and factoring and receivable lending as the appropriate sources.

What is a receivable?

Receivables are created when you sell on terms, when you offer your customer or client credit. You will not benefit directly from this chapter if your business sells its product or service for cash unless you are evaluating the opportunities and costs to generate more sales by offering your customers credit terms.

The real cost of extending credit

Terms are the length of time you extend credit to your customers to pay their bills. Every time you extend credit, you become a customer's banker. If you bought $100 worth of goods today and were told you have 30 days to pay for it, then, in effect, you have borrowed $100 for 30 days. Every time you extend credit, you are losing the value of that money because you have to wait to be paid. For example, the $100 credit you extended to your customer might have been sold for cash and invested in your company immediately rather than at some time in the future.

So extending credit actually costs you money by denying you access to the $100 or the interest that the $100 could have earned if you had just put it into a savings account. Of course, if your customer takes more than your term period to pay a bill, the real cost to you increases dramatically.

Now that you see the costs of extending credit, you must determine whether you want to put that cost into your product or service or absorb the cost for marketing reasons. *You must decide who is going to pay for the cost of credit, you or your customer.*

While it is not the intention of this book to discuss this problem, it is important to bring to your attention the point that extending credit is expensive. And if your customer takes an extra 30 days to pay, the cost to you is even greater.

Terms

Most terms are expressed as "net 30 days," which means you have extended 30 days for your customers to pay their bill. If you see "2% 10 net 30," it means you have extended 30-day terms and also offered a discount of 2% off your invoice to your customers if they pay within 10 days.

If you are cash poor, you may want to offer your customers a greater cash discount as an incentive to get paid quicker.

Some companies offer no terms and expect to get paid as soon as their invoice is received by their customers.

It is customary to start the credit term as of the date of the invoice. But some companies accept the terms as starting on the date of delivery of the product or service.

How to finance those receivables

Now that you have extended credit to your customers and have to wait to get paid for your product or services, you have automatically put yourself in a cash deficit position.

You are in a cash deficit position because your own costs to produce your product or service were paid for before your billing or invoice date. If you are a manufacturer, you might have had to produce shelf stock months before your order. Your suppliers' bills have already come due and now you have extended credit to your own customers. Just about every business that extends credit puts itself into this cash deficit position. Be sure to visualize the precarious position you put yourself into every time you extend credit and understand the cash flow implications it will have for your business.

There is nothing wrong with extending credit. Just be completely aware of the serious cash flow implications and the cost of credit extension. You bought this book because you want ideas about how to get capital for your business. When you look at the real impact of offering terms to your customer, you will see the advantage of receivable financing.

What is receivable financing?

Receivable financing is getting money from either a factor or receivable lender as soon as you ship and bill or invoice your customers. You get your cash when you ship your orders without having to wait for your customers to pay. In some types of receivable financing, you get paid without even taking the risk that your customer might never pay your bill!

The great aspect of receivable financing is that the faster your business grows and the more you ship, the more you will get in receivable financing. *Receivable financing automatically adjusts to your rate of growth because it depends on your invoices to trigger the financing.*

This is a good time to examine the different types of receivable financing sources and the cost and obligations of both the borrower and lender.

There are two main sources of receivable financing: factors and receivable lenders.

Factors are lenders who actually buy your receivables. The factor pays you cash, and what were *your* receivables then become the *factor's* receivables. When you sell your receivables to the factor, you sell them at a discount off the face value. Generally, the factor assumes the credit risk inherent in the receivables and takes responsibility for collections and other credit administration functions.

Credit and collection services

This is one of the great advantages of using factors to finance your receivables. The factor usually provides all credit and collection services, eliminating your costs and concerns regarding credit investigation, tardy payments, and most bad debts. Factors are very experienced at determining credit risks, and since they are detached, they can give impartial credit advice and help you adhere to prudent credit policies.

The following are some of the credit services offered by factors and other receivable lenders:

1. *Assistance in establishing a formal credit limit program.*
2. *Acting as a credit bureau and providing credit information on prospective customers.*
3. *Monitoring the credit of current customers.*
4. *Providing receivable accounting (data entry of all transactions, aging reports).*
5. *Generating financial management reports (sales tracking, history, and analysis).*
6. *Monitoring accounts, issuing late notices, statements, and invoice follow-up reports.*
7. *Serving as a collection agency for long overdue invoices.*

Recourse

There are two ways a factor can buy your receivables: with or without recourse. Recourse means that even though you have sold your invoice to the factor, you still remain legally liable for any deficiency in the receivable, including any amount that the factor is unable to collect. This is called factoring "with recourse."

If a factor buys your receivables "without recourse," you are not legally liable for any collection deficiency experienced by the factor. Thus, if a customer of yours cannot make payments on one of the receivables you have sold to the factor under a "no or without recourse" arrangement, the bad debt is not your problem. The factor takes the loss. A "no recourse" factoring arrangement is actually a form of credit insurance on your receivables.

There is an exception to a non-recourse program. That is when there is a dispute based on the work or service performed. Under those circumstances, the invoice can be returned by the factor for collection.

Read your financing agreements carefully. Some factors and receivable lenders under a so-called non-recourse program include vague clauses giving them a wide variety of exceptions to demand recourse.

The decision to factor with or without recourse may be determined for you by the factors themselves. You may not have a choice. Without recourse will be more expensive, but it will also cut down on all those collection headaches.

Notification

Most factors buy your receivables under a "notification" arrangement, whereby your customer is notified that checks are to be sent to the factor instead of to you.

"Non-notification" means that your customers are not notified that you have sold their obligations and their checks are still sent directly to you. Under non-notification, your customers have no way of knowing you have sold or financed their obligation.

Sometimes, if you insist on a non-notification arrangement, the factor will ask for extra collateral in lieu of notification.

Impact of notification

Before you enter into any type of notification program with either a factor or receivable lender, you should consider the impact notification *may* have on your customer relations. Years ago, factoring was generally considered to indicate that a company's financial condition was unsound. Today, factoring is a very common form of financing even among very substantial and financially sound businesses. But nobody knows your customer better than you do. Just be aware that some people consider paying invoices to another company, be it a factor or any other receivable lender, as a negative reflection on a company's financial condition.

Costs

There is always a price to pay for services, and a factor can perform a lot of services. Factors can pay from 70% to 97% for your receivables, depending on four major conditions:

1. *The financial strength of the customer.* Obviously, if you sell to major companies that have a high credit standing, your cost to factor would be much less than if you sell to very small businesses with weak or poor credit.

2. *The type of industry of both the customer and the borrower.* Certain industries have a reputation for paying invoices slowly. This will affect your cost. Obviously, factors do not want to buy invoices that are past your normal terms. Usually factors will not buy invoices that are older than sixty days.

3. *The financial strength of the borrower.* Your own financial strength is important in recourse factoring arrangements. If the factor can come back to you to collect when the account is not good, your own company must have the financial strength to pay the factor.

4. *Return and credit policies.* The factor's cost may be high if returns or weak credit policies create more costs for a factor to collect the full amount of the invoice.

Cost versus benefits

When deciding whether to use a factor, you should consider the following:

1. *The profitability of your own business.* If you work on a very low margin of profit, factoring might be too costly for you.

2. *The type of customers you have.* If your customer list is entirely made up of poor credit risks, most factors would not even buy your receivables.

3. *Your need for immediate cash.* If you sell to the type of people who take a long time to pay and you have a high profit margin, factoring might be a viable option.

4. *Collection costs.* Relief from the credit administration, collection expenses, and actual bad debt losses may make factoring very worth-

while. Factors are experts at collecting money and will probably be much more effective than you can be.

How factoring works

As you receive orders, you provide the factor with the customers' names, invoice amounts, credit terms, and other credit information. If the factor approves the receivables, then the factor will purchase them from you at the time you ship, deliver, and bill the goods or services.

Each account receivable offered for sale must represent an accurate statement of a bona fide sale, delivery, and acceptance of merchandise or service that has been performed.

How to find factors in your area

Most factors can be found in the Yellow Pages of your phone book under "Factors" or "Finance." If yours aren't so listed, ask your bank for a list of local factors.

How to pick the best factor

Factors have different qualifications depending on the businesses and industries they work with. A factor's cost can vary significantly, so check around and compare. Try to find a factor who knows and understands your type of business. This will save you a lot of time explaining credit and collection practices in your particular industry.

In choosing the right firm, evaluate the professionalism of the factor, check its references, and find out if it has a local office to service your account.

There is always the risk that factors will turn you down for one reason or another, be it creditworthiness or industry preferences. If that happens, try receivable lenders, although they usually require stronger credit from the client than factors.

The advantage of factoring

Factoring is one of the only secured sources that will finance a company starting up or a company with poor credit. This is because the factor is not as interested in the company that gets the money as it is in the company that owes the money. For example, if you were just starting out in business and your first sale were to General Electric on credit terms, there is a good possibility you could factor this receivable even if your credit was bad. After all, the factor is really concerned about the creditworthiness of the company *owing* the money. So factors can take great risks, probably more so than any other secured financing sources or asset-based lenders.

Receivable lending

Receivable lending involves using your receivables as collateral to borrow money. Banks and receivable lending institutions are the two main sources of receivable lending. How much they lend and what it will cost you usually depend on your normal lending criteria. These would be:

1. *Your financial strength.*
2. *The creditworthiness of your receivables.*

Whether you qualify for an accounts receivable loan will depend mainly on your ability to repay the loan and the strength of your receivables. The same qualifications that applied to factoring apply to receivable lending. If your customers are poor credit risks, you will have a hard time obtaining an accounts receivable loan. But keep in mind that the accounts receivable lender is really more interested in your ability to repay the loan than it is in selling off your receivables if you cannot repay the loan. No lender wants to undergo the expense of liquidating any type of collateral, including receivables.

Costs

First of all, most receivable lenders will not lend on receivables that are over 60 days. Second, they will usually lend you only 80% of the value of the receivables. The 20% becomes a reserve for poor risks. Factors also keep a reserve sometimes.

Receivable lending is usually a line of credit that increases or decreases, depending on the activity of the receivables. If your sales go up, you will make more receivables and will be able to borrow more money.

The cost will be the interest rate the receivable lender charges. This will depend again on the following factors:

1. *The financial strength of the borrower.*
2. *The financial strength of the receivables.*

If you can demonstrate that you can repay the "loan" and that your customers pay promptly, your cost of borrowing should be lower. If, on the other hand, you have weak credit and your customers are slow payers, then your cost of borrowing will be higher. If your financial strength is very poor and your customers are financially weak, you may not be able to get any receivable financing at all.

In determining the cost, keep in mind that the receivable lender is tying up all your receivables to be used as collateral and is only lending from 50% to 80% of their value. As those receivables are paid to you, you will eventually get the other 50% to 20%. However, at the beginning and until they are paid, you are not receiving 100% of your invoices.

The difference between factoring and receivable lending

Accounts receivable lending is just *borrowing* from a lending institution where the major collateral is your accounts receivables. Factoring is where you actually *sell* your receivables to a finance company.

Factoring creates no debt on your balance sheet. Under factoring and receivable lending, some money is usually held back in reserve accounts. Many lenders require reserve accounts, which is the 20% that is held as collateral but not funded. Reserves are money withheld from funding to offset unforeseen problems that may arise during the aging process. These include past due accounts, incomplete payments caused by discounts or chargebacks, or disputed accounts. The reserve is usually released after the receivable lender has been compensated for any amounts in question.

Similarities of factoring and receivable financing

Both are self-financing. That is, the more your sales grow, the more money you have to finance your business. Both allow you to finance all or only part of your receivables. Both can offer credit and collection, but factoring almost always offers collection.

Recourse

Under receivable lending, the borrower usually still holds the credit responsibilities of collection, so the lender almost always has "recourse" to the borrower. Some receivable lenders will take over the credit administration and collection responsibilities for an extra fee. But the receivable lender always has recourse to you if your customer does not pay.

Notification

Depending on how the receivable lender wants to structure a loan, you may or may not have to "notify" your customers about using their invoices as collateral for a loan. Sometimes it will be your choice and other times it will be determined by the receivable lender.

How receivable financing works

Receivable financing from an accounts receivable lender is just like any other loan except that there are generally reporting procedures to the lender to keep it informed of your customers. You are usually required to keep the lender informed on a weekly, sometimes daily, basis of any payments you collect on your receivables. As you collect payments, you actually repay the lender that portion of the total you borrowed on your receivables, plus interest.

Where to find accounts receivable lenders

Your first choice should be banks, which do the majority of accounts receivable lending. Chapter 10 shows you how to find a bank that will finance your receivables.

Your other choices are finance companies and those factors that also do accounts receivable lending. Start by looking in your Yellow Pages under "Financing" to find a list of receivable lenders. The Yellow Pages doesn't always have the correct businesses listed under each category, so you will have to make a number of calls to find a company that indeed finances receivables. But it's worth your time.

Advantages and disadvantages

Accounts receivable financing, like factoring, expands as your need for money expands. The only exception is any credit limit the receivable lender puts on the amount of money it will lend you. Even though you may have more receivables available for collateral, most lenders limit the amount of money they will lend to any one business.

Receivable lending is usually less expensive than factoring. There are exceptions to this, so shop around to compare prices and terms.

Of course, the ability to borrow only 80% of your receivables is the biggest disadvantage. Having to do your own credit check and collections is another disadvantage.

How to sweeten the deal to get accepted

If you are having a hard time getting either a factor or a receivable lender to finance you, you might want to offer some extra collateral besides the receivables to support the financing. If you just went out and borrowed on the value of your collateral, it would most likely be reflected on your financial statements. But guerrilla financiers know that by using their collateral, such as real estate, to support only the factor, their financial ratios do not change.

Another advantage of receivable financing is your ability to automatically increase your line by just presenting more sales to finance as opposed to having to reapply for any type of collateral loan.

Don't despair if you are bankrupt. Some factors can, with the court's approval, buy your receivables.

How to choose

Whether a factor or receivable lender is your best source of money will depend on a number of considerations:

1. *Your cash flow requirements.*
2. *Your present cost of collections and credit administration.*
3. *The payment schedules and credit standing of your customers.*
4. *The cost of borrowing against or selling your receivables.*
5. *The source's notification policy.*

If your credit and collection operations are expensive or causing problems, this situation may weigh heavily in favor of factoring your receivables or borrowing from a finance company that notifies your customers and assumes collection operations.

Returns

One other qualification that both factors and receivable lenders look for is your return policy. What percentage of your sales are returned for a credit or refund? If this figure is too high, it could discourage some lenders from financing your receivables.

Spot receivable financing

You don't have to finance all your receivables. You might want to finance just one or a few accounts. This is called spot financing.

Inventory financing

As discussed in the last chapter, you may be able to increase your accounts receivable line from a receivable lender by adding your inventory to the collateral. This way, the receivable lender might lend you 100% of your receivables. This is, in effect, a form of inventory financing. Each receivable lender has its own lending policies regarding what types of inventory it will accept as additional collateral. So you will have to hunt for financing programs and options that fit your needs. Inventory financing is getting harder to find, as most receivable lenders will only do it for their good accounts.

Because it is very expensive to track inventory levels and values accurately, it is difficult to get just pure inventory financing without using your receivables as extra collateral, but there are two ways: flooring and warehouse financing.

Flooring involves an arrangement whereby the lender actually buys the inventory for you and retains ownership until you sell it. Then, as you sell the inventory, you pay off the loan. Usually, only finished durable goods are financed in this manner, such as automobiles, major household appliances, TVs, and VCRs. Typical lenders that do flooring are banks and leasing and finance companies.

Warehouse financing is where the goods being used as collateral are stored at a public warehouse and the receipt for the goods is held by the lender.

Foreign receivables and letters of credit

Some receivable lenders are starting to finance exports by accepting foreign invoices or letters of credit as collateral. In many cases, insurance is available, which makes it easy to finance international accounts. You will have to ask which receivable lenders or factors will accept foreign export paper or irrevocable letters of credit.

How do factors and receivable lenders evaluate your accounts?

Here are some guidelines that the receivable finance community uses to judge your receivables:

1. *Steady, consistent business.* Repetitive, stable business is more desirable than a variable or volatile business in a changeable market.
2. *Creditworthy customers.* Financially strong customers are more desirable than financially weak customers.
3. *A large customer base.* Businesses that sell to a variety of customers are more desirable than businesses that sell to a small, concentrated number of customers.
4. *The individual average size of your receivables.* Do you do 50 invoices at $2,000 each or 1,000 invoices at $100 each? The former would obviously be easier to keep a record of and finance.
5. *The type of industry or business you are in.* It is very difficult to get receivable financing in some types of businesses, such as construction and health care.

When you look for receivable financing of any type, be sure to contact a number of different sources before completing any arrangement. There may be substantial differences in the programs and terms offered by each source. Factors and receivable lenders often have various policies for each industry and use different criteria in determining whether receivables and/or inventory are sufficient collateral to qualify you for financing. Only by contacting a number of sources can you determine what will be the best option for your particular needs.

What to do if they all say no

Not to worry. There are many more chapters filled with other guerrilla sources and techniques to solve your financing problems. Read on and be optimistic.

6
All About Equipment Financing

Equipment financing is using equipment you own or intend to acquire as collateral for borrowing money. The equipment can be new or used.

Every business needs some equipment, even if it is just a desk and telephone. Certain businesses need more equipment than others, such as a printer, who needs a lot of printing equipment. Regardless of how much equipment your business requires, there is a whole world of sources out there ready to finance it. In fact, you can even finance your used equipment. This chapter tells you all you need to know to finance anything that is not nailed down in your place of business.

The basic concept of leasing is that one party (the lessor) offers to rent a piece of equipment to a second party (the lessee). The first party thus gains income in the form of rental payments; the second party gains the use of the property at a minimal cost, saving cash for other needs. There are two ways to borrow money based on the value of equipment.

1. *Traditional equipment financing.* Take possession of the equipment and use it as collateral for the loan.
2. *Leasing.* Let the lender take possession of the equipment and lease (rent) it back to you.

Under the first option, you record the equipment on your books as an asset you own and the loan as a liability. Portions of each loan payment made to the lender are recorded as debt repayment and interest expense, and you depreciate the book value of the equipment over a period of years as prescribed by the tax laws.

Under the second option, while you enjoy the use of the equipment as if you owned it, the equipment does not appear on your books as an asset. There is no corresponding liability, and the payments to the lender are completely expensed.

Which way to finance equipment is better for you and the lender depends on a number of things, such as the type of equipment, type of business and industry you are in, your tax situation, and many others too numerous to discuss. Ask your accountant to recommend the best option for financing your equipment.

Many sources of equipment financing will usually offer you both types of financing — traditional and leasing. You and possibly your accountant will have to decide which is more advantageous.

Advantages and disadvantages of traditional financing and leasing

Both options have advantages and disadvantages. New tax laws seem to give leasing the advantage because you can expense your costs more quickly than is allowed under the new longer-term depreciation schedules.

One of the most exciting aspects of equipment financing is that you can often borrow all the money you need in order to acquire new or used equipment. This 100% financing allows you to get started and operate without equipment costs taking a large bite out of your business. In fact, some of the so-called soft costs, such as down payments, taxes, installation charges, license fees, and insurance, can be included in the lease payment.

Also, equipment financing is usually fixed-rate financing, allowing you to determine the exact cost of your financing.

Leasing allows the financing to be tied to the life of the asset. While most traditional equipment loans are often for periods substantially less than the asset life, leases can be structured to nearly match the asset's economic life.

Leasing has often been called *off–balance sheet financing*. The equipment is not recorded on your balance sheet, but is usually listed under notes to the financial statement. In effect, you are borrowing money without putting any liabilities on your balance sheet. From a financial point of view, not listing the equipment as an asset with a corresponding liability improves your liquidity; your debt-to-equity ratio and current liabilities are decreased. At the same time, the return on investment is enhanced.

Another advantage of leasing is that it acts as a hedge against technological obsolescence. Under a lease, you have the flexibility to upgrade your equipment as new, improved versions are introduced.

Leasing also allows you to test the equipment and evaluate its usefulness before investing in it.

Also, if you only need the equipment periodically, on a cyclical or project basis, it makes sense to lease or even to rent the equipment.

Of course, both types of equipment financing free up money that would otherwise have been spent buying the equipment.

The lease or purchase decision

Your cash flow dictates the decision to finance the purchase traditionally or by a lease. But if you do have some cash and are thinking you might buy the equipment outright, consider these points when deciding:

1. *The length of time until the equipment will become obsolete.*
2. *Any predictable repair and maintenance costs.*
3. *The residual value of the equipment at the expiration of the lease.*
4. *Whether there is a chance to use accelerated depreciation.*
5. *Finally, always consider if the equipment will perform to your expectations.* If it turns out to be the wrong equipment for your purposes, it might be easier to try to get out of a lease than try to return it to the dealer from whom you bought it.

Types of leases

Generally, you have a choice of two types of lease agreements: (1) closed-end, operating, or maintenance leases or (2) open-end, capital, or financial leases.

The operating, closed-end, or maintenance lease is one in which the lessor maintains ownership of the equipment, including all risks and benefits of such ownership, and repairs to the equipment must be made by the lessor.

The operating lease works well for the lessee attempting to avoid the risk of obsolescence. It gives the lessee an opportunity to test a new piece of equipment before purchasing under a long-term lease. Further, at the end of the lease, the lessee is not left with a secondhand piece of equipment that may be difficult to sell.

You can also capitalize on the cost-effective services provided by the lessor as part of the lease contract. For instance, if the lessor specializes in the type of equipment you are leasing (see the later part of this chapter), your leased asset can be more economically maintained and repaired with his trained personnel and complete repair shop (assuming he has one). In addition, replacement equipment can easily be substituted in a timely manner, should the leased asset break down.

Operating leases may contain a cancellation clause that permits the lessee to cancel the lease and return the asset before the expiration of the initial lease term. This provides a great deal of flexibility in case the equipment does not perform as expected or becomes technologically obsolete. However, there may be a penalty or higher lease terms with this option.

Under an open-end, capital, or financial lease, the lessee is responsible for making periodic lease payments and assuming the ownership responsibilities and costs of maintenance, insurance, and taxes. Financial or open-end leases typically cannot be canceled and are full pay-out leases, which means that the lessee makes payments equal to the full price of the leased equipment. Capital leases are treated as a loan, and depreciation is claimed against it.

Differences in the types of leases

With a closed-end lease, when the lease terminates, ownership remains with the lessor. With an open-end lease, the lessee has the option to buy the equipment. A closed-end lease is strictly a rental agreement of fixed payments over a specified period of time. With an open-end lease, you make monthly payments but can purchase the equipment in one balloon payment when the lease expires. The final payment can be based on an estimate of what the equipment will be worth at the end of the lease period or on a predetermined purchase option price.

Also keep in mind that the operating lease is considered off–balance sheet financing and is treated as an expense rather than a liability on the balance sheet.

Types of equipment

Any type of equipment can be financed, new or used. In fact, even leasehold improvements that are permanently attached to buildings are now being financed by some aggressive leasing companies.

Terms

The cost and length of the leasing terms depend not only on the type of equipment but also on your own creditworthiness.

Obsolescence as it affects the cost to borrow

The life span and resalability of the equipment being financed will influence the terms and costs of the lease. Equipment that has a short life or is based on technology that will quickly become obsolete is often more difficult and expensive to finance than durable equipment using mature technologies. Computers, for instance, have a much shorter life span than many industrial machine tools. So by the time you are finished using your computer, there may be little or no market for its technology. Obviously, the cost of leasing computers would be more than to lease machine tools.

Marketability as it affects cost

Marketability affects the resale value of the equipment. Clearly, there is very little demand for obsolete equipment. When the leasing company determines the cost of a lease, it must look at what the resale value will be after the lease is up.

The reality of the leasing situation today, when just about every piece of electronic equipment becomes outdated the moment it is installed, is that most leasing companies assume that the equipment has little, if any, value at the end of the lease and charge accordingly.

For certain types of equipment, however, this would not be true. For example, printing presses and other types of specialized heavy equipment seem to hold their value over time. Here, the leasing company knows that the equipment is marketable and will hardly decrease in value over the length of the lease. Under these circumstances, the cost to lease should be very economical.

Old equipment

Let's say you want to buy a used piece of equipment from a dealer. You can finance it or lease it. If it is the type of equipment that holds its value, it will be easier to get financing. When you want to borrow against equipment you already own, you can do it by using a sale and leaseback arrangement.

Sale and leaseback financing

A sale/leaseback arrangement is a special method of financing equipment you already own. Leasing companies have to own equipment to finance it. So they buy your equipment and then lease or rent it back to you. In other words, you sell your equipment to the leasing company for a cash payment and then the leasing company rents your own equipment back to you according to prearranged terms. This method of financing allows you to get needed cash out of your own equipment while you continue to use it — a guerrilla maneuver if there ever was one.

Upgrading and maintenance

There are several things to keep in mind as you seek equipment financing and negotiate your terms. First, if you are leasing equipment that has a short life span, try to get the lessor to allow you to upgrade or trade up to newer models as they become available. Second, find out if there is a maintenance policy on your equipment and whether it is included in the cost of the lease. A separate maintenance contract can be very costly. Finally, don't forget to understand the buy-out terms at the end of the lease. What will it cost you to own the equipment?

Traditional equipment financing sources

Banks and leasing companies offer traditional equipment financing. Banks are covered in Chapter 10, leasing companies in this chapter.

Leasing sources

The five types of leasing sources are: (1) *general equipment*; (2) *specialized equipment*; (3) *rolling stock equipment sources*; (4) *vendor financing*; and (5) *venture leasing companies*.

General equipment

These sources will finance any type of equipment. They will usually offer the option of either leasing or traditional equipment financing.

Specialized equipment

These sources specialize by types of equipment. The following list notes categories of equipment that usually relate to a specialized financing source:

- Agricultural equipment
- Aircraft
- Automobiles
- Computer equipment
- Construction equipment
- Dry cleaning and Laundromat equipment
- Electronic equipment

- Food service equipment
- Health care equipment
- Heavy-duty trucks and trailers
- Heavy industrial equipment
- Heavy industrial moving equipment
- Machine shop equipment
- Marine equipment
- Office equipment
- Telecommunications equipment
- Trucks and trailers
- Vans

The advantage of using a specialized equipment financing company is the experience and understanding the company will have about your needs when using the equipment. Guerrilla financiers use specialists before going to a leasing company that leases all types of equipment. The specialists usually know more about the problems of financing their industry, and most have a solution. Another key factor is that specialists usually have a very competitive rate.

Always ask for another source

If you are turned down in searching for a leasing company, always ask people to recommend another source. They almost always will. So, in your search for financing, end your conversation by asking if they know of any other company that would finance the equipment you are looking for. It works. Just ask!

Rolling stock

One of the easiest types of equipment to finance is rolling stock, or equipment with wheels. Equipment financing started here and is the most perfected, especially consumer vehicle financing. The vendor or seller of the equipment usually has already lined up a financing source for its equipment. The best place to get financing for rolling stock is from the seller or the seller's financing source. It knows the particular equipment you are financing better than anyone else.

Cars and light trucks are the easiest to finance because most of them are bought by consumers, and consumer equipment financing is the easiest to arrange. But when you get into heavy-duty trucks and trailers and other heavy moving equipment, it becomes more difficult. Then you need to contact specialized commercial equipment financing sources who have a better understanding of that type of equipment.

Vendor financing

Vendor financing means that the equipment manufacturer or distributor has already arranged with a specialized equipment finance company to finance the equipment it is selling. The finance company usually specializes in that vendor's equipment and does not do general equipment financing. Some vendor financing companies exclusively finance one manufacturer's equipment in one industry. Some manufacturers have their own vendor leasing company.

The first place to go for financing is to the vendor or seller of the equipment. Its finance company usually has the best terms because it concentrates only on that vendor's equipment.

How to find the appropriate equipment finance company

Start with the vendor's finance company. If this doesn't work, go to a specialist in the equipment you want to buy, and if that doesn't work, go to a generalist.

The reasoning behind this approach is that the vendor financing company usually has the best financing program for its own equipment. For example, nobody knows how to structure a better deal on a Xerox machine than Xerox's own vendor finance company. If the manufacturer does not have its own financing program, go to a finance company that specializes in copy machines. If you don't have success there, find a company that specializes in office equipment. If that doesn't pan out, go to an equipment financing company that finances any type of equipment. As you can see, when looking for equipment financing companies, *guerrillas work from the specialist to the generalist.*

Venture leasing

This is a new breed of equipment leasing. As the name suggests, venture leasing combines equipment leasing and venture financing. Venture leasing companies concentrate on high-risk situations where there is a chance for a high return. Here, the finance company usually takes an option for equity in the company it finances. Obviously, the risk of financing a new business is high, so this type of equipment financing company offsets that risk by participating in the growth of the company.

Venture leasing companies are few in number and usually only follow traditional venture capital companies. That is, they only finance companies that have already been or are in the process of being financed by a traditional venture capital company. When you get to the chapter on venture capital, you'll see that the venture capital industry is divided into the professional or traditional venture capital community, of which there are probably only two thousand firms in the United States, and the informal venture capital community, which has been estimated at close to one million. The traditional venture capitalists study a business carefully before investing. Venture leasing companies use the same yardstick to decide whether to finance a company. Venture leasing companies usually only finance companies that qualify for traditional venture capital. For now, just keep in mind that venture leasing is usually reserved for traditional venture capital opportunities.

Leasing agreement checklist

Before you sign that lease agreement, work with your accountant. Here is a checklist of key points to consider:

1. *Leasing costs.* How much is each payment? When are payments due? Is there a grace period before all the charges are assessed? What is the actual amount of rental fees (or interest)? What is the total amount to be paid over the term of the lease?
2. *Flexibility.* Are there provisions for skipped payments, allowing you to forgo installments under certain conditions? Are step-up payments, which accelerate the termination date of the lease, allowed?

3. *Extra costs.* Is a security deposit required? Is it returned to you at the end of the lease if the equipment is in good condition? Are any installation charges, license fees, taxes, or other costs to be paid by you?
4. *Penalties.* Are there penalties for early cancellation of the lease?
5. *Service.* Are you responsible for repairs? Is there a guarantee on the equipment? Who performs the maintenance? If the lessor provides servicing, what charges do you have to pay? If the equipment breaks down, do you receive a rebate for the downtime and replacement (loaner) equipment?
6. *Insurance.* Are you responsible for insurance coverage? If the lessor obtains insurance, will you be charged an insurance fee or be billed separately by the carrier?
7. *Equipment upgrades.* Are there provisions for replacing equipment with newer or better models during the term of the lease? If so, what charges are involved?
8. *Residual value.* Decide what the equipment is worth at the end of the lease before you sign the lease. This is called residual value. The estimate of the residual value has a direct impact on the price or cost of the lease.

Where to buy equipment

Leasing companies have become excellent sources for buying equipment, especially vendor leasing companies. Because they have to know the real price of the product they lease, they can either help you with the purchase or actually sell the equipment to you, using their contacts. The next time you need a computer, call a leasing company and see if it can get you a good price. You may be pleasantly surprised.

Where to find the financing sources

First, try your bank. Banks make traditional equipment loans and usually on any type of equipment.

Next try leasing companies that either lease or finance equipment. They can be found in the Yellow Pages of your phone book under "Leasing" and "Financing."

Sound too easy? Wait until you start calling all the companies under "Leasing." You will find that almost 50% of them just lease cars and trucks. So you have to do some phoning to find what you are looking for. Specialized leasing companies sometimes advertise the type of equipment they finance, but, when it comes to business equipment, you usually have to search until you find the appropriate source. Remember to ask each source for a referral if it can't help you.

Vendor leasing companies can be found by asking the vendor; venture leasing companies can be found by asking other leasing companies who does venture leasing or by contacting traditional venture companies and asking them the same thing.

What to do if you need different types of equipment

In this case, you will probably have to go to a general equipment financing company unless the greater part of your equipment needs is one category of equipment.

7
All About
Real Estate Financing

This chapter will help you find your way through the commercial real estate financing maze and introduce you to both guerrilla financing sources and techniques that will save you time and money, get you the best terms, and allow you to get the financing you really want no matter what the circumstances.

What does real estate have to do with business?

What does a book about business financing have to do with real estate? A *lot*. A lot of businesses will get involved in real estate by buying their own building. In fact, guerrillas think first of buying their own facilities. If you made a study of a random group of companies that bought their own building ten years ago and you compared the increase in the value of their businesses to the increase in the value of their building, you would find that the building's value increased *far more than the value of the businesses*. At this point, you may think it better to just forget business and concentrate on real estate. That would be a mistake. The increases mentioned refer to averages and don't reflect the amount of money taken out of the business by the owner over the ten-year period. And of course there is great value in the satisfaction that comes from owning a business.

Buying your own building is not the only time you will need to know how to finance real estate. Many businesses are conducted in residences, such as day care centers, nursing homes, and myriad consulting practices. The real estate is the biggest asset in these businesses, and of course it needs to be financed.

There are also many businesses that evolve in and around real estate, such as project development, real estate management and maintenance, construction, and remodeling. All of them must know how to finance real estate.

What is the definition of commercial and industrial real estate financing?

In this book, commercial and industrial real estate financing covers any real estate financing that is connected with *business* and not for personal purposes. This chapter is not about different ways to finance your home. It is about financing business-related real estate projects. Still, homes will be covered here just in case you buy one as a place to operate your business.

If the credit decision by the financing source is affected by a business's occupying or owning the real estate, then it is a *commercial and industrial real estate financing transaction*. Any income-producing property is also classified as commercial real estate.

What is so difficult about financing real estate?

Compared to financing a business, financing real estate is a snap. This is not to say that any financing is easy. But most financiers agree that real estate is the easiest asset to finance. Why? Because it holds its value better than any other business asset and is easily identifiable. It can also be appraised accurately, cannot be easily moved, and is quite marketable. Even if the business occupying the real estate fails, the value of the real estate itself is usually not affected. And in this country, our laws make it easy to recapture or foreclose in case of default. For all these reasons, there are many sources involved in the business of financing real estate.

What is so difficult about financing commercial real estate?

There is a world of difference between financing your home and financing an income-producing piece of property. With all the standardization of forms and government-backed funding programs, residential financing has almost become a cookie-cutter job. But commercial real estate is entirely customized. *Each and every commercial real estate deal needs a customized financing plan.*

You can't just call a number of lenders for the best rates on your commercial or industrial property as you would for your home. There are just too many factors to consider besides the value of the property and the credit of the borrower, such as zoning, vacancy, licensing of the occupant, and type of business occupying the property. Even national economic factors affect a commercial deal. So, although it may have been easy to get a loan on your home, it may not be easy to get a loan on your commercial property.

Even within the category of commercial and industrial real estate there are varying degrees of difficulty of financing, depending usually on the type of property and the degree of risk involved. The higher the risk, the more difficult it is to find a financing source and the more costly it is to get financing. Risk in commercial real estate is related to the type of building or the type of occupant. For instance, apartment buildings are easier and cheaper to finance than a warehouse. More people need apartments than need warehouses. On the other hand, a warehouse is easier and cheaper to finance than a motel. It is easier to find someone to lease a warehouse than a motel.

Apartment buildings and other conventional real estate usually get the best rates, terms, and conditions. Single-purpose buildings, such as gasoline stations, not only have a high risk and are costly, but very few lenders are even interested in financing them. Lenders look at property that would be the *easiest to unload and sell* if they had to foreclose on it.

Another example of a high-risk situation is a piece of property housing a restaurant. Restaurants have a high degree of turnover (95% go out of business), so the lender will be very cautious, especially if the restaurant is the only occupant. Later, this chapter will evaluate different types of commercial real estate by difficulty of financing.

Environmental pitfalls

Speaking of the difficulties of commercial real estate financing, you should be acquainted with a new liability problem affecting anyone dealing in commercial and industrial real estate. That is the pollution from toxic waste and asbestos.

Once you buy a piece of property, you are responsible for making sure that there is no toxic material or asbestos on or in your building and on or in the ground under the building. If there is, *you* are responsible for cleaning it up.

Real estate financing sources are very aware of this problem and will not finance any property until it has been determined to be environmentally safe. Get a phase one report for land and an asbestos report for buildings. The phase one report will show you who used to own the property and what they did with it. Then you can investigate any potential problems before they occur. Sometimes you can get the seller to pay for these reports.

Help in financing

Guerrillas do not go directly to the source when financing commercial and industrial real estate unless their business is real estate. Residential real estate financing is so consistent and similar that every lender uses the same type of application. Commercial and industrial lenders must look not only at the real estate but also at the creditworthiness of the business occupying and/or owning the real estate. That is why you should use a commercial and industrial mortgage broker to help you finance any type of commercial and industrial real estate. This will be covered later on in this chapter.

When you should buy your own facilities

Let's start with the guerrilla's favorite real estate financing theme: all businesspeople should consider buying their own facilities. It is one of the best investments you can make in your business. First of all, your rent or lease payment is usually one of your largest operating expenses.

By owning your own facilities, you are paying rent to yourself. Also, you are getting valuable tax deductions, and your real estate asset is probably the only asset on your books that actually appreciates in value. Further, real estate financing sources offer the longest terms that allow you to pay back (amortize) your loan — over 25 to 30 years. Consequently, your mortgage payments are often equal to or not much more than your rent payments. Many business owners fail to realize that they can actually afford to own the site where they operate, be it a residence or a commercial building.

If rent is a big part of your expenses and you have to spend a good deal of your money to improve your landlord's property to operate in it, why not pay rent to yourself? After all, if for some reason you have to move, you would be leaving behind all those leasehold improvements. Why put money in your landlord's pocket? The terms in commercial and industrial real estate are usually so favorable that the cost of the mortgage payments is sometimes less than the lease payments.

Even start-ups can own their own facilities

You might be wondering why, when you are just starting a business, you should consider buying your own real estate.

Think about it. Suppose you plan to open a free-standing restaurant that would require constructing a single-purpose building. You're going to be spending a lot of your own money to improve your landlord's property. Everything you want to do will be at the mercy of your landlord. So, if you can swing it, buy it. Here's how.

Office and industrial condos

Even if you need a small amount of space, you can still own it. Haven't you heard of office and industrial condominiums? They're not everywhere yet, but they are coming. Ask your real estate agent about any office or industrial condominiums in your area.

Condominiums are buildings where you own part of the building, not the whole building. In a commercial condominium, each of a number of separate businesses owns a portion of the building. You must have heard of residential condos. Office and industrial condos are just like residential condos. The only difference is that the commercial condo is a place where you work, not live.

When it comes to financing office and industrial condominiums, you usually can only get a 65% loan-to-value ratio. So you have to make a 35% down payment and borrow 65%. It is hard to get financing on a condo because sources don't want to own part of a building if they have to foreclose. For owner-occupied commercial condominiums, the Small Business Administration has an excellent financing program that finances 90% *of the value* of the property. Call your nearest SBA office for details; it is listed in the Blue Pages government listing at the end of the White Pages directory.

Down payment

Most commercial real estate financing sources will finance 65% to 70% of the value of the property, which usually includes leasehold improvements. The SBA program requires only 10% down to buy property for your business.

Usually the lender determines the amount of the down payment based on the cash flow from the property. There must be enough cash flow to cover all costs, including the cost of the financing. To calculate that figure, most lenders use a 3%–5% vacancy factor subtracted from the gross income the property is bringing in. The lenders then subtract all the expenses: taxes, insurance, management, reserve, and maintenance. All the costs of maintaining the commercial property will be subtracted from gross income. The remaining income is called the net operating income (NOI), which is the cash flow that is available for debt service on your financing. Some conservative lenders will even take an additional 5%–10% off the NOI before calculating income or cash flow. This is called a debt-service ratio. With the calculation of the cost of money (interest rate), the lenders will determine what percentage of the property they can lend on, which determines what percentage the borrower must come up with as the down payment.

In calculating the above figures, part of the down payment can be a seller carryback. For instance, you can put 15% of the value of the property as your down payment; the seller can take back 20% of the value of the property, and the financing source can then lend on the other 65%. Guerrilla mathematics.

Should your cash flow service all the debt?

Not always. For instance, suppose you want to buy your own building and you know you don't have the income to service all the debt. In this situation, you would want to get the seller to defer payments, maybe on interest or principal, or both, for a period of time. In this way, the lender calculates that there is enough cash flow to make the loan as long as there are deferred payments.

Other uses for real estate financing

You may already own property that you want to refinance to get a lower interest rate, get better terms, or get more money out of the property. You may want the additional cash for remodeling, expansion, or just to pay operating expenses.

Types of real estate to be financed

The following are some of the different categories of real estate financing, arranged by difficulty of financing and risk involved to the lender. The types of property at the top of the list are much easier to finance than those at the bottom. The riskier the proposal, the harder it is to finance. Lenders measure risk in real estate financing by the danger of default on mortgage payments and/or the loss that might occur by foreclosure proceedings. The harder it is to sell the property after foreclosure, the more difficult it is to finance. As you study this list, you will see that the properties at the top are more multi-use and the properties at the bottom are more single-use. Multi-use properties are more marketable than single-use properties.

- Residential homes
- Apartments
- Mixed-use buildings
- Residential subdivisions
- Office buildings
- Shopping centers

- Medical/professional buildings
- Office/warehouses
- Industrial
- Office condominiums
- Industrial condominiums
- Mobile home parks
- Mini-storage
- Hotels/motels
- Recreational vehicle parks
- Convalescent homes
- Restaurants
- Single-purpose buildings
- Raw, undeveloped land

Just about all the techniques and sources discussed in this chapter will help you finance some of these types of properties.

Single-purpose property

Commercial and industrial properties are usually classified in one of three categories for funding purposes: single-purpose, multi-purpose, or mixed- or split-use. A single-purpose property can normally be used for only one purpose. Examples include motels, hotels, gas stations, specialty restaurants, and similar facilities that are built for only one use. In general, single-purpose properties are the most difficult classification to finance. This is easy to understand. If the owner of a bowling alley is unsuccessful and cannot make the loan payments, the lender will foreclose on the property and be left with very few choices. It can sell the bowling alley to someone else with the hope that the new owner will be more successful, even though the new owner will run the same type of business at the same site. Or the lender can write off the investment in the bowling alley and tear it down so that the land can be redeveloped for another use. Lenders face similar risks in financing any single-purpose property. If you need financing for a single-purpose property, consider the following:

1. Your loan-to-value ratio will be lower by about 10%.
2. Give yourself extra time to find a lender.

3. Make certain your financing proposal is as strong as possible.
4. Use a commercial mortgage broker to find the best lender and terms.

Multipurpose properties

Multipurpose properties include buildings that are suitable for any number of different businesses. Two good examples of such properties are office buildings and warehouses. If the owner of a small business buys an office building and then runs into trouble and cannot make the loan payments, it is relatively easy for the lender to repossess the building and sell or lease it to someone else who may be involved in a totally different type of business. Accordingly, properties in this classification are much easier to finance.

Mixed-use or split-use properties

A mixed-use or split-use property is one that can be used for two or more distinct purposes at the same time. A building with apartments on the second floor and retail stores on the ground floor is a good example. As you can imagine, the resale market for these semi-specialized properties is not as good as it is for multipurpose properties, such as office buildings, but it is not as limited as the market for highly specialized single-purpose properties. In general, the difficulty of financing a mixed-use property falls somewhere between that of single-purpose and multipurpose properties.

Where to find sources to finance real estate

For residential real estate financing, there are many sources. But for commercial and industrial real estate financing, the choices are narrow. This is because the government sponsors the concept of buying your own home and has developed many ways for you to get financing for it.

On the other hand, commercial and industrial real estate financing sources must consider many more factors besides the inherent value of the land and building and the creditworthiness of the owner. They must also carefully examine the creditworthiness of the occupier of the property, which is usually not the owner. It is one thing to analyze an individual's credit and income, and it's another to study the creditworthiness and income of a business. Also, the financing sources must study such things as zoning restrictions, licensing and utility requirements, type of business occupying the property, and even long-term economic factors that would affect the occupant's ability to meet loan payments.

Commercial and industrial financing sources

Just because commercial and industrial financing is more complicated than residential financing doesn't mean it can't be done. Some sources specialize in this type of financing. Let's cover them one at a time.

Savings and loan associations

Because of the recent crisis in this industry, these financial institutions are now extremely careful when lending on commercial real estate. Nevertheless, they are still a prime source of capital for business real estate financing. Just look under "Real Estate Loans" in your Yellow Pages to find a savings and loan association.

Keep in mind that savings and loan associations tend to make their lending decisions based more on the value of the property than on the cash flow.

Banks

Banks are a good source for business real estate financing. In fact, they are a better source than savings and loan institutions when the cash flow of the property is stronger than the value of the property. Banks know real estate and business, while savings and loan institutions usually know only real estate. Banks tend to focus on the creditworthiness of the business more than on the value of the property. If your project is more business-oriented than real estate–oriented, try a bank before going to a savings and loan.

One of the best uses of bank financing for relatively small real estate transactions is the Small Business Administration's Loan Guarantee Program. Under this program, a business can buy its own property for only 10% down. Use this method of financing if you want to buy your own building and will occupy at least 51% of the property. This whole program is discussed in detail in Chapter 8.

Thrifts and loan companies, finance companies, and credit unions

These institutions do make real estate loans on commercial projects. Usually they can secure the loan with personal and real property. The problem here is that their lending limits are very low and usually will help fund only a very small real estate deal or part of a deal. These lenders are more interested in the creditworthiness of the borrower than in the value and type of property used as collateral for the loan. Use these lenders for your more difficult deals and for unusual and undesirable types of properties, such as single-purpose properties and restaurants. They are more costly than other lenders, but they take more risks.

Life insurance companies

Life insurance companies finance only quality commercial real estate deals. They usually won't touch a deal under $2 million. Their advantage is that they have the best terms and rates of any real estate financing source. Since this book is geared to smaller types of financing, it will not dwell on this source other than to say that if you have a really clean big real estate deal, insurance companies are the natural source.

Pension funds

Pension funds will take greater risks than insurance companies, but, like insurance companies, they concentrate on larger deals. Pension funds like to finance intermediaries instead of the borrowers directly. For example, pension funds are a good source of capital for hard money lenders and venture capital firms. Pension funds will look for high-yield situations and high-risk situations, but usually will not fund over 65% loan-to-value ratio on any commercial real estate.

Foreign investors

Foreign investors are becoming an increasingly large source of funds for large real estate investments, but they are generally more interested in owning properties than in making loans to finance properties. Sometimes they might make a loan just to get an equity position in a property. Also, they are a good source to join in a venture with another lender on a very large deal.

Mortgage bankers and brokers

This book refers to commercial real estate mortgage brokers and bankers as if they were the same. From the borrower's point of view, that is true. In reality, the mortgage banker can be a direct source of funds and not just a broker. Both types of firms are excellent places to look for commercial and industrial real estate financing.

In fact, in commercial and industrial real estate financing, you *always* start by seeing a commercial mortgage broker or banker first. Why? Unlike the standardization of residential real estate financing, commercial and industrial real estate financing is extremely complex, with every transaction being unique. Unless you are an expert in this field, you need to hire such an expert to have any decent chance of securing the best possible terms. The expert you need is a good mortgage broker who will represent your interests. Experienced mortgage brokers, who have worked with many lending sources on many different transactions, are in the best position to know which source is likely to give you the best terms on the particular property you want to acquire or refinance. Commercial mortgage brokers and mortgage bankers make it their business to know each lender, what types of properties each lender is willing to finance, and what kinds of transactions each lender likes to structure. Brokers carry much more weight with a lender because of the volume of business they bring to the lender. Because of this, they can actually get a much better deal for the borrower than the borrower can as an individual.

The average mortgage broker and mortgage banker are actively involved in the real estate market on a daily basis. They can provide a vital link between borrower and lender. The mortgage broker and banker are constantly aware of the most competitive rates and can help in shaping, structuring, and negotiating the transaction.

How to find a commercial mortgage broker

Practically every city in this country has at least one mortgage brokerage firm with at least one person who specializes in the commercial side of real estate financing. Start by looking under "Real Estate Loans" and "Loans" in the Yellow Pages. Most mortgage brokers listed in the Yellow Pages are residential mortgage brokers, but some firms may state that they specialize in commercial loans.

Most residential mortgage brokerage firms have one or two people who specialize in commercial deals, so you will have to ask if a firm has anyone who handles commercial and industrial properties or the type of property you are looking for.

Start by contacting the brokers who are *closest to the property* you want to buy or refinance. Brokers near the property will know the lenders who are willing to finance properties in that geographical area. Be sure to contact more than one broker. Discuss your real estate interests and business operations, then select the broker who understands your circumstances and will work in your best interests. Let the broker find a number of sources. Compare their rates and other terms. Commercial and industrial financing sources have different requirements and degrees of enthusiasm about financing particular properties and businesses, so you should always be able to select from a choice of sources.

The broker will charge a commission, but it is well worth it.

Venture real estate sources

These people finance the riskier real estate deals and can be neatly put into two categories: (1) hard money lenders and (2) private investors.

Hard money lenders

The term *hard money* in real estate usually means expensive money. A hard money lender can be a company or an individual who lends directly or arranges for others to make hard money loans. They are lending strictly on the value of the property, not the credit of the borrower. They do high-risk real estate loans and are considered a lender of last resort.

Hard money lenders are usually private sources of capital looking for a high return. A hard money broker operates like a mortgage broker by arranging real estate loans but specializes in hard money lenders. Brokers will charge high rates to compensate their investors, and they will also charge a high amount of points to cover their own overhead and profit.

Hard money lenders usually will not lend over 65% of the value of the property.

The advantages of hard money lenders are:

1. They ask few credit questions and confine themselves to the value of the property. They make loans to people who do not qualify from other, more traditional sources. They are true guerrilla financing sources.
2. They can sometimes deliver a loan within a few days.
3. They can usually do a quick drive-by appraisal.
4. They can be used for short-term bridge financing.
5. They can be used to save a property from foreclosure.

   Their disadvantages are:

1. They are expensive and charge from 3 to 15 points.
2. Their loans are usually only for a short term — one to three years.

Needless to say, from the borrower's point of view, hard money is a very expensive way to finance real estate. Sometimes, however, it is the only available source. When considering using a hard money loan, be careful that the cost of the money is part of your profit calculations. Sometimes the cost of money is just too expensive to conclude a deal.

How to find hard money lenders

If you check the Yellow Pages under "Real Estate Loans" or "Loans," you will have to make a number of calls to find a hard money lender because while every residential mortgage broker is listed, hard money lenders or brokers don't advertise themselves as such. But when you speak to a mortgage broker, ask if it knows of any hard money lenders. Most mortgage brokers are familiar with at least one hard money lender.

Hard money lenders and brokers sometimes advertise in the newspaper. Look in the classified section under "Real Estate Loans," "Money to Loan," or "Capital Available." If you can't find a hard money lender, try placing an advertisement yourself in the "Money Wanted" section. You might attract a hard money lender or private investor. Your ad should read like this: "Need $100,000. Will give mortgage on well-secured apartment building, call. . . ." People with money to loan read the financial pages and *will* call. See Chapter 12 for more on how to place classified ads for money. And be prepared to shop around for the best rate and terms, because you will find that they vary considerably.

Private venture investors

Private venture investors can either lend to or invest in a commercial real estate transaction. They are different from a hard money lender in that they usually take some equity or ownership position in the real estate project. The private investor will always take the greatest risk and, therefore, is usually offered the greatest chance of gaining from the investment. Whereas a hard money lender may look for a 20% to 30% return, a private venture investor may look for the same high return *plus* equity in the property.

How to find a private venture investor

There are many ways to find and attract private investors, including private and public syndications. Public syndications are usually sold by a licensed securities brokerage firm, which looks for investors for your real estate project. The cost of this type of financing makes it prohibitive for small businesses. Limited private partnerships can be used for a private syndication very effectively on small deals and can be sold by the principals themselves. Both methods are a special and legal way to offer ownership in a real estate transaction. But someone must find the investors, no matter what type of technique you use. Consult a real estate securities attorney and Chapter 13 for advice.

The ideal situation is a private venture investor who takes equity only. More equity in a real estate deal makes it more likely to succeed, since no debt payments have to be made.

A very easy and inexpensive way to attract a private investor for a real estate deal is to advertise in the classified section of a newspaper under "Business Opportunities" or "Capital Wanted." It may be difficult to raise large sums of money this way, but it is an excellent way to raise small amounts.

Even more financing techniques

Guerrillas also use these techniques to find real estate capital:

1. *Debt.* There are many ways to create a mortgage, and you should rely on the lender to find the best vehicle for financing a particular project and suggesting the most appropriate method for your situation.
2. *Private partner.* Private partners usually want a very high return or an ownership position in the property. Taking equity or ownership in the property, of course, requires taking the highest risk, from the investor's point of view, but offers a larger share of the profits from the deal. Again, there are many different tools to use, from private to public securities. Your legal counsel and securities underwriter can be most helpful on a private partner financing transaction.
3. *Participating mortgages.* Here, the financial source obtains a share

of the property's income and/or sales price without assuming an equity interest in the property. This is an ideal instrument to use to convince a lender to go into a risky real estate transaction.

4. *Seller financing.* Always try to get the seller of the property to take some amount back and hold a note for it. Economically, this method is very advantageous for the borrower. The seller is usually anxious to sell and will offer terms and rates on a loan that most lending institutions cannot match.

5. *Sale and leaseback.* The owner of a property sells the property to an investor and at the same time leases it back. The owner thereby frees up his or her investment into cash, and the investor gets the depreciation.

6. *Contributions of land by the landowner.* An additional source of financing is the contribution of land by the landowner to a partnership in lieu of the purchase of land. The owner can contribute the value of the land to help in the financing and take an equity stake in the project.

7. *Lease of land.* Instead of buying the land, you may consider leasing the land and just own the buildings on it. In most cases, the property would revert to the lessor at the end of the term of the lease, but the term is usually of sufficient length for the borrower to realize substantially all of the economic benefit from the project. You must obtain a lease of about 35 years or more to qualify for this type of financing, and it must be assignable to the lender. This is a difficult type of financing for which to find a source, but it can be done.

Commercial real estate terminology

You shouldn't have to become an overnight expert in real estate to raise capital for commercial and industrial real estate transactions. But if you are dealing in this type of financing, you should become acquainted with the following terminology.

Interest rate. Rate refers to the percentage used in calculating the interest you will have to pay on the money you borrow.

Maturity. Maturity refers to the number of years you have in which to repay the loan. If the loan's maturity period is 25 years, you must repay the entire loan within 25 years. If a loan matures, or comes due, in 5 years, you must repay the entire loan by the end of the fifth year.

The amortization period. The amortization period is the number of years used as a basis for calculating the amount of your periodic loan payments. *Amortization schedule* refers to the schedule, or table, of monthly payments you must make on the loan. If the amortization period is 30 years, for instance, 30 years (or 360 months) will be used as your theoretical repayment period for the purpose of calculating the amount of your monthly payments. Keep in mind that an amortization period of 30 years *does not mean* that the lender will give you 30 years to repay the loan. It means only that 30 years was the length of time used in calculating the amount of each monthly payment. The number of years the lender will give you to fully repay the loan is its *maturity period*, not its amortization period.

Maturity period and amortization period are often not the same. For instance, a lender may offer financing with a 30-year amortization period and a 5-year maturity. This means your monthly loan payments will be calculated as if you were paying off the loan over 30 years, but the 5-year maturity means that you must repay the entire balance of the loan at the end of the fifth year, as a final balloon payment. Lenders refer to this as "thirty due in five." A "fully amortized" loan is one where the amortization period is equal to the maturity period, such as "thirty due in thirty." While fully amortized loans are the norm in residential lending, they are rare in commercial and industrial lending. Pay attention to the distinction between amortization period and maturity period so that you will fully understand the terms being offered.

Balloon payments

A balloon payment comes about when you are intentionally not paying enough on your principal to pay off the loan when it becomes due. When the loan matures, comes due, you still owe a substantial amount on the loan. This onetime large payment is called a balloon payment and usually occurs when your maturity date is different from your amortization date. You may amortize the loan over 30 years, but your loan may mature in 10 years. In this case, you will still owe a considerable amount upon maturity. *Be prepared for such payments well in advance.* You don't want to look for financing when you have only a few months until your balloon payment is due. Business real estate loans take time.

Commercial real estate financing is so individual that it is difficult to determine the actual length of time it will take to get financing, so give yourself plenty of time to arrange for it, at least 90 to 120 days.

Loan-to-value

The loan-to-value (LTV) is a ratio showing the maximum amount of money a financing source will lend on a property. It is not 100% of value because of the costs of foreclosure. It is therefore the ratio of the amount of the loan to the value of the property.

Residential lenders can sometimes lend up to 95% of the value of the property. Here, the loan-to-value would be 95%. But the usual loan-to-value on residential property is 80%.

Commercial and industrial property's usual loan-to-value is 70%, which means, in order to buy a commercial property, you must put 30% down and can borrow 70%.

Raw land has a loan-to-value of only 50%.

Refinancing

Refinancing is when you pay off your existing mortgages with another mortgage that has better terms, or you pay off your existing mortgages to get some cash out of your property, or perhaps a combination of the above. Unless you desperately need the cash, there is no sense in refinancing unless there is a clear and definite economic reason to do so, such as getting better interest, longer maturity, or longer amortization on the new loan.

Construction financing

Construction loans are special-purpose short-term loans designed to finance the construction of a building. They are usually made by banks and are for the duration of the construction only. The money is advanced as the contractor needs it. For example, if it takes 12 months to build a hotel, the construction loan might consist of twelve monthly payments until the building has been completed. Most lenders will not fund a construction loan until the borrower has obtained a "take-out loan commitment" or a long-term loan from another lender. You must secure your long-term financing before the construction lender will start to disburse the construction funds. The long-term lender "takes you out" of the construction loan. That is, it pays off the construction lender upon completion of the project.

Construction lenders will take an interest reserve out of the loan so that the borrower will not have to make interest payments during the course of the loan. They will also take out a contingency reserve to cover any contingencies or overages that may arise during construction. You pay interest only on the money you borrow.

Check out your lease

Now that you are learning about financing commercial real estate, you might want to examine your current lease agreement to see if the owner allows you to buy the property. Most renters don't realize that some leases have this option. Check it out!

Your real estate as a source of funds

Remember, as your own property appreciates in value, the property itself will become a growing source of cash or collateral. Through additional borrowing or refinancing on your property, you can help fund the growth of your business.

8
All About
Government Financing

Welcome to one of the largest single sources of funds available to small businesses. Here is your chance to get back some of those hard-earned tax dollars. Tap into government or quasi-government programs that offer the entrepreneur financial assistance. Look at *all levels of government* — federal, state, and local.

Know up front that state and local programs and agencies are as active as the federal government when it comes to financing assistance for small businesses. But don't knock the generous federal programs in the United States, including the Small Business Administration's Loan Guarantee Program, which today, regretfully, requires substantial collateral for you to qualify. But don't fear, there are lots of other programs available.

Guerrilla financiers realize that federal, state, and local government financing sources have funds for multitudes of small businesses. At the federal level alone are 1,078 programs administered by 57 different agencies. Read here about the more popular programs, then read how to find out about *all* of them. You will be surprised by the number and variety of agencies and programs available to citizens at all levels of government.

You may have heard horror stories about how difficult it is to get financial assistance from any government program. The stories may be true, but they do not necessarily mean that you will tell the same story. Some people get SBA loans in weeks. Others take years. Sometimes it is what you know, who you know, or just a matter of luck — preparation meeting opportunity.

It is true that there is no easy way to get financing assistance from the government, but there are ways to do it. The process will usually be long, paper-ridden, cumbersome, and time-consuming. You'll need patience and persistence, but there *is* money available. There are *bil-*

lions of dollars in federal, state, and local government programs, funds specifically set aside for small businesses. There is more money in these programs than is actually loaned!

There is a good likelihood that the program for which you apply will be well funded. You will have to investigate to find the right people to talk to at the right time, but the wait can be well worthwhile.

Public financing could be private financing

Government programs are not only public programs. They may also include government-sponsored programs that are managed and operated by *private* organizations.

As you begin to contact these agencies, you will learn that many of them are not part of any government but are private companies that use some government-backed guarantee to fund their loans to small businesses. You may think you are talking to a government official when in fact he or she is just another private businessperson.

Whether these private organizations involved with government programs are for profit or are nonprofit is really not relevant. What is important is that some government organization does exist to help you get money. Getting your fair share is what matters.

What this chapter isn't

This chapter *is not* a listing of every program that is available. Such a listing would be out of date as soon as it is printed because new agencies and programs are being created every day in every state in the Union. Not only are many new programs created, but many old programs are constantly being phased out. Most of these changes are due to changes in the leadership of the various government agencies.

This chapter *is* a way for you to learn what government financing is all about — its aims and goals, understanding the range of programs and services, and how you can apply and qualify for a program suited to your needs. This chapter is basic training for guerrillas.

Don't take no for an answer

Alas, in this great country of ours, the government's right hand does not always know what its left hand is doing. For example, if you request assistance from a particular program and one person tells you no, don't take that no as final. Check with another person in that program. If the second person also says no, you can acknowledge that the answer really is no. If you get a no from the government's right hand, check with the left hand before you give up on that particular program or agency.

Don't be afraid to talk to the director of a program. Go directly to or telephone the department director's office. A woman was waiting for money from a disaster loan for her business. The government agency told her the money would be there in four weeks. She made some calls to the head of that particular agency and was able to get her money in a few *days*. Speak up. Remember your taxes are paying their salaries.

With so many government assistance programs covering so many areas, it is difficult to imagine that your business is somehow not eligible for any of them. Ultimately, there is nothing magical about getting financial assistance from the government; your success will depend on finding the right program and persevering until you get the funds you need. If there is one thing that separates the winners from the losers in pursuing government assistance, it is perseverance.

Two points to consider when dealing with the government

1. Don't assume that one agency at the state or federal level is aware of what any other agency is doing.

2. Before beginning any loan application, ask the agency or institution the number of applications submitted and the number of loans made last year. If, considering the number of applications, there have been relatively few loans, it may not be a good investment of your time to seek help from that particular funding program.

Think local

When it comes to government financing, every entrepreneur thinks of the SBA, which is the best known federal small business financing program in America. But what is *not* well known is that when you consider all the other federal, state, and local government financing programs, the SBA is just a drop in the bucket.

Many programs at the city and county level are especially exciting as potential financing sources because they are often new and operated by local people who want to help small businesses in their own communities. It is almost always easier to present your proposal to a neighbor than to some unknown government official.

Guerrillas start their inquiries about government financing at the local level and work their way up to the state and federal levels.

Most local government sources are private development companies that work in conjunction with government agencies and programs to provide funding and other types of assistance to small businesses. Just about every major city and county in the country has one of these development companies or agencies. Their job is to help develop more business, jobs, and revenues for the communities and counties in which they operate. Surprisingly, perhaps, you will usually find them anxious to listen to your proposal because they want to find businesses they can help.

Successful businesses encourage economic growth, which translates into more jobs, stronger communities, and increased tax revenues. Local governments feel that if they can provide enough incentives for business development, businesses will be attracted by these programs and operate in their jurisdictions.

How many times have you noticed almost overnight development in an otherwise run-down part of town? Local government was at work giving incentives to businesses that wanted to locate in these areas and rebuild the city.

Many cities and counties have established industrial development authorities to issue tax-exempt bonds. These are industrial revenue bonds that promote new and expanded business. Some government groups are called industrial development agencies and are considered public benefit corporations under the state's municipal laws. Other communities have established downtown development authorities, which are responsible for tax-exempt notes to be used for commercial revitalization.

Some areas have created locally operated revolving loan pools that are controlled by city or county governments.

There should be something set up to help you, regardless of the type of financing used by your community.

How to get local assistance

Contact your city and county or township governments to find out what assistance they have for you. Elected officials, such as a mayor, are usually *not* the people to start with. See the people who actually run the local governments. Try the city manager — just about every city has one. Chambers of commerce and local bankers are also rich sources of information about local funding programs and agencies.

Guerrillas have good luck finding funds because they know the guerrilla's funding source book: the phone book. Start by looking in the white pages under local governments. Look for an agency that has *industrial development* or *economic development* in its name. Turn to the white pages under the name of your city or town and your county, and again look for an agency that has *industrial development* or *economic development* in its name.

A telephone call will probably yield the initial information you need, some descriptive literature, and an appointment for a follow-up interview. By contacting a number of people and explaining your unique situation, you may get referrals to other agencies and programs of interest — then, finally, money.

The rules to follow

As you contact local development companies and agencies, keep several important things in mind. Even though there is an agency in your city, you do not have to limit your efforts to that agency. It is a good idea to contact agencies in neighboring cities and counties. A neighboring agency might offer you a better deal. Also, remember that you are looking not only for sources for *funding* but also for sources of *information* that might lead you to other sources of funding. The more people you talk to, the more leads you will find, and the more you will learn about the ways in which government at all levels is trying to help small businesses.

Setting up your own agency

If for some reason there is no local development corporation or industrial development agency in your area, try setting one up yourself! Usually you would incorporate as a nonprofit organization with public or quasi-public objectives to make financial assistance available to companies in your city or county. Check for any state or federal financial help that is available to help your *development corporation* get off the ground. Your funds will come mainly from your local city officials because they want the new jobs and added tax revenue. Attracting new business, holding on to existing businesses, and even just encouraging local businesses to expand are the goals of every development organization.

State programs

State governments are really gearing up to help small businesses get established in their state. In all fifty states you now have a choice of *hundreds* of agencies and programs to help small businesses raise capital. Their motives are not purely altruistic, of course; new jobs and a healthy economy are the prizes for any community or region that can attract new business. Some states have developed attractive inducements for businesses to move into their states. As we enter the twenty-first century, a state's main objective is to offer incentives in the form of both financial and technical assistance aimed at encouraging business growth and bringing new investment and business into the state.

The incentives at the state level fit into four categories: (1) direct financial incentives; (2) tax benefits; (3) technical assistance; and (4) incubators.

Direct financial incentives

1. *State direct loans.* Most of the states offer direct loan programs. Most of them are aimed at providing fixed-asset financing, such as equipment and real estate financing, but there are some state programs that are unsecured and will finance working capital needs. Many loans are provided in the form of revolving funds in order to make the most of the state's limited allocation of capital. Sometimes the state's direct loans are part of a package that includes a commercial loan from a bank or finance company, with the state making another loan that is subordinated to the commercial loan. A state's direct loans usually carry a below-market interest rate.

2. *Loan guarantee programs.* A loan guarantee is not a direct loan but a guarantee that a loan made by a financial institution will be paid by the state in the event of default by the borrower. This type of financing is very popular because the state does not have to actually use any funds, only guarantee the loans. The problem with this type of financing is that the borrower must not only qualify under the state guarantee program but also under the actual lending institution's loan program.

3. *Security deposit programs.* Here, funds are deposited into the financial institutions that agree to provide low-interest loans to businesses specified by the state. This is an interest-decreasing program that encourages private lenders to make loans to small businesses at rates more favorable than those available on the open market.

4. *Industrial development bonds.* IDBs are the most common financial incentive for business at the state level. *All fifty states issue IDB bonds.* The interest earned on an industrial development bond is federally tax exempt so that the states can easily sell the bonds.

   The money from the sale of these bonds is loaned to businesses at low rates to subsidize the financing of land, site development, or other large fixed assets. These loans are usually fairly large and are an ideal source for a company that wants to buy or build its own facilities.

5. *Umbrella or pooled industrial development bonds.* These bonds are used to meet the financing needs of several small projects. The loans are grouped into a package, and the bonds are sold when a certain minimum is reached. This way, small business loans can

be provided for projects too small to qualify for the general revenue industrial development bond program. Again, the loans from this program are usually made to help companies finance the acquisition of land, buildings, machinery, and equipment. Borrowers usually pay below-market interest rates for long-term maturities.

6. *Grants.* A grant is the most lucrative form of direct financing because it usually does not have to be paid back. As you might have guessed, state grants are not as common as the other sources of state funds we've mentioned. Most often, states give grants to communities to underwrite the various costs of economic development, such as building or improving the physical infrastructures of buildings, supporting research and development projects, and supporting local development projects.

7. *Equity venture capital programs.* A new trend in state financing is the equity investment program, where the state provides risk or venture capital to assist business start-ups and expansion. This program is geared to provide financing for firms with rapid growth potential or firms that produce innovative products or processes that would not be eligible for conventional financing. You might call this guerrilla government financing.

8. *Target programs.* Some states have target programs for small, minority, or disadvantaged businesses. Ask about them.

Tax incentives

Tax incentives are provided to new and developing companies in a state to reduce the company's tax burden, thereby increasing its chances of survival. The incentives consist of tax credits, tax deductions, and even tax exemptions. Sometimes you can get a tax abatement or tax rate reduction.

A good example of tax assistance is the creation of "enterprise zones." An enterprise zone is usually a distressed area of the state that is looking for economic growth; any business locating in that zone receives certain tax advantages.

Technical assistance

Here the state, through various agencies, provides technical and management assistance and entrepreneurial training to help and encourage small business enterprises. Many states have opened small business assistance offices as part of their development agencies. These offices provide personalized assistance, seminars, management training, and loan assistance.

Incubators

A new approach to helping small businesses is the creation of incubators by the state. The incubator is the creation of shared facilities and services below market rates. The incubator leases space to specific tenants qualified by the state and offers management support and other services such as secretarial, fax, copying, and answering services. Many times these incubator facilities are near a university, enabling the new entrepreneurs to tap into facilities normally not readily available, such as computer services, patent searches, libraries, and other technical expertise.

Business development corporations

Business development corporations (BDCs) are chartered by the states to make loans to small businesses. They are probably the most flexible and innovative quasi-governmental lending institutions you'll ever discover. They are owned by private individuals, financial institutions, and even large corporations. Funding for these corporations is generally provided by individual financial institutions and corporations whose interests are served by making small business loans and increasing the availability of jobs.

The BDCs can do any or all of the following:

1. Make conventional loans, secured or unsecured.
2. Enter into purchase/leasebacks where they might buy or build, then lease back a plant for a small company.

3. Make SBA-guaranteed loans.
4. Provide venture capital.

Where to find state financing

Start with your library's research department under State Agencies. Or consult your friend, the white pages of your or any other state capital's phone book. Listed under the state's name will be all the development and economic agencies. Next, contact the state chamber of commerce. It will have a list of state programs and agencies. Remember to look for the words *development, industrial,* and *economic.*

For a list of Small Business Development Centers, contact:

Association of Small Business Development Centers
1050 Seventeenth Street N.W., #810
Washington, D.C. 20036
202-887-5599

For a list of incubators in your area, contact:

National Business Incubation Association
One President Street
Athens, Ohio 45701
614-593-4331

If these sources don't supply the money you need, contact your local state representative for advice and information.

Federal financing programs

At last you come to the big spender, the federal government. How can you get money from the federal government? Ask! Yes, ask everyone you will come in contact with as you search through the various programs and agencies that are available to you. As you know, the government is into everything. What you may not know is that the government is into helping small businesses raise capital.

Many government loans and loan guarantees, even though they are funded at the local or state level, come from federal agencies. Here are the major programs and agencies, starting with the SBA.

The Small Business Administration

In 1953, in an effort to stimulate the growth of small businesses and to encourage entrepreneurs, Congress established an independent federal agency called the Small Business Administration (SBA). The SBA's sole purpose is to assist small business concerns. It does this partly by providing management and technical assistance services, but mainly by helping small businesses obtain money on reasonable terms. Its Loan Guarantee Program provides loan guarantees to small businesses that lack creditworthiness and/or access to larger capital markets.

Since its inception, the SBA has expanded considerably and has become a significant force in the growth and development of small business in this country. One small peanut farmer in Georgia received an SBA loan; he went on to become the president of the United States.

The scope of the SBA's programs is vast, and the number of businesses that stand to benefit from them is enormous. Some 95% of all the businesses in the United States qualify as a small business as defined by the SBA. Yet too few businesses take advantage of the SBA, perhaps due to widespread misconceptions concerning its policies and functions.

The big misconception is that people think the SBA makes mostly direct loans. That is incorrect. Most SBA loans are made by banks and other special lending institutions. All the SBA does is guarantee repayment to the lender if the borrower defaults. So the bulk of the SBA's lending program is really *only a guarantee program, not a direct loan program.* The two most popular SBA programs are the 7(a) and the 504 programs. The rest are very specialized programs for specific situations.

SBA loan programs

A list of most of the available SBA programs is presented here for the serious entrepreneur.

Guaranteed loan program. In this excellent program, the loans are made by private financial institutions and guaranteed by the SBA. These lending institutions take more of a risk and offer better terms to the borrower because of the federal guarantee. Your local SBA office would have a list of lenders under this program. This is the most popular program of all the SBA programs. Its two main categories are:

1. *7(a) Program.* Working capital, equipment, and real estate lending program. Under this broadest and largest of all the SBA loan programs, loans are made by lending institutions approved by the SBA and range from $50,000 to $1 million. Always start with this program because it is the most flexible. Contact the SBA for a list of active 7(a) lenders in your area.
2. *504 Program.* This is a participating program where both the lending institution and the SBA participate in the loan. It is used for real estate and heavy equipment. Loans can go up to $3 million and more. Contact the SBA for a list of 504 lenders.

Direct loan program. You must apply directly to the SBA for these loans, and they are very hard to get. The following is a brief description of some of them. For more information, contact your local SBA office.

1. *Economic opportunity loans.* Loans to socially or economically disadvantaged entrepreneurs or minorities.
2. *Handicapped assistance loans.* A direct loan program for those individuals who are handicapped.
3. *Disaster loans.* Loans to help victims (businesses) of natural or economic catastrophes.
4. *Small business energy loans.* Loans to small businesses engaged in the manufacturing, selling, installing, servicing, or developing of specific energy measures.
5. *Contract loan program.* Open to small construction contractors, service firms, and manufacturing companies providing a specific product or service under an assignable contract. The loan is made to fulfill the terms of the contract.
6. *Pollution control financing guarantees.* Loans to small businesses engaged in the planning, design, or installation of pollution control facilities.
7. *Surety bond guarantees.* Guarantees to private surety companies to help small contractors obtain a contract.
8. *Certified development company loans.* Construction and real estate development loans where the project costs are funded by not more than 50% from federal dollars.
9. *Displaced business loans.* Loans to businesses that suffer economic injury from federal, state, or locally assisted construction projects, such as businesses that have to relocate because of a highway or housing project.
10. *Economic injury loans.* Loans to businesses that have losses as a

result of complying with standards established under various government health and safety acts.

11. *Economic dislocation loans.* Assistance to businesses that have suffered substantial injury as a result of so-called economic dislocation, generally caused by a shift in the purchasing power of their customers.

12. *Export revolving line of credit (ERLC).* Financing pre-export production and marketing development. A company must be in business for more than one year to qualify.

13. *Pool loans.* Loans to corporations formed and capitalized by groups of small businesses, which pool their resources in order to purchase — for use in each separate business — raw materials, equipment, inventories, supplies at quantity discounts, research and development, or new facilities for that purpose.

14. *Coal mine health and safety loans.* Loans to businesses that suffer economic injury as a result of complying with the Coal Mine Health and Occupational Safety acts.

15. *Consumer protection loans.* Loans to businesses that suffer economic injury as a result of complying with the Egg Products Inspection Act, the Wholesale Poultry Act, or the Wholesale Meat Act.

16. *Occupational health and safety loans.* Loans to businesses that suffer economic injury as a result of complying with the Occupational Health and Safety Act.

17. *Strategic arms economic injury loans.* Loans to businesses that suffer economic injury as a result of cutbacks or the installation of certain federal projects and programs.

18. *Base closing economic injury loans.* If a federal military installation closes or is severely reduced in size and scope, causing economic injury to your firm, you may be eligible for these loans.

19. *Air pollution control loan program.* Loans to businesses that suffer economic injury as a result of complying with the requirements of the Clean Air Act.

20. *Water pollution control loan program.* These loans are open to just about any business likely to suffer economic injury as a result of meeting any water pollution control requirement.

21. *Emergency energy shortage economic injury loan program.* Available to small firms that have suffered, or are likely to suffer, from shortages of fuel, electrical energy, or energy-producing resources, or shortages of raw or processed materials resulting from energy shortages.

22. *Loans for veterans and disabled veterans.* Special loan programs have been developed for veterans of recent wars or combat missions.

Advantages of an SBA loan

1. *Long maturities.* Only through the SBA program can you get a 7-year working capital loan, a 10-year equipment loan, and a 25-year fully amortized real estate loan. Real estate loans only require a 10% down payment, versus a 30% down payment for a private commercial and industrial real estate loan. You can even combine all three uses of the money and get a 15-year working capital, equipment, and real estate loan. Imagine having 15 years to pay off a working capital loan! Just calculate your return on the value of that money each year and you will see the tremendous advantages of an SBA loan. No private program can match these terms.
2. *Competitive interest rates.* SBA loans usually carry rates that are lower than market rates.
3. *Capital leverage.* Banks usually only offer a debt-to-equity ratio of 2:1, while the SBA can go up to 4:1. In other words, for every dollar of capital you put into your business, you can borrow four dollars. SBA loans allow you to increase the leverage on your money.
4. *No prepayment penalties.* If you decide to pay off part or all of your loan, there is no penalty to do so.
5. *Easier eligibility.* This is the biggest advantage. When a bank turns you down, if you can get an SBA guarantee, that same bank might make the loan because of the protection of the federal guarantee.
6. *Unique collateral.* Aggressive SBA lenders use all kinds of interesting things as collateral, including personal collectibles such as paintings, jewelry, classic cars, and antiques.

Disadvantages of an SBA loan

1. *Collateral requirements.* SBA loans are not giveaways. Most loans are secured with some sort of collateral. Just because the federal government is guaranteeing up to 90% of the loan doesn't mean

the institution actually making the loan will not heavily qualify the borrower as to credit and secondary collateral to support the loan. Today, the majority of financial institutions making SBA guarantee loans require that at least 50% of the loan be collateralized by real estate or some other very good collateral. Most SBA lenders require close to 100% collateralization. It is rare to find an SBA lender that will make an unsecured loan.

2. *Paperwork*. It never ends, but it is not as bad as you might expect. Use an SBA packager to do the work for you. The packager helps put together all the legal documentation necessary. Packagers know the ropes and can make the entire process easier for you. Your local SBA office can recommend a qualified SBA packager.

3. *Time*. This has improved dramatically, but an SBA loan still takes longer than a private loan.

4. *Restrictions*. Besides personally guaranteeing the loan, the SBA will place certain restrictions on your freedom to run your business. How much you can spend and what you can use it for will be closely monitored by the institution making the SBA loan. Also, you will have to report your financial condition to the lender every year. Many of these restrictions would also apply to non-government-sponsored loans.

5. *Double requirements*. You have to go through two qualifications to get an SBA guarantee loan. First, you have to qualify under the financial institution you are applying to, then you have to be approved by the SBA.

Though an SBA loan is a participating loan made by a financial institution with a federal government guarantee, the lending institution is still going to require the borrower to meet its normal lending requirements plus the SBA's lending requirements. So to get an SBA guarantee loan, you have to meet two sets of financial requirements.

The value of an SBA loan

After comparing all the advantages and disadvantages, if you can qualify for an SBA loan, take it. Except for straight real estate financing, the terms of an SBA loan are almost always better than you could get privately.

Aggressive and conservative SBA lenders

Keep in mind that when one SBA lender turns you down, another might accept you. Among these lenders, as in any market, there are aggressive and conservative lenders. Even though the SBA qualifications are the same, the actual lender's qualifications may vary. Some SBA lenders might want 100% real estate to support a loan, and some might want only 50%.

How do you find out? First, get a list of the active SBA lenders from your local SBA office. Then submit your package to a number of lenders to find out who is aggressive and who is conservative.

How do I know that I qualify as a small business?

Don't worry about being eligible as a small business to apply for an SBA loan. Nearly 95% of all businesses in the United States are eligible to apply for an SBA loan.

How to get in touch with the SBA

There are SBA offices throughout the country. Look in the white pages of your phone book under "United States Federal Government." If the SBA is not listed, call the federal government information number for the nearest office. Or contact the SBA directly:

U.S. Small Business Administration
1441 L Street N.W.
Washington, D.C. 20416
800-368-5855 or 202-653-6570

Other federal agencies

The SBA is only one federal agency that offers financial help to small businesses. The following is a list of some of the other major federal programs and agencies offering help.

The Office of Small and Disadvantaged Business Utilization (OSDBU). A disadvantaged business is a business, more than 50% of which is owned or controlled by one or more socially and economically disadvantaged persons. They are socially disadvantaged because of their identification as members of certain groups that have suffered the effects of discriminatory practices or similar insidious circumstances over which they have no control. They include women, black Americans, Hispanic Americans, Asian-Pacific Americans, American Indians, and Mexican Americans. For more information, contact:

Office of Small and Disadvantaged Business Utilization
400 7th Street S.W., Room 9410
Washington, D.C. 20590
202-366-5335

Minority Business Development Agency. The following programs are administered by this agency:

Minority Business Development Center Program
Export Development Program
American Indian Program
Rural Assistance Program
Franchise Assistance Program
State and Local Government Program
Volunteer Managing Support Program
Research Information Program
Minority Trade Association Program
National Minority Supplier Development Council Program
Advocacy Assistance Program
Interagency Working Group for Minority Business
Minority Business Opportunity Committee Program
Information Clearinghouse Program

If you feel you may qualify, contact:

Minority Business Development Agency
U.S. Department of Commerce
14th Street between Constitution & E Streets N.W.
Washington, D.C. 20230
202-377-1936 or 202-377-2414

Overseas Company Promotion. Here, the government helps in exporting and importing. The loan program is limited to businesses that have been in business for at least twelve months. Contact the SBA or Department of Commerce.

Department of Energy Loans. The following are some of the energy-related loan programs:

Research and Development in Energy
Research and Development in Fission, Fossil, Solar, Geothermal,
   Electric Storage Systems, and Magnetic Fusion
Basic Energy Sciences, High Energy, and Nuclear Physics
Advanced Technology and Assessments Projects
Electric and Hybrid Vehicle Loan Guarantees
American Indian Energy Production and Efficiency
Biomass Loan Guarantees
Coal Loan Guarantees
Geothermal Loan Guarantees

For more information about any one of these programs, contact:

U.S. Department of Energy
1000 Independence Avenue S.W.
Washington, D.C. 20585
202-586-8000 or 202-586-8210

Export-Import Bank. These are financing programs for U.S. exporters that enable them to compete effectively in other countries. For information, contact:

Office of Exporter Credits and Guarantees
Export-Import Bank of the U.S.
811 Vermont Avenue N.W.
Washington, D.C. 20571
800-424-5201

Small Business Innovation (Investment) Research Program (SBIR). This program offers working capital grants from $50,000 to $500,000 to companies completing a research and development project or commercializing a proprietary product developed for the U.S. government. See Grants, later in this chapter.

Department of Housing and Urban Development. Mortgage loans for builders of housing and renewal projects are available. For more information, contact:

U.S. Department of Housing and Urban Development
451 Seventh Street S.W.
Washington, D.C. 20410
202-472-3947

Maritime Administration. These loans promote the construction of merchant vessels. Contact the U.S. Department of Commerce.

Overseas Private Investment Corporation. It makes direct or guaranteed loans to businesses doing business with friendly developing nations. Contact:

Overseas Private Investment Corporation
1615 M Street N.W.
Washington, D.C. 20527
800-424-6742 or 202-457-7200

Farmers Home Administration. See Chapter 9.

Department of Commerce's Economic Development Administration. Get to know about it.

1. *Business development assistance program.* Helps businesses in redevelopment areas finance the cost of land, buildings, equipment, and working capital.
2. *Protection from imports.* This program makes loans to businesses adversely affected by the increased competition from cheaply manufactured goods imported from overseas.
3. *Special economic development and adjustment assistance program.* Grants to businesses in regions threatened with economic deterio-

ration due to the loss of a major employer or a succession of smaller employers, whether that loss is due to relocation, depletion of natural resources, compliance with environmental regulations, the closing of a military installation, or some other related cause. Contact:

U.S. Department of Commerce
14th Street and Constitution Avenue N.W.
Washington, D.C. 20230
202-377-2000

Commodity Credit Corporation. Helps entrepreneurs produce and market agricultural products abroad. Contact:

Commodity Credit Corporation
U.S. Department of Agriculture
14th Street and Independence Avenue S.W.
Washington, D.C. 20003
202-447-8732

Aid for International Development (AID). Specific export financing to specific countries.

Guerrilla Financing has listed only a small number of programs. For a complete list and more information on each program, you can order the following documents:

Catalog of Federal Domestic Assistance
Office of Management and Budget
Superintendent of Documents
U.S. Government Printing Office
Washington, D.C. 20402

Small Business Guide to Government
U.S. Small Business Administration
Office of Advocacy
1441 L Street N.W.
Washington, D.C. 20416

For more information about federal programs, call 202-472-1082.

Federal grants

Sometimes you can get money in the form of grants or money that does not have to be paid back. These are not bailouts or charity programs. They are carefully designed federal government assistance programs to encourage the growth of small businesses. In order to get a grant, you must fill out an application. Usually these applications are very long and detailed and force you to think out your project in great detail. The bad news is that 90% of all federal grant proposals fail, mainly because the applicants failed to do their homework. When looking for any grant, government or private, hire an expert, a grant consultant, to help you plan your project. This person will help you fill out your application correctly and make your project sound more reasonable, thereby increasing your chances of getting the grant and often increasing its size.

Federal grant programs

Just about every department in the federal government has many grant programs going at the same time. Write to them and ask for a list of their grants. From a business point of view, research grants are the most lucrative. The most aggressive small business federal grant program is called the Small Business Innovation Research Program.

Small Business Innovation Research Program

This federal program requires federal agencies and departments to allocate part of their research and development budgets to qualifying small businesses. The nationwide program supports creative advanced research in scientific and engineering areas. It is designed to encourage the conversion of the research and development into technological innovation and commercial application.

The real objective of the program is to stimulate high-quality research and to increase the incentive and opportunity for small firms to undertake cutting-edge, high-risk, or long-term research that has a potential payoff if the research is successful. The program fosters research that explores advanced ideas that can lead to important technology breakthroughs, innovative products, or to the next generation of a product or process. It funds the gap between a research-based idea and a prototype that can then be supported by private sources.

This program is *not* an assistance program for small businesses. It is highly competitive and based on merit.

The grants range from $50,000 to $500,000 and do not have to be paid back.

Be sure to understand that faulty compliance on your part to the vast body of disclosure and reporting requirements of the U.S. government can cause you to lose some or all of your ownership rights to the product or technology you develop under this program.

How to apply for the Small Business Innovation Research Program

Following is a list of the government agencies and departments that award these grants, and their phone numbers:

Department of Agriculture	202-475-5022
Department of Commerce	202-377-1472
Department of Defense	202-697-9383
Department of Education	202-357-6065
Department of Energy	301-353-5867
Department of Health and Human Services	202-634-1305
Department of Transportation	617-494-2051
Environmental Protection Agency	202-382-5744
National Aeronautics and Space Administration	202-453-2848
National Science Foundation	202-357-7527
Nuclear Regulatory Commission	301-443-7770

Write to the SBIR Program Director of each department or agency, or contact:

Office of Innovation Research and Technology
U.S. Small Business Administration
1441 L Street N.W.
Washington, D.C. 20416
202-653-6458

Preferential procurement programs

Books on how to get government money for your business are usually talking about *doing business with the government*. It is true that the federal government buys a lot of goods and services, and a certain percentage of those goods and services by law must be bought from small businesses. To find out what preferential programs would be right for your business, contact your local SBA office. There you can learn how your company can provide appropriate products and services needed by the government. You can request information on government buying methods, the products and services bought, the agencies that buy them, and the necessary steps in getting on bidder lists. You can also get involved with the SBA's Certificate of Competency program to demonstrate to the government your company's ability to provide a satisfactory product or service.

Once you have established yourself with the SBA, you can take steps to get involved with the SBA's Procurement Automated Source System (PASS). This computerized referral system informs government agencies and prime contractors of your company's services.

To find out what government contracts are available at the local and state levels, contact your local and state departments of commerce.

Federal programs for women and minorities

If 51% of your company is owned by a woman or a minority or a handicapped individual, there are preferential programs for the company. The four main programs are:

The Small Business Set-Aside Program. This program is geared to give small businesses an advantage when bidding on government contracts or requesting government assistance. To find out if you qualify, contact your local Department of Commerce.

Labor Surplus Set-Asides. These are contracts awarded to companies located in areas of high unemployment. Again, contact your local Department of Commerce.

Small Business Innovation Research Program Set-Asides. Most federal agencies have a Small and Disadvantaged Business Department. Check with them to see if you qualify for a percentage of the research grants.

Minority Business Set-Asides. Small minority businesses get preferential treatment in obtaining a government contract. The SBA can help you find out if you qualify.

State and local programs for women and minority businesses

Most states and communities across the nation have policies to ensure equitable opportunities, or even preferential treatment, for disadvantaged individuals or minorities and women. To see if you qualify for these Small and Minority Business Advocacy (SMBA) programs, contact your state Department of Commerce, your local economic development office, your local Chamber of Commerce, or your local Office of Minority Business Development.

The SMBA program requires state and local government contractors to involve small and minority businesses in their subcontracting and procurement activities.

Finding federal government assistance through government bookstores

Each year the department offices and agencies of the federal government prepare and release thousands of publications, many of which concern themselves with financing programs. An excellent place to start is your local government bookstore, called Government Printing Office Bookstores and Distribution Centers. Your nearest major library can tell you where it is, or write to:

Superintendent of Documents
The U.S. Government Printing Office Bookstore
Washington, D.C. 20402

Two important publications that are available from the government bookstores are:
The Annual Catalog of Federal Domestic Assistance. A list of all federal programs.

The States and Small Business: A Directory of Programs and Activities. A list of the most active state and local programs.

Accessing federal funds through the Department of Commerce

Another bountiful source of information is the local office of the Department of Commerce. The department has offices in every state, and you can get a list from your library or write to the Department of Commerce at:

U.S. Department of Commerce
14th Street and Constitution Avenue N.W.
Washington, D.C. 20230
202-377-2000

If you still can't find help, contact your federal legislators, your congressman, or your senator. After all, you are a voter and taxpayer. They usually can get you the information you require. If you still need help, you can write to:

Chairman
U.S. Senate Small Business Committee
U.S. Senate, Room SR-428A
Washington, D.C. 20510

Chairman
U.S. House Small Business Committee
U.S. House of Representatives, Room 2361 RHOB
Washington, D.C. 20515

Guerrillas turn to their governments for financing help. And because they are aware of so many local, state, and federal sources, you can be confident that they get the money they need to use as they want.

9
All About Agricultural Financing

Agricultural financing is *not* just for farmers; it is open to any business involved in agriculture or the production of commodities. Even if you don't generally think of yourself as a farmer, don't overlook agricultural sources of financing. The Department of Agriculture helps all kinds of businesses in rural areas, towns, or cities with a population below 50,000. The Farm Credit Administration can help a business of any size.

The two main sources of funds are the Farm Credit Administration, a federal agency that administers a cooperative association of private lending institutions, and the Farmers Home Administration, a subdivision of the Department of Agriculture that covers many farm and rural programs.

The Farm Credit Program

The Farm Credit Program is set up to help small businesses involved in a wide range of commodity and agricultural operations. In fact, this program offers short-term and long-term financing to just about any type of agricultural operation, including those that produce tree, vine, and row crops, livestock, dairy animals and products, and nursery stock and cut flowers. It also assists commercial fishing operations. Small businesses involved in the production of just about any commodity may receive financial assistance through the Farm Credit Program.

The Farm Credit Administration

The Farm Credit Administration is the federal agency that administers the Farm Credit Program. The program contains a nationwide network of cooperatively owned lending institutions and associations that are private organizations directed by members of credit cooperatives. The small business borrower actually becomes a member of the cooperative as part of the lending agreement by investing in the stock of the association in proportion to the size of the loan.

The Farm Credit Program consists of two organizations, the Federal Land Bank Cooperative Associations, which provide long-term loans, and the Production Credit Associations, which provide short-term loans.

Federal Land Bank Cooperative Associations

Federal Land Bank Cooperative Associations provide long-term loans, mainly for the purpose of purchasing agricultural real estate. However, these loans may also be used for other purposes, including capital improvements, vineyard and orchard development, land improvements, and the purchase of such things as production machinery, irrigation equipment, and storage facilities.

Production Credit Associations

Production Credit Associations provide short-term loans for operating expenses and working capital needs. These loans are usually granted for a 12-month period to cover such costs as feed, seed, fertilizer, labor, harvesting expenses, chemicals, livestock and poultry expenses, rent, taxes, insurance, and even family living expenses. The loans may also be used to finance commodity processing and marketing expenses. In fact, almost any expense related to running an agricultural business qualifies as a legitimate use of Production Credit Association funds. The loans are usually structured to allow the borrower to draw funds as necessary to meet expenses and to repay the loan according to a schedule based on projections of income from product sales.

How to qualify for farm credit financing

The basic requirements for either long-term or short-term agricultural financing are demonstrated experience and a history of sound financial and operations management. The associations evaluate the financial strength of the borrower and examine cash flow history and cash flow expectations based on the borrower's production and marketing projections. Because agricultural production can be unexpectedly and adversely affected by the weather and other factors, the associations require that the borrower's financial condition be sound enough to withstand some adversity. As you may expect, the loan must be used for purposes that are constructive and beneficial to the borrower's business. And the associations require some type of collateral to secure their financial position.

Farmers Home Administration

The Farmers Home Administration, a subdivision of the Department of Agriculture, provides loans to small enterprises in agriculture and to small businesses in rural areas. A variety of programs provide supplementary sources of credit that are intended to be used as an addition to private sources rather than as a replacement for them. The FHA provides a series of guaranteed loans to develop the economies of communities of up to 50,000 persons.

Department of Agriculture loan programs

- Commodity Loans and Purchases
- Dairy Indemnity Payments
- Emergency Conservation Program
- Export Programs
- Feed Grain Production Stabilization
- Forestry Incentives Program
- Grain Reserve Program
- Grazing Association Loans
- Irrigation, Drainage, and Other Soil and Water Conservation Loans

• National Wool Act Payments
• Rice Production Stabilization
• Rural Clean Water Program
• Storage Facilities and Equipment Loans
• Water Bank Program
• Wheat Production Stabilization

How to contact these programs

Get in touch with your nearest Department of Agriculture office for the address of the Farmers Home Administration and the Farm Credit Administration. Every state has federal Land Bank Associations and Production Credit Associations. Look under Department of Agriculture in your state capital's phone book. Your library's reference department can also give you the names and addresses of whom to contact.

You can also contact the Department of Agriculture at:

Farmers Home Administration
Business and Industrial Loan Program
U.S. Department of Agriculture
14th Street and Independence Avenue S.W.
Washington, D.C. 20250
202-447-7967
or call their general number:
202-447-8867

Do guerrillas obtain agricultural funding? Do scarecrows scare crows?

10
All About
Aggressive Bank Financing

Why waste time with banks?

You are probably reading this book because your bank turned you down
for a loan. Or you may be angry at a particular bank that just called
your loan or told you it won't renew your loan.

So why talk about banks? Because banks make the majority of business loans in this country. The question is, who gets these loans and is
there a chance for you to get a piece of the action?

Is it just a matter of searching for the right bank, the right banker,
and the right time when money will be available for financing? In some
cases, the answer is yes, but in most, it's no. Unless you meet the
qualifications listed in this chapter, you are usually wasting your time.
But if you are on the border, there may be an aggressive bank with an
aggressive banker who will finance your business. It may sound like a
tough task, and it is, but if you are willing to try, this chapter will show
you how.

Why are banks so conservative?

Banks operate the way banks should. Banks are places to keep your
money safe. Would you want your deposits loaned to a small business
without all the safeguards? Absolutely not. Let's face it, the failure rate
of small businesses is extremely high, so why should a banker risk your
deposits in a small business, even *your* business?

Banks and risk are at opposite ends of the spectrum when it comes
to small business financing. You can ask, what about all those loans to
South American countries that defaulted? What about all those loans
to leverage buyout large corporations that then went bankrupt? What

about all those junk bonds bought by banks? There is no logical answer. It is just the way things are in the banking world. What makes you think that financing always makes sense? Banks like to take large risks, not small risks. The small business is a small risk.

What are the uses of a bank loan?

Focus on exactly what types of loans banks make.

Banks are willing to finance just about any asset or for any logical business reason except for starting a business. You may get a bank loan to start a business if you have all the credit and collateral in the world to cover the loss if you don't make it.

You can also apply for an accounts receivable loan, an inventory loan, an equipment loan, a working capital loan, or even a real estate loan.

Why you want the money is not that important

The reason you want the money is really not as important to the bank as much as the risk involved. Whether you want the money to increase assets or to pay off liabilities, the bank is more interested in your ability to repay the loan and your secondary collateral. Secondary collateral is something of value that the bank can use for security if you don't pay the loan back. So you can use the money for just about anything, as long as you can prove you can pay it back and secure it.

What is the length of a bank loan?

The length is directly related to the type of loan. Short-term loans include loans for receivables, inventory, and working capital. Longer-term loans are for equipment and real estate. The term or maturity of the loan is directly related to the type of loan. This makes sense if you understand that the bank wants you to pay the money back as it is used up in the business for the purpose for which it was loaned.

For example, an inventory loan usually finances a seasonal need of a business and should be paid off in 12 months or less when the seasonal need is no longer required. An equipment loan might be for as long as the expected life of the equipment. When the equipment is no longer valuable to the business, the loan for its purchase should have been paid off. Of course, loans for real estate have the longest terms, due to the long-term obligation of the company to pay off the mortgage. Just remember, the length of the loan will depend on the use of the money being borrowed.

Six reasons that can get you a bank loan

Now that you know you can use a bank loan for just about any business purpose, the question is, *how do you get the loan?* To answer that, you have to know what the bank is looking for.

The six top reasons that a bank makes a business loan, in order of importance, are:

1. *Proper evidence of a historically strong cash flow.* Notice the words are *cash flow*, not profits. Your profits may be great, but if you can't collect on your receivables, you just may go out of business. Cash flow is the key.
2. *Collateral that will hold its value throughout the duration of the loan.* A 5-year bank loan can't be collateralized by receivables and inventory. Receivables and inventory are usually financed through a line of credit that must be paid off (cleaned up) for one month each year. But some equipment and all real estate will be around for 5 years, so equipment and real estate secure longer-term loans. Keep in mind that the collateral you use to secure the loan must hold its value throughout the term of the loan.
3. *Historical trends showing a consistent increase in profits and retained earnings.* Where the company is going means a lot to a banker. If the borrower is losing money, why should the bank lend to a loser? Banks want to lend to profitable companies that shouldn't have trouble paying them back. The bank wants to know that those earnings will end up as retained earnings each year, not as a new Cadillac in the owner's garage. Bankers want you to keep the money in the business.
4. *Large financial interest in the business by the owner.* In other words, a high net worth–to–debt ratio.

Is the owner keeping the profits in the business? Does the owner have a large stake in the outcome of the business? If the assets are all pledged, there is not enough equity to support more debt, so why should the bank lend any more money?

5. *Credit.* Does the owner pay his or her bills on time, both personally and in the business? Poor credit is a killer for most bank loans.

6. *The high personal net worth of the owner outside the business.* A strong personal net worth shows that the owner did not blow the profits from the business but used them to build his or her estate.

Of course, there are many more reasons for acceptance, including a large average bank balance. After all, the more you can keep on balance, the more the bank can make on your money.

Five reasons that you can't qualify for a bank loan

The five top reasons that a business bank loan is rejected are, in order of importance:

1. *Poor and/or inconsistent cash flow.* A couple of good months doesn't cut it; your cash flow must be consistent month in and month out.

2. *Insufficient or inappropriate collateral.* Even if you show a good cash flow, poor collateral will kill a deal. Bankers always look at the downside risk. What if you can't make your loan payments? The banker tries to sell off the collateral.

    Suppose you want to finance computers and explain to the bank that it should take the computers as collateral. Most likely the banker will say no because computers lose their value almost the instant they are bought. Bankers or other financing sources don't want to try to sell a computer to pay off a loan. It costs money to foreclose on anything, including real estate.

3. *Historical trends showing inconsistent and/or decreasing profits and retained earnings.* Why should the bank lend to a company with decreasing assets?

4. *A history of the owner's taking all or most of the profits out of the business, producing a low net worth.* The business needs capital

to grow. If you don't invest in your own business, why should the bank?

5. *The minimal net worth of the owner.* You can hide a lot from Uncle Sam, but you can't explain away a small personal net worth and at the same time a large unrecorded cash flow! If you tell your banker that your tax return doesn't reflect your true earnings, you had better have a strong personal net worth. The money has to end up somewhere.

The four C's debt sources want

In going for bank or almost any debt financing, the overriding consideration that determines approval is your ability to repay the loan. Bankers and other debt sources have used the four C's as an expression of criteria for approving loans. It's kind of corny, but you should understand how most bankers think:

Character/credit. Does the borrower appear to have the reputation and good credit history to ensure repayment of the loan?

Capital. Does the borrower have a sufficient amount of equity funds invested in the business?

Capacity. Does the borrower have the skills needed to manage the business profitably?

Collateral. Does the borrower have suitable assets to pledge as collateral?

How do I get money from a bank?

Now you know the in's and out's of what most bankers want. How can a small business qualify, especially a business with weak qualifications? The answer is, you go to an aggressive bank and find an aggressive banker.

Aggressive and still prudent

Aggressive banks do not necessarily take risks. There is a big difference. Aggressive means the bank may lower its qualifications just a bit to make the loan, but not much. Just a bit can mean all the difference in the world, but it still does not mean taking more than a prudent risk.

An aggressive bank is hungry for deposits or loans or both. Who fits that category? Mostly small local banks. The small one- or two-branch bank is ideal. You can almost automatically call this type of bank aggressive because it is usually hungry for new business. It needs your deposits.

The value of your deposits

Banks need deposits to survive and grow. A business with any kind of sales will be making a deposit in a bank. Those deposits have value to the bank. Banks earn money on deposits by lending them out or investing them in some kind of security, such as bonds and U.S. Treasury bills.

The concept is that deposits provide a kind of float for a bank. If you made a deposit today, not all of it is going to be spent from your checking account. Some will constantly remain in the account and be known as the average daily balance. That is the amount of money on which the bank is earning money. The larger your average daily balance, the more the bank values your account. Money that stays in the bank makes money for that bank. Presumably, the larger your sales volume, the larger your deposits in the bank. That is why banks like big customers who make big deposits.

But for a small bank, every deposit is big. It doesn't have the money to spend on aggressive marketing, so it needs deposits and needs to make money on those deposits by investing them or lending them out at a good markup. Therefore, the larger your sales, the more the bank will be interested in considering a loan, sometimes just to get your deposit business.

Why don't small banks just raise their interest to offset the risk?

Most banks, as a rule, don't charge more than three or four points over prime, and they couldn't charge enough interest to offset the risk of losing their depositors' money. Banks just can't charge enough to compensate for those risks.

Finding an aggressive banker is the real secret to getting a bank loan

It is not enough just to find an aggressive bank. You must find an aggressive banker who understands your business and what you are trying to do. Banks don't make lending decisions, bankers do. Banks have loan policies, but the right banker can do wonders with those policies.

The right banker, no matter what bank he or she is in, can work *miracles*. Of course, an aggressive banker in an aggressive bank is the ideal combination.

How to find an aggressive banker

Where are these bankers? How do you spot them? They are out there, in small and large banks anywhere in this country.

Look for a banker who understands your business and has made loans to people in your industry. Even if the aggressive banker is in a large bank, there is a chance that, if he or she likes your business, you will get the money you need.

The real truth is that finding the right banker is more important than finding the right bank.

Check out your local one- or two-branch banks. Visit them and ask for the senior lending officer. If the first thing you are asked is how long you have been in business and how much collateral you have, you are wasting your time. On the other hand, if the banker shakes your hand, gives you a chair, and says, "What can I do for you?" you may just have met an aggressive banker.

Find a banker with clout

The problem today is that very few bankers have the authority to make the final lending decisions. Just finding a banker who knows and likes your business is not enough. That banker must have enough clout to get your loan approved through the bank's loan committee. Sometimes, in a very small bank, the banker you are talking to *is* the loan committee. Always try to meet the senior loan officer. He or she is the one at the bank who usually makes the final lending decision. An aggressive bank's policy is to *find a way to make a loan* if at all possible. There are more and more innovative and creative bankers coming along to give entrepreneurs the opportunity they so justly deserve. You just have to keep hunting for the right person.

How to tell when a bank has money to lend

There are times that banks run out of money or their reserves get low, and they have to tighten their lending standards. When you are talking to banks, find out if they are making business loans; ask about the availability of money. There is no sense exerting your energy with a bank that has reached its lending limit.

You may have met the right bank and the right banker, but if money gets tight, you may as well forget it and try another source.

Tight money just means that the cost of money, the interest, is going up and the supply of money is going down.

Effects of tight money

Tight money not only reduces new loans, it also can hurt the existing borrowers. One man had a loan with a major San Francisco bank, which changed presidents. A few weeks later the new president announced that he was tightening up on the bank's loan portfolio due to what was happening in the economy. The president looked at the man's company financial statement, saw that the man had never missed a payment, but said that this ratio and that ratio were out of line. Soon the man got a letter saying that he had 60 days in which to repay the loan. The loan had been "called." Every loan agreement has provisions allowing the bank to call the loan if the borrower's financial ratios are not kept at a certain level. This owner's company was growing and his ratios had dropped below the allowed levels. No one minded until the new president took over and started to weed out the so-called weak loans.

Every day, companies are being forced out by their banks, companies that have been with major banks for 30 years or more. This type of treatment is a big mistake, yet it is still going on all over the country. With the deregulation of the banking industry, the smaller banks will be bought out by larger banks, making it even more difficult to get financing for small businesses.

Every once in a while, a large bank announces that it wants small business customers, but usually that is just advertising for more deposits. As soon as money tightens up again, it drops its small business accounts like hot potatoes.

What if you have little collateral and weak credit?

The beginning of this chapter said that most small business owners will have difficulty getting bank financing unless they meet or are very close to the bank's lending criteria. If you have little collateral and weak credit, you are too far from a bank's criteria to get any sort of meaningful financing.

On the other hand, you may be able to swing it if you can find that right banker and bank. You will have to spend a lot of time and effort searching. That time and effort can be used trying other sources mentioned in this book. At some point you have to decide to stop trying banks and start trying other avenues.

If you have made up your mind to try for bank financing, do what guerrillas do:

1. *Get the best loan package possible.* If available, hire an accountant or business consultant to prepare the package. See Chapters 14 and 15 on how to prepare your written and oral financing presentation.
2. *Hire a financing consultant who knows some aggressive bankers*

and banks. Get help. If you try to do it yourself, you are going to waste a lot of time tracking down banks and bankers.

3. *Search for a banker who understands your business.* Try to find a banker who understands your business before you look for a bank to make the loan.

4. *Look for a small bank that needs the business.* Look for a banker at a small bank that seems to be more aggressive than large banks.

5. *Give it all you have, and if it doesn't work out, try the other sources and techniques mentioned in this book.* If three or more banks turn you down, your situation is probably not close enough to meet the banks' lending criteria. Don't fret; there are plenty of other choices in the guerrilla financing community.

11
All About
Traditional Venture Capital

Venture capital is risk capital. And who takes risks when it comes to financing businesses? *Venture capitalists.* These investors are not interested in securing the assets of your business. They *are* interested in the cash flow and profits it will generate.

Most of the sources discussed so far are interested in some type of tangible asset to secure the financing. The venture community, however, is interested in *intangible* assets and in how those assets will produce future profits.

The venture capitalist uses equity or debt as the actual investment vehicle. Either way, the risk is very high. It is true that the other sources mentioned may take high risks, but usually their risks are protected to some degree by a lien on a tangible asset. Venture capital's risk is usually protected only by intangible assets such as management expertise, patents, and success formulas.

What you don't hear about venture capital

Most entrepreneurs looking for venture money don't realize that there are two major categories of venture capital: traditional/professional and nontraditional/informal. As you will see, they are as different as night and day.

Most people are surprised that what they know about venture capital covers only a minor percentage of the venture capital sources available. Everyone has been led to believe that traditional or professional venture capital represents the entire venture community. In fact, it represents only 10% of the community but takes credit for 100% of the financings. Every time the media talk about venture capital, they are referring only to the traditional venture community, which represents only the institutional sources and is the *most conservative* source.

A good analogy is the media's coverage of small business in this country. Some 97% of all the 18 million businesses in the United States are small businesses, but you don't read many stories about them in the business section of the newspaper. Hardly anyone spotlights them.

The same goes for informal venture capital. The media are aware only of the professional venture community, so that is what they write about. But 90% of venture capital is created by the nontraditional venture sources, the vast pool of guerrilla venture capital, of which few people are aware!

The main reason that the media and the public have a false view of small business and venture capital is that there is no lobby or spokesperson for small businesses or for the informal venture capital community. Nobody communicates what is *really* happening.

The tragedy is that the average potential entrepreneur reads about how difficult it is to get venture capital and decides not to develop that new technology or introduce that new cost-cutting device. Thus the economy suffers because of misinformation.

Traditional vs. nontraditional

As you read this comparison, you might jump to the erroneous conclusion that, since traditional venture capital would not be appropriate for your situation, you should skip this chapter and go on to the next, which covers the nontraditional venture community. Nothing could hurt your chances more for *nontraditional venture capital.* The more you understand where the traditional venture capitalists are coming from, the more effective you will be in communicating with the nontraditional venture capitalists.

Professional/traditional venture capitalists

These firms are usually partnerships that are funded by large institutions, such as pension funds, insurance companies, major corporations, foundations, and even the government. They are institutionally funded firms staffed by professional money managers who have a fiduciary responsibility to their funding sources to preserve their capital and take only prudent risks.

Professional venture capitalist firms consist of the following types: (1) venture capital firms; (2) venture capital subsidiaries of banks; (3) venture capital subsidiaries of major corporations; (4) Small Business Investment Companies (SBICs); and (5) Minority Enterprise Small Business Investment Companies (MESBICs).

Statistics that are hard to believe

Of the approximately $30 billion of private venture money invested in businesses in the United States each year, approximately $3 billion, or only 10%, comes from the traditional venture community. If that surprises you, the following statistics are going to be downright shocking!

The total number of traditional venture capital firms in the United States is fewer than 1,000, and these firms fund only about 2,000 businesses each year. One third of those 2,000 have received venture financing before, which means that each year, out of the 18 million businesses in this country, only 1,400 companies receive traditional venture financing for the first time! To make matters worse, only 15% of the 1,400 are early-stage or start-up companies, which means that *fewer than 250 start-up businesses* get traditional venture capital each year.

Isn't that outrageous? The media cover only traditional venture capital. That is all that the entrepreneurs in this country know of, and only 250 start-ups in the entire country are funded each year! It seems that entrepreneurs in this country are being led up the wrong path to obtaining capital, since their chances of getting traditional venture capital are astronomically low.

But don't panic. Guerrillas know how to get funded in spite of these gloomy figures.

Nontraditional or informal venture sources

This category represents 90% *of all venture capital*, and very few people know anything about who has it, where it is, and how to get to it! The informal venture community is made up of private investors who put up their *own* capital and don't have to report to anybody except their own conscience. They are the *real* venture capitalists in this country today. Call them *adventurists* because they are the type of people who enjoy the adventure of taking risks. They are the real pioneers in the venture capital world.

Though the informal venture capital community will be covered in detail in the next chapter, you should be aware that this category is actually made up of two groups: the investors (angels) and the advisers to the investors (intermediaries). So that you will know who they are, here is a guide.

Informal venture capital intermediaries
1. Investment banker (underwriter)
2. Venture investment banker (boutique investment banker)
3. Merchant banker
4. Financing consultant
5. Financial planner and adviser
6. Loan broker/money finder
7. Venture clubs
8. Networking organizations

Angels (informal investors)
1. Professionals: doctors, dentists, lawyers, accountants, and other professionals
2. Middle managers
3. Entrepreneurs
4. Associates
5. Relatives and friends

Thank goodness for these statistics

The informal venture community invests over $27 billion in ventures each year, and approximately 50% of that money goes into early-stage businesses! More good news: while only 31% of traditional venture capital goes into financings under $1 million and only 13% into financings under $500,000, the informal venture community invests 90% in financings under $1 million and 82% under $500,000!

The secret to getting any kind of venture financing

Even though the odds of getting traditional venture capital are very slim, to understand the nontraditional marketplace, first understand how the traditional venture capital business operates. When you understand that, the informal venture market becomes a more clearly defined marketing target.

Marketing is the right word, because obtaining any type of venture money, traditional or nontraditional, is much more related to persuasion than to the cold facts of the asset-based debt financing covered up to this point. So far, you have read about the types of tangible assets used as collateral for banks, factors, receivable lenders, leasing companies, real estate lenders, and government agencies. Now you enter the world of *projections*, where little or no historical figures exist and all investment decisions are based on estimates, or, more accurately, "guesstimates." The idea is that you must sell your business idea to another person to get the money. Selling is marketing and marketing is persuasion, so you must think creatively to convince the venture community to invest in your business idea.

Keep in mind that although fewer than 1% of the applications for traditional venture capital are actually funded, you could still be in that 1% if you play your cards right.

Don't worry about how to approach either the traditional or nontraditional venture communities; that will be covered in Chapters 14 and 15. Just sit back and learn about the world of private equity money and how you can get it.

Who Finances Entrepreneurs?
Money Invested in 1988

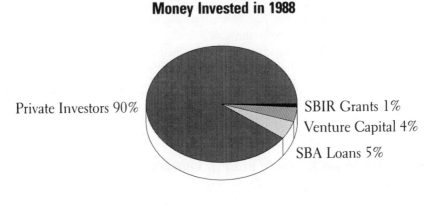

Private Investors 90%

SBIR Grants 1%
Venture Capital 4%
SBA Loans 5%

Prepared by: The Capital Institute

Why are the odds of getting traditional venture capital so low?

Attitude! The venture spirit has gone out of the traditional venture capital community. The managers of these firms are very rarely investing their own money anymore. They are investing their institutional clients' money, so they no longer want to take risks; they are looking for a sure thing. Instead of investing in start-up situations, traditional venture capital is concerned mostly with financing strong, emerging, existing companies (*mezzanine financing*) or the leveraged buyout of strong companies. There seems to be little or no venture left in traditional venture capital.

The big hit

Understand that one of the reasons traditional venture capital is so hard to get is that only about one company in ten in the portfolio of a traditional venture firm will make the "big hit." The portfolio of a venture firm is all the companies that have already received funding. The big hit is an investment that will average an annual return of 100% or more of invested capital over the life of the investment. Of every ten companies receiving professional venture capital, about half will probably not make it at all, and the other half will come in with an average return of 20% to 25%. The venture community wants a return of at least 20% to 25% annually over the life of the investment. When you take into account that one third of the money invested each year by the traditional venture capital community goes to companies that have *already received venture funds*, you can start to see some of the reasons that fewer than 1% of the proposals submitted to standard venture capitalists are ever funded.

Venture capitalists are not magicians. They shoot for the big hit and know they will end up only with an above-average return.

What do you need to attract traditional venture capital?

What does your project need to have to be the one in one hundred that gets funded? Recall that traditional venture capitalists do not invest in small businesses. They invest in large businesses that are just getting started! With that in mind, here are the qualifications they are looking for.

1. *Proprietary product or service.* The company seeking funds must absolutely have a proprietary product or service protectable by patents, copyrights, formulas, trade secrets, or know-how.

   The exception would be a company that is the first in a market with a lead time of at least 12 months over its competition. Lead time means a head start over the competitors' products plus the ability to maintain a monopoly position for as long as possible.
2. *Growth potential.* The company must have a potential market of from (get ready for a shock) $50 million to $100 million and be able to reach those figures within 5 to 10 years of funding.

   That is not a misprint. You must be able to become (at a minimum) a $50 million company in a relatively short time. Is your business in an industry large enough to reach those gross revenue figures? Obviously, if your project has only a regional market, you will have a hard time meeting the above sales projections.

3. *High return to investors.* On top of those sales figures, your company has to average an annual return of at least 20% to 25% each year — and that includes the start-up years. Since few companies will achieve maximum returns in the first few years, you must project substantial returns after your first few years of operation to average a *minimum* of 20% to 25% return. Notice that this is only *minimum* returns. Some traditional venture firms look for 30% *to* 40% *average* returns from every deal.

4. *Management.* Venture capitalists tend to invest in *people* rather than ideas, markets, products, services, or technologies. *The strength of the management team is the most crucial element in raising traditional venture capital!* Each member of the team should have a demonstrable ability in his or her field, with depth and credentials showing a familiarity with the market and previous experience managing a somewhat similar business. A successful track record means not only being associated with a successful company but also being personally responsible (in part) for the success.

   Seasoned management is the most important qualification the professional venture capital community looks for in a proposal. It has been said many times that a professional venture capitalist will invest in a second-rate product or service with a top-flight management team before it will invest in a first-rate product or service with a secondary management team.

Management characteristics

The traditional venture capital firms look for these characteristics in management: (1) experience, (2) competence, (3) character, (4) energy, (5) commitment, (6) honesty, (7) realism, (8) high achievement, (9) the ability to work under stressful conditions, and (10) the ability to work as a team.

Team is the key word

You don't just need a manager, you need a management *team.* The typical independence of the entrepreneur works against getting traditional venture capital, for that type of entrepreneur is not a team player.

The following positions on the team are absolutely necessary, and they may or may not include the founder or founders.

1. *Chief executive officer (CEO)*. The person who is the real leader and manager of the managers.
2. *Chief operating officer (COO)*. The organization person who manages the operations and administration of the business.
3. *Chief financial officer (CFO)*. The person who controls the money and makes sure the company has enough to meet its commitments.
4. *Chief marketing officer (CMO)*. The person who will be responsible for people buying your product; no profits are generated by a business until it sells something.

When venture capitalists say, "I'll back you," they are really talking about *you and your team, not your business.* They must be convinced that you and your management team can help the idea fly and make lots of money doing it. Your task is to explain why you and your team are the ones who can actually make it happen.

What the venture community is *really* looking for

It is looking for a profit opportunity, an opportunity to make a lot of money in a very short period of time — 5 to 10 years. Not many companies meet that criterion.

It is looking for good ideas that will make money. There are many good ideas, some of which could improve the nation's standard of living or lifestyles considerably, but the only question the venture community asks is, "Will it make money?" Not only must your idea make money, but, to reach the professional venture capital community, it must offer a *very large* profit opportunity, not just "make a profit." It is not interested in faith, hope, or charity. Most professional venture capitalist firms are just managing someone else's money, so they must produce a profit or lose their access to capital. Therefore, if you are offering *anything other than profit, you should not approach the traditional venture capital community.*

Is the traditional venture capital community interested in product or service companies?

Traditional venture capitalists are usually much more interested in companies with products than in companies selling services. The informal venture community is more likely to invest in service-oriented companies. Don't let that statement scare you if you sell a service. It just means you have to be more creative in your efforts to finance it.

Isn't it ironic that the United States economy is a service economy, while the traditional venture community, like the traditional lending community, is mainly attracted to manufacturing industries? That is why you have to use guerrilla sources and tactics to get any funds for your service business. Guerrilla financing is paramount.

What types of products do traditional venture capitalists like and dislike?

These classes of products describe the life cycle of an industry, along with what the traditional venture firms like and dislike.

1. *Revolutionary* (DISLIKE). Revolutionary products create a market where there wasn't one before. Examples of such products are the first light bulb, TV, camera, computer, and many more breakthrough inventions. This type of product is difficult to raise capital for because the source is investing in a pioneering situation. How would you like to invest in a company before the public knows or even understands what the company's product can do? Also, creating a market for your product can be very expensive. Who knew what a spa, fax machine, or a waterbed was when it first came out? It took years before they were accepted into the marketplace. An example of a revolutionary brand would be Sperry Rand's first computer.
2. *Innovative* (LIKE). Innovative products are the next generation of a product when the market has already been established. Here, you have a much better chance of getting traditional venture capital since investors can understand what you are selling. Good exam-

ples of such products are instant cameras, personal computers, and color TVs. A brand example would be Apple's personal computer.
3. *Evolutionary* (LIKE SOMEWHAT). These products are 1 year ahead of the competition, not 5 or 10 years ahead, such as a cheaper version of an existing product. Combine an evolutionary product with an excellent management team and you can attract substantial venture capital. A good example of a brand would be Commodore's cheaper personal computer.
4. *Substitutions* (LIKE SOMEWHAT). This is a repackaged product or a similar product (clone), such as substituting fast chicken for fast burgers or repackaging an old product with a new approach. It is more difficult to attract traditional venture capital to these situations than to innovative or evolutionary product companies, but not as difficult as financing a revolutionary product company. Good brand examples would be all the IBM personal computer clones.

The stages of venture capital

To understand where you fit in the cycle of venture capital investments, be aware of the various stages of growth most companies go through.

Early stage. This is the start-up stage, where the concept is unproven and no revenues have been produced. The type of investment at this stage is called *seed financing,* which means planting the original seeds of capital to get a business started. Traditional venture capital is rarely interested at this stage, whereas nontraditional venture capital is definitely interested. There are three substages in this category:

1. *Concept stage.* At this stage, entrepreneurs sit around the kitchen table and develop the concept or idea for the business and start to work on a business plan. At this stage, there is no monetary investment in the project.
2. *Research and development stage.* Now the first prototype of the product or service is developed. Time and money are being spent on the development of the project before any market testing.
3. *Prototype stage.* At this stage the prototype of the product or service is finished and tested. The company starts to sell small quantities for a market test and works out of a small building, office, or

even a garage. Estimated sales and costs can be formulated at this stage, and the management team is put together.

First stage. The product or service is ready to be marketed and now goes through debugging and modification to improve consumer acceptance; production capability is increased and a follow-up servicing program established. This stage usually includes the first year of business. Traditional venture capital is now a possibility, but only to a small degree. Nontraditional venture capital is very active at this stage.

Second stage. This is the initial growth and expansion period and is the stage where the product or service has been on the market for a period of time and has achieved some degree of success. The company turns profitable, and the projections of revenues, expenses, and profits become highly predictable. The venture capitalists can accurately measure the success of the company and the return on their investment. *It is at this stage that most traditional venture capital is invested.*

Nontraditional venture capital is also active at this stage, but to a much lesser degree, because it starts to compete with asset-based debt sources, covered in earlier chapters.

Third and fourth stages. These are mature stages, indicating a profitable success story with very little venture or risk left in the project. Financing at this point is usually called *mezzanine financing* and can include some form of debt financing. Traditional venture capitalists love this stage of little risk and high profit. Traditional debt financing institutions are the most active at this stage, with nontraditional venture financing becoming almost nonexistent. Some companies go for venture capital at this stage, even though bank loans are usually available, because they want to leverage the debt. The more equity a company has, the more it can borrow, so venture equity money at this stage is used to increase the borrowing capacity of a company. This type of financing is most effective in a rapid growth situation that requires a large amount of capital.

Other special stages. The following stages are funded almost equally by both the traditional and nontraditional venture sources.

1. *Bridge financing.* This happens when capital has been promised to the entrepreneur but there is a time lag before the funds are actually delivered. The two major types of bridge financing are: (a) prior financing to an initial public offering (IPO); (b) prior financing to a leveraged buyout (LBO).

2. *Leveraged buyout.* Money is made available to take over control of a company, using venture financing as one source of capital to complete the financing.
3. *Acquisition.* Obviously, this refers to the use of venture funds for one company to acquire another.
4. *Turnaround situations.* They occur when a company in trouble, maybe even in bankruptcy, turns into a profitable enterprise with the injection of venture financing and a new management team.
5. *Research and development.* Companies formed to market university and industrial research come under this category. Sometimes, as products are created or made practicable by research and development, the *spinoff* possibilities become very important. This is a very small part of venture capital and very difficult to arrange financing for without the help of some outside institution, such as the government. Sometimes it consists of partnerships of large companies, universities, government agencies, and traditional venture capitalists.

Do traditional venture capitalists require collateral?

The answer is no. Traditional venture capitalists almost never ask for collateral. The only exception is when a government-sponsored venture firm makes a loan along with an investment in a business, in which case the loan might require collateral. These government-sponsored venture capital companies are discussed later in this chapter.

Ownership in your business

Venture capital companies offer financing to businesses in return for an opportunity to profit from the growth of the business. Their right to profit is represented in their part-ownership, or equity position, which they buy by providing financing. No matter how you slice it, venture capitalists want to share in your profits, and the only way to do that is to be a part owner.

Traditional venture capital as a partner

Not surprisingly, traditional venture capitalists are probably the best business partners you could possibly have. The value you get from a traditional venture capitalist who invests in your business might far exceed the actual dollars that go into your bank account. They will offer you expert management advice, excellent contacts for credit purposes, and as your needs expand and your company grows, valuable assistance in attracting top personnel.

Misconceptions about traditional venture capital

Venture capital is for start-ups only. Absolutely incorrect. Some 30% of traditional venture capital goes into existing portfolio companies, firms that have already received venture financing. The traditional venture capitalists usually have to make sure that their investment returns a profit and, sometimes, in order to keep their old investments on track, they may have to invest more money. Only about 15% of traditional venture funds go into start-up situations. In fact, a start-up is the hardest stage to finance using traditional venture capital. Most professional venture capitalists are presently investing in mezzanine financing, companies that have already shown a profit and need expansion capital.

Most venture firms want to control your company. This is just not true. Many business owners, particularly small business owners, are very wary of giving away part-ownership in their business. This fear may be based partly on horror stories, tales about equity partners taking control of a business away from the original owners. It would be inaccurate to say that such takeovers have never occurred. But it would also be inaccurate to say that they usually occur. Professional venture capitalists *do not* want to take away the incentive from the founders of a company.

Most traditional venture capitalists, contrary to popular belief, are not interested in running your business. They have too much to do just keeping up with their existing investments and seeking new ones. They will only want to take control if the management does not live up to its promises to protect their investment. Therefore, the terms of the financing agreement may allow them to take control if and when the management does not live up to the expectations stated in the business plan.

The product or service is the main ingredient for attracting venture capital. False. The main attraction is management, not the market or the product.

Venture capital is only looking for companies in the high-tech and biotech fields. This is not the case. A large part of traditional venture capital goes into nontechnical ventures such as retail and distribution companies. In fact, there is really no industry that is inherently unsuitable for venture capital. Venture capital is interested in any high-growth situation that will make money.

Each venture capital company only invests in the industries listed in the venture directories. Not always. The traditional venture capital industry produces volumes of literature describing what types of opportunities each venture firm is looking for. However, things change so fast that these publications are out of date the minute they are published.

So if you read that a certain firm finances only high-tech companies, you may call them and find out that they are now financing low- or no-tech companies. Investors come and go; investment objectives change; portfolios are restructured; the availability of funds fluctuates; and many other factors change constantly and unexpectedly, so you never know what industry will appeal to what venture firm at any given time. Most traditional venture capital firms will consider any good profit opportunity at any time — no matter what is printed in any venture capital directory. Call the venture firm before you submit any proposal to find out what it is *currently* interested in.

You must have an introduction to the venture community to obtain financing. It helps, but a well-prepared business plan is the best introduction you can have. Obviously, the best combination would be an introduction from a person trusted by the venture capital firm *plus* a first-rate business plan. Guerrillas always try for the best.

Exit strategy

Traditional venture capital companies don't want to be your partner forever. Usually they want out within 3 to 5, or even 7 years. Sometimes they will stay for 10 years if a lot of research and development will take place before the company's product or service goes to market.

Exit strategy means the ways investors can get their money out of the business. There are really only two possible exit strategies.

1. *Going public.* By offering stock to the public, the company makes a fluid market for its shares and lets the marketplace determine the value of the company. Investors can then eventually sell their shares on the open market to liquidate their original investment. This is called "a liquidity event," the event that causes the investors to get out of their investment and back into a liquid cash position.
2. *Private sale of shares.* The only other possibility is to sell shares in the company to another business or perhaps even to the management of the company.

Professional or traditional investors like to know, before they invest, what exit strategy is being considered. There must be a possibility of a liquidity event.

The whole idea of traditional venture capital is to invest in the stock of a young company for as little as possible and to sell it for as much as possible while owning it for as short a time as possible.

The advantages of professional over informal venture capital

Deep pockets of investors. Usually, if the company needs more money later on, the professional investors either fund it themselves or know where to get it.

Professional management. Traditional venture capitalists have a lot of experience in helping small, emerging companies. They have the contacts to attract experienced management to fill in the gaps in a management team. Professional venture capitalists receive résumés from top managers all the time and often refer them to their own clients.

What are sharks?

In the venture financing business, sharks are people who want to take the deal or company away from you. There are a few among traditional venture capitalists, but many among the informal venture community. They may lead you to the edge of financing and then insist on control for some vague reason at the final moment. Most of the time it is very hard to spot a shark. When something doesn't sound logical or seems contradictory, *watch out*. Use common sense and good judgment, and always have third parties review the terms of a deal. Your lawyer should be able to catch a shark before he or she bites.

Patents

Don't wait for a patent to be filed or processed before looking for venture money. It is true that traditional venture capitalists love to see some sort of patent protection, but patent protection is not always the answer to competition. Statistics show that most patents are not defensible and disclose the technology to the competition anyway. Most professional venture investors want to give you enough money to capture a major position in the market before your competition catches up — patents or no patents. Patents are nice, but market share is much better. You should plan improvements in your product or service so that by the time your competition catches up to you, you have already improved your product or service enough to counter it.

Government-sponsored venture capital firms: SBICs and MESBICs

These are privately owned traditional venture capital firms, specifically licensed and partially financed by the Small Business Administration. They are called Small Business Investment Companies (SBICs) and Minority Enterprise Small Business Investment Companies (MESBICs are SBICs that must invest in minority-owned businesses). The fact that they are regulated by the government should not affect your relationship with them when looking for capital. Treat them as you would any traditional venture firm. The only difference between these government-sponsored venture firms and the private venture firms is that (1) the government-sponsored firms tend to make loans and investments in venture opportunities, and (2) they are legally prohibited from taking control of your company.

State government sources of venture capital

Besides the SBA's SBIC and MESBIC programs, some states are starting to set up their own venture funds to help small businesses get capital. Government resources are shifting from the quick fix of generous industrial incentive packages to capital earmarked for applied research, product development, and commercial venturing. These new state venture programs are usually geared to stimulate private investments instead of using direct state investment funds. Sometimes they operate by giving local lending institutions incentives to fund smaller and riskier companies than they normally would. These days, some states now offer tax breaks to private investors in state-approved venture capital funds.

Founders' investment: sweat equity

The venture community will always ask what you have put into your project so far. Your answer will revolve around your own money, time, and effort. Time and effort are called *sweat equity* in venture capital terms, and it does have value when it comes to negotiating what percentage of your company you will end up with after the financing.

Though the time, effort, and income you have lost during the initial stages of growth will be considered, traditional venture capitalists will not finance past debts that have been built up by the founders over the early stages. Venture people want their money to be used to improve the business, not to pay off old debts.

Try to stay close to home

When looking for traditional venture capital, begin your search in your own area. Most venture capitalists like to provide management assistance as well as capital and tend to invest in companies in their region. Starting in your own backyard may not be practical or effective, so you may have to start with some distant source, but try to find a venture firm that would be sufficiently interested in your company to recruit a local venture firm to sponsor your financing.

What hard documents do you present to traditional venture capitalists?

Though this is explained in detail in Chapter 14, here is a brief rundown.

1. *Business plan.* You must have an effective document that communicates what you want the money for and why it is an excellent investment.
2. *Concept paper.* Used more and more, this is a summary of the important points of a business plan, without the backup material but with some projections.
3. *Executive summary.* It's a one- or two-page summary of the business plan listing who, what, when, where, and why.

Tips about your business plan (for more, see Chapter 14)

1. Don't overemphasize the technical aspects of your product or service. Keep that type of information as a footnote or reference material at the end of the plan.
2. Don't overdo market research data. Again, keep that type of material in the back or as a footnote.
3. Don't forget to prepare visual aids that can be used when you present your oral presentation to the prospective funding sources.

4. Always include a cover letter telling how you learned about the venture sources and how they can get in touch with you.
5. Put in the negative aspects of your business. Tell the investor all the risks that are involved. This honesty will impress any venture source. Honesty and ingenuity are hallmarks of the true guerrilla entrepreneur.

The first two questions to ask venture capitalists

1. Are they actively looking for projects in which to invest?
2. Are they interested in your industry? Don't waste time if they say no. Try to get a reference to a more appropriate firm.

How to reach the traditional venture capitalists

They are easier to locate than you might imagine, as demonstrated by these four tactics.

1. *Study the venture capital directories.* Even though traditional venture capitalists have very stringent funding qualifications, the firms themselves are easily identifiable. Not every traditional venture capital company is listed in some database for public inspection, but you can find a majority of them by asking the following organizations for their list of venture capital firms:

National Venture Capital Association
1655 North Fort Meyer Drive, #700
Arlington, Virginia 22209
703-528-4370

Western Association of Venture Capitalists
3000 Sand Hill Road, Building 1, #90
Menlo Park, California 94025
415-854-1322

Pratt's Guide to Venture Capital Sources
Venture Economics Inc.
16 Laurel Avenue
Wellesley Hills, Massachusetts 02181
617-431-8100

International Venture Capital Institute
Box 1333
Stamford, Connecticut 06904
203-323-3143

And for the government-affiliated venture capital firms:

National Association of Small Business Investment Companies
1156 15th Street, #1101
Washington, D.C. 20005
202-833-8230

2. *Get an introduction.* Get to know somebody who can introduce
   you to a venture capitalist or who can at least arrange for the venture capitalist to review your business plan, concept paper, or executive summary.
       How do you get an introduction? Ask around, talk to successful
   entrepreneurs, bankers, investment bankers, merchant bankers,
   lawyers, accountants, and consultants who perform some of the
   "due diligence" for the venture firms. Some other ways to meet
   venture capitalists in person are to attend conferences and meetings where they congregate, such as: (1) local venture capital
   clubs, (2) venture capital conferences, and (3) networking meetings
   discussing financing techniques.
       While your business plan has to stand on its own merits, an in-
   troduction from a credible source can ensure it more than a cur-
   sory review and can result in meaningful feedback if the venture
   capitalist decides not to invest.
3. *Direct mail to specific firms.* First, call the firms you feel would be
   most interested in your financing proposal. Find out who handles
   your industry. Try to talk to this person first; be brief, describe the
   project, and answer any questions. Explain that you will be putting something in the mail. Then mail your plan, concept paper,
   or executive summary to these selected firms. Wait a few days,

then call back the person you originally talked to. If you can't get to speak to an appropriate person, at least get a name so you can address your plan properly.

4. *Buckshot approach.* This should be your last choice, but it does work. Mail as many plans, concept papers, or executive summaries to as many firms as you can. The problem with this approach is that some venture firms are turned off if they find out you did a mailing to all their competitors. But if you are like most people and lack contacts to the "old boy network," you are just going to have to let your business plan speak for itself, and the buckshot approach is the best way to get your plan in front of every venture capitalist.

Always try to find out why your proposal was turned down. After about a week, call the people you sent it to and try to find out what they did or didn't like about it.

After reading this chapter you may think, My God! You've got me so depressed by telling me the truth about traditional venture capital that I know I don't have a chance! What do I do?

Stay cool. You will now learn about the nontraditional venture capital world, where *most* of the action takes place. Guerrillas know the truth of the following statement: *"There is not a company in America with a viable market that can't be financed using nontraditional venture capital."*

Open up your mind and enter that brave new world, *the world of adventure capital.*

12
All About
Informal Venture Capital

If all the guerrilla financing sources listed in this book so far do not meet your needs, you can use another source, the largest and easiest source of financing to obtain and the essence of guerrilla financing.

State-of-the-art sources and techniques

In this chapter and the next you will learn about the most innovative aspect of guerrilla financing. This information is not available in any other book, textbook, or any source material in any bookstore or library in the country. You are about to learn state-of-the-art small business financing techniques that have been developed for the growing community of American entrepreneurs. You are about to learn unconventional financing methods at the extremes of guerrilla financing. You are about to embark on an adventure.

Adventure versus venture

The rest of this book refers to traditional venture capital as *venture capital* and nontraditional or informal venture capital as *adventure capital*.

Adventure capital is guerrilla venture capital.

Guerrilla venture capital

Now that you have learned how extremely difficult it is to get venture capital, you will be pleased to know that it is *much easier* to get adventure capital. The first reason is that there is more adventure capital available. For every dollar of venture capital there are approximately ten dollars of adventure capital.

Second, there are more adventure than venture capitalists. It has been estimated that there are close to one million adventure capitalists in the United States. This easily represents a 1000:1 ratio over traditional venture capitalists. The ratio of companies receiving adventure capital versus venture capital is approximately 300:1. Finally, the adventure capital market sees over two million proposals for capital each year and funds approximately 20%! That's 400,000 small businesses that get the money they want.

The odds of your getting adventure capital, rather than venture capital, are excellent — if you're a guerrilla. All the hype and glamour you have been fed by the media about how the traditional venture capital community funds the pot of money at the end of the entrepreneur's rainbow is not true. The real pot at the end of the rainbow is the informal venture community. It operates far from the spotlight, preferring to work alone or in small groups. But it is the backbone of risk venture capital in this country.

This chapter divulges the secret of getting your hands on private venture capital, guerrilla venture capital. You will learn who these adventure capitalists are, how to get to them, and what they are looking for. You will learn how to match your entrepreneurial dream with their investment dream, and their dollars.

By now you should have a good understanding of what traditional venture capital is all about. Without this background, you would not appreciate what you will learn in this chapter.

A second look at venture capital

Before getting started, it is important to review the differences between the two types of risk capital: *venture* and *adventure*.

The venture community is very small, only about a thousand firms nationwide. It is a very close-knit community, and everybody knows one another pretty well. Venture capitalists frequently talk to one another and invest jointly in a majority of their deals. It seems that, even with all their due diligence, no one venture capital company wants to take all the risks in any one deal. For example, in a typical $3 million financing, there may be six venture capital companies that each put in $500,000. One of those six firms would be considered the lead investor, whose job it is to find the deal and convince the other five to join in.

The money for venture capital comes from large insurance companies, pension funds, and major corporations. Venture capitalists are the professional managers of these funds. They are like any professional money managers, such as managers of mutual funds, pension funds, and large investment funds.

The early venture capitalists usually came from operating backgrounds in business and sometimes invested their own money. But today's venture capitalists usually specialize in particular fields — technology, biotechnology, distribution, manufacturing, and the like. Many of these venture capitalists have had very little experience running a business.

Here is a small group of professional people investing large amounts of other people's money with very little operating experience. No wonder they have become so conservative! Under these circumstances, would you risk other people's money as you would your own? Of course not, and that is exactly what has happened to the venture capital community. What was once a group of highly aggressive risk takers has become a community of risk managers, even risk *avoiders*. This is not to criticize any particular venture capitalist, but only to explain the dramatic change that has occurred in the venture community.

Adventure capital

Adventure capital is any type of risk capital investment made by individuals or firms other than the thousand publicly known venture capital firms. This includes anyone who invests in a business but who does not make a living by investing in businesses.

Yes, Virginia, there are angels

The adventure capital community is divided into two groups. The first group is the investors, who are known as angels. The second group is the advisers to the investors, who are called intermediaries. The terms *adventure capitalist, adventurist, angels,* and *investors* may be used interchangeably. They all refer to the nontraditional, informal venture capital community.

The term *angel* was born on Broadway, in New York, and used to describe individuals who put up the high-risk money to launch a Broadway production. Now the term refers to those individual investors who back emerging entrepreneurial ventures. They are also called business angels. *They are the largest source of real risk capital in the country and the least understood.* In fact, outside the major financial centers, they are virtually the *only* source of risk capital for the entrepreneur! There are approximately one million investors, or angels, in the United States who invest equity capital into business opportunities each year. This figure includes relatives, friends, and associates of the entrepreneur, but one third of these angels were strangers to the entrepreneurs.

Probably the most famous recent angel is the billionaire Texas industrialist H. Ross Perot, who plunked a mere $20 million into Steven P. Jobs's new company, called NeXT. You may not recall that in 1903 five venturesome angels invested $40,000 in a small new automobile company called Ford. Their investment earned them $145 million over a period of 16 years!

The angel market, like any market, is composed of suppliers (angels) and demanders (entrepreneurs) who engage in transactions (investment deals). There are also middlemen, or intermediaries, who bring both parties together.

A good percentage of the angels have a high net worth, usually over $1 million. In the United States, there are more than two million households with a net worth of $1 million, and more than 90% of them made their fortunes by starting their own ventures.

However, the majority of angels are not millionaires, although their incomes are above average. The average annual income of an angel is $90,000. Close to 70% of all angels are business owners or middle managers and are generally twenty years older than the entrepreneurs they finance. Best of all, more than 85% of angels don't seek voting control! In other words, they don't want to take over your business. All in all, the adventure capitalists are the modern Johnny Appleseeds, planting their seeds of capital in small entrepreneurial companies. A few years back, these investors might have been financing real estate or oil and gas limited partnerships to shelter their income for tax purposes. Today, with the change in the tax laws, these same angels are much more interested in investing in emerging growth companies that will increase their investment.

The second group is the advisers and consultants to the angels, the intermediaries or middlemen. You can go either directly to the angel or through an intermediary, or go to both at once.

What is so different about adventure capital?

The difference is the level of sophistication of the investor. Venture capitalists are professionals who make their living by using their investment skills. Adventure capitalists are people just like you who have discretionary capital that they prefer to invest in private business opportunities. The adventurist has much less skill at investing and is much easier to convince. There are also other differences between venture and adventure capitalists.

1. *Their own money.* Adventure capital is *not* other people's money. It is an adventurist's *own* personal money put directly into business opportunities.

   An interesting twist is that there are some venture capitalists who will invest their own money in riskier deals. When they do this, they qualify as adventure capitalists.
2. *Small amounts of money.* Since it is the adventure capitalist's own money, it is difficult to raise more than $100,000 from any one individual. Over half of all adventure capital investments are under $50,000. The average angel invests about $37,000 in any one company. Yet adventure capitalists are known to go into deals together where up to $500,000 or more has been raised. Raising over $500,000 is difficult using adventure capital. Only 18% of adventure capital deals involve financings over $500,000.

   Even though the average adventure capitalist invests less than $50,000 in one deal, the average start-up using adventure capital raises approximately $150,000, so it usually takes *more than one angel* to finance an adventure deal.
3. *Angels love start-ups.* Where the venture community invests only

15% of its capital in start-ups, the adventure community invests over 60% in start-ups.

4. *Easier to sell.* While the venture capital companies like to study a financing project thoroughly from top to bottom, a process called due diligence, adventure capitalists usually evaluate an opportunity based on sketchy evidence. Their investment standards, requirements, and qualifications are much less stringent than those of the venture capitalist, and their decisions are likely to be based on emotional issues rather than pure facts.

5. *The decision to invest is much quicker.* The decision to invest is made faster than that from the venture capitalist. Venture capitalists usually take six months to investigate a company, while the adventure capitalist may take only a few weeks, if not days!

6. *Easier to contact.* Venture capitalists are hard to meet. As you may expect, they are very busy people and usually won't see anyone without first reviewing their business plan. The adventure capitalist, on the other hand, is much more accessible. In fact, there is a whole network of intermediaries between the adventurists and the companies looking for money.

7. *There are a lot more of them.* One million angels are much easier to find than approximately five thousand traditional venture capitalists. Since adventure capitalists are all over the country, the money is available in a wider range of locations and industries than venture capital.

8. *They are local.* Adventure capitalists are everywhere. They could be your neighbor, doctor, lawyer, or accountant. *It has been estimated that there is one angel for every 250 adults, so in a city of 250,000 people there are approximately 1,000 angels!*

What do I need to attract adventure capital?

To understand what you need, you must understand what the adventure capitalist is looking for in an investment. You will notice some similarities and differences from what the venture capitalist is looking for. The angel looks for these characteristics when investing in an entrepreneurial company:

1. *Viable business concept.* Angels are not stupid. They may be somewhat unsophisticated compared to professional investors

when it comes to investing in private deals, but they know a good business deal when they see it. They look for real products or services, not hype, and a clearly identified market niche.

2. *Minimum annual return of at least 20%*. Just like venture capitalists, adventure capitalists are looking for a high return on their money. Both types want the same return, at least 20% to 25% annually on their money. In four years or so, the adventurists expect to get their investment back. This is a minimum figure. Many adventurists want a return ranging from 30% to 40%.

3. *Local company*. Adventure capitalists don't want to invest in companies too far away. They want to touch, smell, feel, and see their investments. Most angels like to invest in opportunities within 50 miles from their home or work or at least within a day's drive.

4. *Management integrity and commitment*. Angels are more concerned with integrity and commitment than competence. When it comes to management, they look for such characteristics as honesty and dedication more than career experience.

5. *Image*. They like the prestige of owning a piece of a business. Owning a popular restaurant, for instance, brings status to angels. They can tell their friends they own part of it and invite them to eat there. They might actually own only 10% or 15%, but it is something to discuss at parties. You could say the same for owning part of a new high-tech company, retail store, franchise — many kinds of enterprises.

6. *The excitement of psychic income*. Many angels are bored with their own jobs or careers and invest in local business opportunities for the excitement of belonging to something new or different. Angels' hot buttons are quite different from those of the venture capitalist. Many hot buttons are not financial rewards: investing in civic or social responsibility issues satisfies a sense of obligation to reinvest in the system that helped them succeed.

An angel's enthusiasm to invest often comes from something other than the normal financial risk/reward characteristics of an opportunity. The psychic income from investing may be partly financial and partly from the satisfaction and stimulation of playing entrepreneur.

There is even a romantic notion behind the angel's motivation, especially older entrepreneurs. One entrepreneur begets another entrepreneur, one generation fuels the next, relishing the aura of uncertainty that they vividly remember from the early days of their own ventures.

Is that all there is to it?

You may ask, "Is that all there is to it? What about patents, proprietary products and services, national markets, growth potential, experienced management?"

All these qualifications might be important for some deals but not for others. If you are looking for $50,000 to expand your gasoline service station, grocery store, or restaurant and you can show a healthy profit, you have an excellent chance of attracting adventure capital.

On the other hand, if you are looking for $200,000 to start a technical manufacturing business, you should meet some of the qualifications used by venture capitalists. Your particular endeavor fits somewhere in the spectrum of financing from unsophisticated to very complicated businesses. In attracting adventure capital, the more money you want and the more complicated your business, the closer you will have to come to matching the qualifications for financing set by the traditional venture capital community.

There is a big difference between looking for capital for one retail store and finding capital for a national chain of retail stores. That goes for distribution, manufacturing, and service businesses. The more sophisticated your business, the more qualifications you will have to meet to attract adventure capital. A well-written business plan helps you attract it. Chapter 14 tells you how to write it.

How do you find adventure capital?

Although adventure capital is made up of almost one million angels, they are not listed anywhere. Venture capital firms are listed in directories, but the adventure community of angels and intermediaries is very hard to find. But it is *not* impossible. Here is how guerrillas reach both the angels and the intermediaries.

Adventure capital intermediaries

Adventure capital intermediaries are groups of people and firms who are the confidants or advisers to angels. They perform the screening job for the angels, their due diligence. Who are these intermediaries? Many will sound familiar to you.

Investment bankers. Investment bankers are not bankers at all. They do not take in deposits and they do not lend money. Investment bankers are firms that raise debt or equity capital for their clients through the sale of private and public securities. Most investment bankers *do not* get involved in adventure capital because it is not cost effective for them. They work on financings of over $3 million to $5 million, which leaves out approximately 95% of all adventure capital. Investment bankers are not a good source for adventure capital.

Boutique investment bankers, merchant bankers, financing consultants. A new type of investment banker is popping up all over the country. They are called boutique investment bankers, merchant bankers, or financing consultants. They specialize in raising small amounts of capital, usually between $100,000 and $5 million. They have a network of adventure capitalists who invest in the deals they find, and they are an excellent link to the adventure capital community. Their job is to screen out inappropriate financings before presenting them to their clients, usually wealthy individuals looking to invest in small business opportunities. They also can arrange some debt and overseas financing.

It is not easy to find boutique investment bankers, merchant bankers, and financing consultants. These people are in a new category, and they are very difficult to locate. Look for them in the Yellow Pages under "Investment Management" and "Financing Consultants." Bruce Blechman's firm, the Capital Institute, is considered one of the top boutique investment banking firms in the country. See the last page in this book.

Financing planners and advisers. These people manage the investments of individual clients. Usually, they work through a brokerage firm that decides what kind of securities they can sell to their clients. But if you look hard enough, you can find a financial planner and adviser who may invest a client's capital in an entrepreneurial opportunity. These planners and advisers are not a good source of adventure capital because they concentrate too much on avoiding taxes and protecting capital, and not enough on capital appreciation. By nature, they avoid risk, like the venture capital community, because they are investing other people's money. But if you want to scout for the exceptions, look in your Yellow Pages under "Investment Advisory Services" and "Financial Planners."

Loan brokers and money finders. These are usually small operations that *claim* to find money for their clients. Do not confuse them with mortgage brokers, who arrange loans based on real estate. Loan brokers and money finders usually find money for real estate *and* business opportunities.

Most loan brokers and money finders are not qualified to give their clients enough of the financing advice they need. They have little to offer except a few sources and contacts. They do little consulting work for the client and, instead, shuffle paperwork from one source to another. The only advantage of these intermediaries is that they will try to help their clients look for deals requiring less than $100,000.

Be cautious when dealing with these types of intermediaries. Make sure you check their track record and references before using their services.

They can usually be found in the classified section of your newspaper under "Money to Loan" or "Capital Available."

Venture capital clubs. More and more, so-called venture capital clubs are being started all over the country. They offer a forum for both venture and adventure capitalists and intermediaries to convene once a month. They represent a hit-or-miss approach to finding any type of capital, but they can be a good place to learn about the local venture and adventure capital community. Contact the following organization for a list of clubs around the country:

Jim Jensen
Association of Venture Clubs
265 East 100 South, Suite 300
Salt Lake City, Utah 84110-3358
801-364-1100

Venture Capital Network. There is a new network of adventure capitalists as a result of the work of Professor William Wetzel at the University of New Hampshire. It is a kind of dating service for angels and entrepreneurs. It calls itself the Venture Capital Network and introduces entrepreneurs to adventure capitalists using a computerized matching system. (It uses a confidential database of entrepreneurs and adventure capitalists.) In a two-stage process, it submits to adventure capitalists those investment opportunities that meet the angel's screening criteria. Both the entrepreneur and the investor remain anonymous throughout the process and are only introduced when the investor expresses an interest in a particular entrepreneur's project.

These groups are located in only a few cities and have a limited number of members. The promise to match entrepreneurs with private investors sounds great, but the actual track record of putting deals together has been very spotty so far. If there is a venture network in your area, it is nonetheless worth contacting. For a list of the nearest venture capital groups, call or write to:

Venture Capital Network
Box 882
Durham, New Hampshire 03824
603-862-3558

Who are the angels?

Angels are the ultimate source of adventure capital. They're the people who invest the capital, the actual adventure capitalists. They are the ones who put their own money on the line. Angels can be divided into two major categories: affiliated and nonaffiliated. Affiliated would be anyone who knew or was associated with the entrepreneur looking for capital. Examples of affiliated angels are relatives/friends and associates.

Nonaffiliated angels are strangers to the entrepreneur. They can be divided into three subcategories: professionals, middle managers, and entrepreneurs.

Affiliated angels

Relatives and friends. You don't need this book to show you how to find these people. They're often the first source approached.

Associates. This includes anyone, other than a relative or friend, who is acquainted in some way with the entrepreneur. Examples are professionals who provide services for you, such as your doctor, lawyer, and accountant. They are also business associates, suppliers, customers, noncompeting companies in the same industry, service companies, and employees. Since this is an excellent source of adventure capital, it merits further attention.

Suppliers are owners of companies who are the suppliers or vendors of the entrepreneur. Their ulterior motive in investing in the entrepreneur's business is to tie the entrepreneur to the supplier's product or service. For example, a manufacturer looking for outside adventure capital might approach one of his largest vendors to invest in his company.

Customers are angels who own companies that are also customers of the entrepreneur. An original equipment manufacturer may have a customer who depends on the part he or she makes. There may be a chance that the customer wants the product enough to help finance your company.

Noncompeting similar companies own companies in the same industry but do not compete. A good example is two regional companies on opposite sides of the country. Each may help the other by sharing information and even investing in each other.

Employees can be investors. Suppose you need capital and you also need a new sales manager. You might be able to do both at once by looking for a sales manager who is willing to invest in your business for a piece of the action.

Service companies are businesspeople who service your business — your lawyer, bookkeeper, consultants, whatever. These advisers make good investors or may know of some prospective investors.

How to find an affiliated angel

These are the easiest angels to find and get to invest in your business. They know you or know of you. You are aware of them and are possibly using some of their services. Few guerrillas need encouragement to approach them for an investment. List all the possible affiliated angels you may already know. You will be surprised at how many there are. Even if they are not interested, they may know someone who is. You will never know unless you ask.

Many affiliated angels have extra reasons to invest in your business. Professionals and suppliers want your business.

Affiliated angels make great partners and are much easier to approach than nonaffiliated angels. Try all your affiliated contacts before contacting your nonaffiliated contacts. When looking for money, try the shortest and quickest way first. Then work your way up.

Since you already know these people, you don't need an introduction; you can just call them for an appointment. Even though you know or are acquainted with these people, prepare your business plan before meeting them. A professional business plan always impresses angels.

Nonaffiliated angels

These people are absolute strangers to you. They can be professionals, middle managers, or entrepreneurs.

Professionals. Professionals include anyone in the medical field (doctors, dentists), lawyers, and accountants as well as other professionals such as architects and consultants. It's a long list. Professionals themselves are either non-business-oriented or business-oriented professionals.

Most non-business-oriented professions, such as medicine or science, leave their investment decisions to their financial planners, lawyers, and accountants. Most business-oriented professions, such as law, accounting, engineering, and consulting, like to study their own deals.

Middle managers. These angels are people in middle management or managerial positions in large corporations, people close to the top. They have enough discretionary income to invest in small entrepreneurial opportunities.

These middle managers are often bored with their jobs and want to have some fun investing in a small business. They might also be interested in covering their income in case they are phased out of their jobs, or they are thinking of leaving their jobs and want to explore other possibilities without having actually to leave yet.

Entrepreneurs. These angels own successful businesses and enjoy investing in other businesses. Nonaffiliated entrepreneurs own companies that have been successful enough to have the capital to invest in other entrepreneurial companies. The best entrepreneur and middle manager angels are people who are working or have worked in the same or similar industries as the entrepreneur looking for money.

How to find nonaffiliated angels

You know it's a cinch to contact affiliated angels, but complete strangers? Impossible? Absolutely not! There are four extremely effective ways to find, contact, and convince perfect strangers to invest in your business or project. Each way has been tried, tested, and proven.

Don't worry if you are not successful at attracting strangers right away. You can practice on angels forever and never run out of people to contact.

There are actually five ways to find nonaffiliated angels. One is to go through intermediaries. There are also four direct ways to find nonaffiliated angels: classified advertising, dialing for dollars, business brokers, and *Investor* magazine.

Classified advertising

Classified advertising is the most cost-effective guerrilla method for finding financing sources for small businesses. Of all the techniques to find money discussed in this *entire book,* classified advertising is the single most cost effective because it is all of the following:

Cheap. An ad in Sunday's paper asking for a partner costs less than $150 anywhere in the United States. Hundreds of thousands of dollars are raised using this simple method.

Simple. Who can't write an ad for their own project? Some of these ads receive over three hundred responses.

Quick. You can place an ad in your local newspaper today and get a phone call from a prospective angel tomorrow. How's that for quick?

Effective. You will be delighted when you discover the activity in the Sunday classified Business Opportunity section of your newspaper. Every day, thousands of people read these ads looking for businesses to buy. Many entrepreneurs receive remarkable results using classified advertising to attract private partners.

Too good to be true

You're probably thinking that this all sounds too good to be true. It *is* true. And few people are aware that placing a classified ad for capital is so effective. *It is the least expensive and most successful method of raising less than $100,000.* Ads in the classified section of the *Wall Street Journal* are known to raise much higher sums.

Who reads the classifieds?

People with money to invest read the classified Business Opportunity section of every newspaper in the country. Who are they? They run the gamut from people with $10,000 to $25,000 who'd like to put a little money into a small business to professionals wanting to sink hundreds of thousands of dollars into a venture. Many people read the classified section just for the fun of it. Some are serious buyers and some are not. The point is that this section of the newspaper attracts people who are thinking of parting with various sums of money in order to own a business or *part of a business*. That's right, *part of a business*. You don't want to sell all your business but might consider selling part of it. That is what this is all about, bringing in a partner to buy part of your business.

The people looking through the classified ads are looking for an opportunity. Whether that means owning 100% or 20% of a company, the opportunity and how they can benefit are the most important things. The object of the game is to convince the buyer that it is better to buy, say, 30% of *your* business than 100% of some *other* business. The buyer's motivations and how to satisfy them are covered later in this chapter.

How to place a successful classified ad

To be effective in classified advertising, there are some definite ground rules. If you have a friend who has tried it unsuccessfully, it was not because the classified section is not effective; it was probably because your friend did not know the proper ground rules. They are:

Proper placement
Effective heading, copy, and close
Effective screening of responses
Proper presentation of opportunity
Good negotiating techniques

Proper placement. Where you place your ad is extremely important. Guerrillas place it in *only* two sections of the classified: Business Opportunity and Employment.

Business Opportunity is where people who want to sell their business place an advertisement. The people who read this section, therefore, are people who want to buy a business. And people who want to buy a business usually have *money*. The people who read the Business Opportunity section usually have between $10,000 and $100,000 to invest or have access to that much capital.

The important thing to be aware of is that the Business Opportunity section, especially on Sundays, is the best place to attract an angel to invest in your business. If for some reason your newspaper doesn't have a Business Opportunity or a Business Offerings section, place your ad in the Money or Capital Wanted section. Some newspapers call that section Investments or Financial Investments.

The next best place for your ad is the *Employment section.* Who looks there? People looking for employment. *But* some of those people just might have some capital and be interested in owning part of the business. If you had a choice between a job at which you had no ownership or a job that also offered ownership, which one would you choose?

You may wonder how you can advertise for an angel in the employment section. Very easily. Simply think of the area of *your* business or proposed business that needs help. It could be management, marketing, sales, administration, production, distribution, or any other area. But whatever it is, place an ad in the section for which you are looking for help. Suppose it is sales. Your ad may read as follows: **SALES MANAGER**. Rapidly growing manufacturing company seeks sales manager; equity position available to qualified individual. Call *(your number)*.

What you are saying is that you are looking for a sales manager and, to the right person, you are willing to offer a partnership in the business! You can catch both talent and money at the same time. This is an extremely effective guerrilla financing technique.

If you happen to be looking for more than $100,000, try a national paper like the *Wall Street Journal* or *USA Today*.

Perhaps you don't need a sales manager or another key person. But if you need the money, you may have to create the position, especially if you can attract a talented, experienced person who knows your field and is willing to invest in your business.

Before you learn how your ad should read, you should know the legal aspects of classified advertising for angels.

The legal aspects of classified advertising

First, get your lawyer's opinion before you try what you read in this chapter. Not all lawyers agree, so you might have to get two opinions if the first opinion is not agreeable.

There is only one legal way for you to advertise for a partnership, and that is to advertise for an active general partner. There is no securities law in this land that says any business owner cannot place an advertisement in a newspaper for an active general partner. Soliciting individuals to join you as active general partners does not involve the sale of a security.

Suppose you are a limited partnership or a corporation. Any legal entity can be in partnership with any other legal entity. So if you are a corporation, your corporation can have a general partnership with an individual or with another partnership or even another corporation. Even a limited partnership can add more general partners.

You *cannot* advertise in a newspaper for a limited partner, a passive partner (investor), or to sell stock in your business. You can only advertise for an active general partner.

What is an active general partner?

It is up to you and your legal counsel to decide what constitutes "active" for you. An active general partner can usually be defined as someone who has a significant voice in the management of the business. One day a week or a few hours a week may be considered active. If a partner does not have a voice in management and has no liability for any debts, then the partner may be considered a limited or passive partner, and you are not allowed to advertise for limited or passive partners. The exception to this is when you register your company for a securities sale. Ask your legal counsel for advice on this issue.

Should the angel be experienced in your business?

The angel you attract from advertising may turn out to be experienced in your field and a great asset to your business. Even if the angel is not much of an asset the angel's money *is* an asset. Experience is, as they say, helpful but not necessary.

Don't be fooled by what you read in the papers

If you look in the classified section of your newspaper, you will probably see ads with the following headings:

• Investors
• Investment Opportunity
• Inactive Partner
• Silent Partner
• Associate
• Entrepreneur
• Need Capital
• Venture Capital Wanted
• $100,000 Wanted

Just about all of the people who use those headings don't realize they may be doing something illegal. But probably no harm will be done and the law will most likely not be enforced on these types of ads.

The danger in using the above headings in your ad is that if your business or project loses money for the angel, the angel may have the legal right to get his or her money back just because you broke the state or federal securities laws by improper advertising of a security.

Heading, body, and close
Now that you understand that classified ads are legal and effective, you should know how to write an ad that pulls responses. In using

classified advertising to find angels, the object is to get as many responses as possible, then to screen them to find appropriate partners.

There are three distinct parts of a classified ad: the *heading*, the *copy*, and the *close*. The *heading* is important because most newspapers place ads alphabetically by heading, and if your heading is "Tom's Plumbing Store," your ad will be in the "T's," near the end of the section. The *body* tells and sells the story, and the *close* tells the reader what to do if interested.

Headings. Remember that this is an ad, and, like any other ad, the object is to attract the right attention. The heading is the first word or few words of the ad and is usually in bold capital type. Your heading is very important; you should concentrate on it before you create the copy. Your heading should attract the kind of person you are looking for. Some of the headings that have worked for others are:

MANUFACTURER. Expanding manufacturer of machine parts looking for partner. Call ———.

TEMPORARY PERSONNEL AGENCY needs expansion capital. Will accept partnership. Call ———.

RETAIL CONCEPT, new with unlimited potential, equity position available. Call ———.

ELECTRONIC manufacturer needs start-up capital. Substantial equity position available. Call ———.

Copy. This is the heart of your ad. If the heading is designed to attract angels, the copy is designed to sell angels on your project, enough that they'll call you. The copy explains and sells at the same time. It convinces the readers to do what you want them to do.

Here are some more examples that have produced outstanding results:

GROWING SERVICE BUSINESS seeks expansion capital. Looking for a partner who is interested in owning part of an exciting local business. Call ———.

PRESTIGIOUS RESTAURANT, with experienced management, requires additional working capital. Substantial equity available. Call ———.

TRUCKING company needs partner. Established company seeks capital to finance truck purchase. Investment collateralized by trucks. New customers already in place. Call ———.

JEWELRY STORE, two-store profitable chain needs expansion capital. Substantial equity position offered. Call ———.

VIDEO STORE, start-up, great location with excellent potential and return. Substantial equity position available for partner. Call ———.

GRAPHICS FIRM, showing a 76% growth rate, with exceptionally strong management, needs expansion capital. Call ———.

WHOLESALE ORIENTAL RUG DISTRIBUTOR, ten-year-old profitable distributor of handmade rugs from China needs expansion capital to import directly. Looking for partner. Call ———.

COFFEE SHOP needs partner, low cash required, excellent growth prospects. Call ———.

RECREATION BUSINESS in romantic and adventurous industry. High growth potential. Looking for partner. Call ———.

AUTO REPAIR & BODY SHOP needs expansion capital. Six-year-old profitable shop with over $500,000 in sales looking for partner. Call ———.

PHOTOGRAPHIC PORTRAIT STUDIO, well established, needs capital to implement proven marketing program. Will offer substantial equity position. Call ———.

An ad for a start-up

ELECTRONICS COMMUNICATION DEVICE: Inventor with experience in products for the handicapped is seeking investment in new device for audio communication. Product has been evaluated professionally and patent is pending. Substantial equity position available for right partner. Call ———.

An ad to buy a business

EQUIPMENT RENTAL BUSINESS: 37-year-old established firm showing excellent cash flow. Looking for partner to buy the business. Owner taking back note for 63% of the asking price. Call ———.

Ads placed in both business opportunity and employment sections by the same company

Business opportunity section

TROPICAL FISH STORE. Experienced management seeks partner. Call ———.

Employment section

STORE MANAGER. Tropical fish store, new store concept seeks manager. Will consider partner. Call ———.

Business opportunity section

SECURITY SERVICE COMPANY. Entrepreneur with long successful career in the security and allied industry is seeking an investment in start-up company with new concept in demonstrable high-demand market. Looking for partner. Call ————.

Employment section

SALES/MARKETING MANAGER. New remote electronic surveillance company, substantial equity position available. Call ————.

Ad placed in the employment section of the Wall Street Journal

CEO/PARTNER. Expanding processor of electronic scrap material headquartered in the San Francisco Bay Area looking for CEO/INVESTOR/PARTNER. Excellent opportunity to direct rapidly growing national company. Call ————.

Close. You always want the reader of the ad to call you. Addresses and post office boxes just don't count when it comes to shopping for an angel. You want action and you want it fast. The phone is the best way to get what you want. Buyers of businesses make up their mind very quickly. You don't have time to exchange letters. You want to talk to that prospective angel and either set up a meeting or get off the phone quickly. So always end your ad with your phone number. You should always have an answering machine to take a message if you are not home or at your office. If necessary, use a temporary answering service just to handle responses to your ad.

What if the ad doesn't pull responses?

If your ad does not attract enough people, rewrite it. Your chances of getting the correct ad, one that will pull a strong response the first time you place it, are only about 50-50. You might have to rewrite the ad two or three times to get the kind of response you want.

You don't want the ad to be too long or too short. It should say just enough to elicit a phone call. Ads that get a small number of calls are just not written well. It has little to do with the type of business you are in. Sure, if you are producing a movie or TV show, maybe that is glamorous enough by itself to attract investors. But the bottom line is, a well-written ad will pull responses for any type of business in any industry.

Remember, the goal of the ad is to get as many responses as possible so that you can discuss your proposal with as many potential partners/ investors as possible and select those most compatible with your interests.

What is a good response?

You may get one or two good phone calls that turn into very interested parties, or you may get ten poor responses that don't meet your partnership criteria at all. You will always get your share of flakes, but that is par for the course.

A good ad should pull about three to five responses. Sunday's paper is the best place to run the ad, but if you need the money fast, run it every day for a week or two. It doesn't cost much more than running it only on Sunday.

Effective screening of responses. The object is to tell the inquirers what you are doing and find out if they are compatible and have enough money to make it worthwhile to meet. You should be selective in the initial phone call. It should help you decide if you want to meet with the potential investor/partner/angel. Be cordial and try to let the other person do most of the talking. You want to present the best aspects of your business proposal and determine if you have a serious enough investor to set up a meeting. This initial phone conversation should *not* be used as a negotiating session, but only as a screening session to determine if both sides have enough interest to pursue the subject.

Remember, you are looking for a compatible partner who may be very active, or inactive, in your business. You may find that you are talking to a retired accountant, banker, attorney, or business manager who can assist you with your business operations. Usually, after a few minutes on the phone, you can tell if you want to pursue the conversation.

You will probably receive calls from business brokers who want a listing. Keep their phone numbers. You'll see how to get angel money using business brokers later in this chapter. You will also probably get some real loony types of calls. They are typical, and you should be able to spot an undesirable contact right away. Be cordial but firm in all your phone conversations, and be prepared with the information a potential investor will want to know.

Don't set up a personal meeting until you have enough information to determine whether the caller has enough money to swing all or part of the deal.

Avoid long phone conversations. If you have an interested party, you should set up an appointment to meet.

Proper presentation of opportunity. A face-to-face meeting is the next step in handling classified responses. Meet at your business or even at a local coffee shop. Don't use your home for the first meeting. You have never met this person, and it would be more professional at your office or at a place like a coffee shop.

The object of the meeting is for you to get to know the investor and to explain your business or project in greater detail. Don't discuss terms at this first meeting unless the angel shows a very strong interest in investing right away. Ideally, you will have prepared a business plan and, if you are both still interested after the meeting, personally hand the angel a copy of the plan.

Try not to mail business plans to investors from classified ads. You should only hand them to an interested investor/partner after you have met. First impressions are extremely important in these encounters. Study Chapter 14 carefully. *Don't even place an ad until you have created your business plan and thoroughly studied this book.*

Good negotiating techniques. At the first meeting you and your angel will get to know each other and you will give the prospective angel a business plan to analyze. The second meeting should be to discuss and negotiate the specific amount of money the angel would be willing to invest and under what terms. Terms in these cases usually revolve around what you are willing to give up in equity for an investment. Terms in traditional venture negotiations are much lengthier and complicated, not only because more money is involved, but because other people's money is being invested. Here, you are talking about an individual investing his or her own money in your business or project.

Negotiations will be discussed in Chapter 16, but for now, always try to negotiate an agreement that offers the best terms to both parties. It should be a win-win situation if the partnership is to succeed. Both parties should walk away from the negotiating table feeling that they got what they wanted and that the agreement is fair. If your negotiating sessions don't seem to go too well at first, don't be alarmed. In the beginning you may lose some prospects, but there are more out there. Negotiating for money is a new experience for most people, and it may be stressful at first. It will probably include some trial and error before you feel effective and comfortable. In the end, negotiating good terms involves common sense more than anything else. As the meetings progress, you may want someone to be with you during negotiations: a friend, consultant, accountant, or even an attorney. However, usually it is best to negotiate and settle the terms of the agreement yourself and then ask an attorney to put everything in writing.

Attitude

This is the all-important aspect of getting the best responses and partners attracted to your proposal. In all your phone conversations and personal meetings with potential angels, you should be confident but not haughty. Act as though you have something to offer without expressing how much you need the money. Let the other party assume you have many offers and are deciding which one to take. Be confident you can meet the projections you have put down in your business plan. If you are not confident, change your plan to make it more realistic.

Classified can be fun

The process of using a classified ad to raise money may seem weird or far-out at first, but it is an inexpensive way that thousands of entrepreneurs have used to raise the capital they needed for their businesses. It is guerrilla financing at its purest.

Dialing for dollars approach

Here is the second direct way to find angels: call them on the phone. The dialing for dollars approach is definitely more difficult than the classified approach because it involves more persuasive techniques. Whom do you call? You can buy lists of people in your area who have invested in business opportunities or partnerships, or you can create your own lists of potential angels.

Calling affiliated sources

Start with all the affiliated contacts you know. Go back over your list of all the affiliated angels and start calling. You will have the most success in attracting affiliated angels by contacting other entrepreneurs who wish to maintain their interest in the same product line or industry as you do. Contact individuals whose business expertise gives them a special appreciation of your industry or product or service. You should know who these people are already. If you run out of affiliates, the next approach is to cold call.

Cold calling

Cold calling strangers is a tough way to raise capital, but it is being done by entrepreneurs all the time.

A young man raised $500,000 for a restaurant using this approach. He didn't buy a list; he made his own. He visited all the grand openings of restaurants that he could, and asked for the names of the investors. He called these people and told them about his project. He used one person to then recommend another. He constantly looked for lists of people with money. He checked the society pages and called the people mentioned. He called local celebrities and anyone he thought might be interested.

The bad news is that it took him about twelve months to raise the capital, and he had to speak to over three hundred people in order to attract fifty investors. The good news is that he is now the proud owner of a successful restaurant.

Many companies sell lists of wealthy people. All you have to do is look up "Mailing Lists" in the Yellow Pages. The list brokers will get you virtually any combination you desire. The best list would be wealthy people who invest in business opportunities. Always go for local people or for people who live close to your place of business.

But be warned, cold calling requires skin five feet thick because the rejection rate is so high. It is difficult to engage in cold calling for more than four hours at a time if you're to retain any sanity or self-esteem. No pain, no gain, truly applies here.

Be creative: Make your own list

You can also, like the restaurant owner, make your own list. Be creative; call the owners of similar companies outside your trade area. Look for people who have made it, preferably in the same business you are in. Studies have shown that people with a strong sense of social responsibility are likely candidates to be angels. Maybe you should look at the board of directors of local nonprofit organizations. Creating your own list comes under the category of *networking*.

Networking

Create your own list, or even sometimes meet the potential investor directly, by networking. Networking just means getting out there and meeting lots of people. You can start with your local chambers of commerce and work your way into all the other local clubs and organizations, Rotary, Elks, and the many others. This is an inefficient and time-consuming way to build a list, but it is effective if you are sociable.

What to say on the phone

When you have a *hot lead* that is a referral, a phone conversation is much more relaxed and informal. Basically, it is the same as handling a response from a classified ad. On the other hand, *cold calling* for investor leads requires more persuasive skills. Introduce yourself as the president, founder, or investor. Explain how you have obtained the person's name and what you are trying to accomplish. Take a very positive attitude; this will be reflected in the tone, pitch, level, and sound of your voice. Smile as you talk. It will also be reflected in the sound of your voice. Use the same techniques as those given for handling telephone inquiries from classified ads. Get the person's interest. Then set up an appointment to meet.

The conversation may go like this:

"Hello, my name is ———. I am the owner of ——— company.

We manufacture widgets. I got your name from a list of investors I purchased. The reason I am calling is to see if you would be interested in a unique investment opportunity with my company."

Of course, this technique requires telemarketing skills. If you are going to make the calls yourself, you must be emotionally prepared to handle a lot of rejection. If you find this difficult, hire a professional telemarketer or telemarketing company to do it for you. You are not selling any security. You are just looking for an active general partner for your own business. The telemarketer or telemarketing company's job is only to screen people who are interested in meeting or talking with you. They should not go into any details other than gathering information about the investor.

Business brokers

The third guerrilla financing technique for contacting angels directly is the toughest because it requires the cooperation of the business brokerage community, which has been slow to adopt it. As this method is used more and more around the country, more business brokers will cooperate, endorse, and help to implement it.

The owner of a large business brokerage firm received over 5,000 inquiries in one year, and only from his branches in northern California. His firm contacted 5,000 potential angels because every phone call was from a person with money who wanted to buy a business. Out of the 5,000 inquiries, they negotiated 400 sales. Which means there are at least 4,600 entrepreneurs out there still looking for a business to buy. This is an enormous amount of adventure capital.

Obviously, most of the 5,000 people who contacted his firm had money. All he had to do was to find out which ones would be interested in buying part of businesses he had for sale.

This technique for finding angels usually only works with ongoing and profitable businesses. It is not effective for attracting capital to a start-up situation.

Approach a business broker to sell part, not all, of your business. Usually you will have to give up from 25% to 49% of your business to make it worthwhile for the broker. The broker searches his or her files for potential buyers, then contacts them and tells them he has found an expanding company with strong existing management that wants to sell a substantial ownership position to an active party. The broker is key in this type of arrangement, because he or she must convince the buyer that it is better to invest in an ongoing profitable business with existing management than to risk everything buying 100% of a business and being responsible for running it. The argument is that it is far less of a risk to buy into a profitable ongoing business where the management stays than to take over a profitable business where the management is leaving. The broker may also mention that the new partner can still have the fringe benefits of owning his or her own business. This is an ideal arrangement if the new partner understands the industry involved and can add management skills to the company.

Most business brokers are not very keen on this idea of selling only a part of a business. Still, the technique works. You may have to convince the business broker to give it a try. You may have to ask quite a few business brokerage firms before you find an aggressive one that will cooperate and try this technique. Eventually, many business brokers will come around to this guerrilla concept.

Besides getting past the broker, the most difficult part of this approach is convincing the investors that it is better for them to own, say, 40% of a going business with experienced management, where they will be free of the sole responsibility for running the business, than to own 100% of a business where they will be assuming 100% of the responsibilities.

Sometimes it is easier to convince the buyer than it is to convince business brokers. They are not used to this sort of transaction. Business brokers can be found in the Yellow Pages under "Business Brokers."

Advertise in a special magazine for angels

There is still another way for you to reach the informal venture community: *Investor* magazine is for investors in private companies and is mailed to thousands of informal investors and intermediaries all over the country. The magazine has colorful, clear articles about private companies that are seeking capital. The articles cover companies in all stages of development, from start-up to going concerns. The companies are described in editorials that are paid for by the entrepreneur looking for capital. They are called advertorials. No solicitation for capital appears in the article. It is an effective way to get your message directly to both angels and intermediaries in the informal venture market. The magazine has regional issues for every area of the United States, so your article can reach angels right in your own area. To find out if you qualify for an article in *Investor* magazine, call 1-800-748-6951.

Setting partnership criteria

What type of partner should you look for when seeking nonaffiliated angels? Partnerships are like marriages, so look before you leap. It should be someone you would be comfortable working with, for you are going to have to give up some of your business to this angel.

Check the references of potential investors/partners. You will need to open your books and plans to them, and they should be willing to give you sufficient references and other pertinent information. Know the person or people with whom you are about to get involved.

The best way to get them to know you is to "get into bed with them." If there is time, have them spend a few weeks at your place of business. Pretend they are owners. See what happens. You can learn a lot by studying a person at close range. And vice versa.

Partnerships are not necessarily forever

A lot of people are afraid of bringing on a partner, especially a stranger, because they don't know how they will get along. When guerrillas prepare partnership agreements, they agree to disagree. They agree to dissolve the partnership or arrange for a buy-sell arrangement whereby one partner can buy out the other if they can't agree to continue. Buy-sell agreements backed up by insurance are also necessary in case of the death of one partner.

How to close a deal

When you are preparing the partnership with an adventure capitalist, you may want to do what the venture capitalists do. You might not like this idea because it puts the burden on the entrepreneur, but if you put it in your agreement, it has a tendency to close the deal with the investor.

This means making an agreement whereby the investor can take control of the company if the projections are not being met. As long as you are meeting or coming close to your projections, the investor will not interfere with the operation of your business. But if you are consistently missing your projections by a wide margin, the investor has a right to come in and take over the operation of the business. This may be a hard pill to swallow, and if the investor does not bring it up there is no reason for you to, but if the negotiations are bogging down and you want to close the deal, this type of agreement just may be enough to do it. After all, it shows your confidence in your own projections. In effect, you are putting the control of the company on the line. You are putting your money where your mouth is.

Checklist for dealing with private adventure capital

1. *Designate responsibilities in your partnership agreement.* Don't forget to spell out exactly what each partner is responsible for so that there won't be any later disagreement as to who is responsible for what.
2. *Be prepared.* Don't waste your time and money on an ad unless you are prepared to make an effective oral and written presentation of your business project. Implement Chapters 14 and 15 before you contact any financing source.
3. *Be positive.* Investors will be buying your concept and *you.* First impressions are lasting impressions. You never get a second chance to make a first impression.
4. *Talk to principals only.* Over the phone, screen out loan brokers and everyone else who says they can help you get money from a third party. You want to spend your time talking to qualified investors/angels only.
5. *Don't be too specific over the phone.* Present the project you want to finance, but only in enough detail to encourage an investor's interest. Definitely do not be specific about what you are willing to give up in return for the money. That is a matter to be discussed in detail only in person with prime prospects.

6. *Listen carefully over the phone.* You need to pick up details in order to judge whether you want to spend your time meeting the person on the other end of the line.
7. *Be open to suggestions from your prospective partner on how to raise money.* Investors may have not cash but enough collateral to get you a loan. Many people are sitting with equity in their homes and don't know they can use its borrowing power.
8. *Very active partners should add something to the business.* A partner who is active beyond the legal qualification should contribute the expertise that is so essential to your success. You don't want an active partner who is watching you work and looking over your shoulder all the time. All partners should be allowed to review your books from time to time, but they should not be allowed to participate in the daily operation of your business unless their skills are necessary.
9. *Be selective.* Don't try to peddle an equity interest in your venture to anyone who will sign a check. Finding the right investor is crucial to the future of your company. You might have to go through some very tough times together, so you need an investor who not only has financial resources to bankroll you but has the know-how and emotional experience to hang in there.

Do I want one partner or several?
And how much can I realistically raise?

You may not have the option of choosing just one partner. Classified advertising usually does not attract large investors but is very effective for small investors. If you are looking for more than $100,000, try *Investor* magazine, for you may have to bring on a number of partners. In your ad, don't state the amount of money you are looking for because most people will assume that you require the whole amount from one person. If you're looking for $50,000, you may be able to attract five people to put in $10,000 each much quicker than you can one person with $50,000. If you had stated in your ad that you were looking for $50,000, the people with just $10,000 might have never even called.

The same idea is true when you are talking to prospective investors on the phone. So as not to scare a smaller investor away, if you are looking for $50,000 and the investor has only $10,000, you might mention that you will consider a number of partners and that one investor does not have to come up with all the money.

The group approach

When you can't get one or two investors to provide all the money, another approach is to contact all the smaller investors as a group. As responses are coming in, take down the names of all the people who are interested but do not themselves have enough money to fund the entire deal. Then call back the smaller investors and invite them to a *group investor meeting*. Group presentations can be very effective. The investors at the meeting feel they are not alone and that there is sufficient interest in your project to attract more than just one investor. At one group presentation you may be able to raise all the money you need. Using more than one angel to invest in a company has become so popular that this technique has been called using a *choir of angels*. The group presentation is discussed in detail in Chapter 15.

"Last person in" technique

Nobody likes to be the first person to invest in a deal. Everyone feels more comfortable if other people have already committed. A very effective guerrilla financing technique is to tell each investor separately that he or she doesn't have to come up with the cash until there has been a commitment to a majority of the investment.

As you talk to individual investors, explain that you are only asking for a commitment *if* you can raise a majority of the money, say 60%. The investors are only asked to commit when 60% has already been committed.

Guidelines to the ideal investor

It helps to know what defines the ideal angel/investor. No single angel will ever fit this guideline, but it is something to shoot for. The perfect angel is:

1. Experienced with seed capital and start-up situations.
2. Experienced in related fields of business or technology.
3. Aware of the risks involved, and emotionally as well as financially able to bear those risks.
4. Aware of the inevitability of unforeseen delays and other small business problems.
5. Prepared to invest additional funds if the venture succeeds and/or realistic about the cost of additional outside equity capital.
6. Able to have exit expectations consistent with those of the entrepreneur and the cash flow requirements of the venture.
7. Ready for active participation in management compatible with the needs of the company and the entrepreneur.

Gaston's cast of angels

Robert J. Gaston, a man who has studied the angel market extensively and written a book on the subject (*Finding Private Venture Capital for Your Firm*, New York: John Wiley, 1989), has created a somewhat humorous and exaggerated definition of different types of angels. Studying these different characteristics of angels should help you be cautious and avoid the pitfalls of entering into a partnership with the wrong person. Although some of these descriptions are complimentary, some are definitely not. But there is a lot of truth in them.

1. *Devils.* Devils are angels who get voting control of the firm away from the entrepreneurs. Devils are hard to detect. Usually they express their desire for control right away. They have a low education level and lower than usual income levels. They almost always want to participate in the operation of the firm.
2. *Godfathers.* These are successful, semiretired consultants and mentors. They are usually older, with higher incomes and more experience than the entrepreneur. Godfathers are the best of all the angels; they seldom want control and they bring valuable experience to each investment.
3. *Peers.* Here are active business owners who want to help new entrepreneurs, with a vested interest in the market, industry, or individual. This is the largest group of angels. They are sensitive to management talent, unlikely to seek control, and patient about liquidation or payoff of their investment.

4. *Cousin Randy.* This is obviously a family investor. He doesn't operate "at arm's length" because of his family relationship. The good aspect of a Cousin Randy is that he doesn't expect much of a return on his investment and is fairly easy to satisfy.

5. *Dr. Kildare.* This describes professionals such as M.D.'s, accountants, lawyers, and others. They are relatively inactive in the daily operation of the firm and rarely seek control. They also don't expect a high return on their investment.

6. *Corporate achievers.* These are frustrated middle managers who "jump ship" by buying into a small firm and who often take over. They are looking for a career change and want to occupy a key management position. They usually have one of the lowest income levels and invest small amounts of money but get control from the entrepreneurs in the majority of firms in which they invest.

7. *Daddy Warbucks.* These investors have a net worth of $1 million and more. They make up a substantial percentage of all angels, and their investments are the largest. They are usually successful owners of businesses themselves and do not want to take control away from the entrepreneur.

8. *High-tech angels.* They are angels who invest only in firms that manufacture high-tech products. They're usually experienced businesspeople who invest in capital-intensive firms and like to be active in the firm's operations, often adding invaluable experience to existing management, rarely obtaining voting control, and often receiving small amounts of ownership for their investment. Also, they seem to be more patient about getting their money out than the other types of angels.

9. *The stockholder.* He or she is any angel who does *not* participate in the firm's operations. These angels are definitely passive investors only. Their investment is usually small, and they like to share it with a number of co-investors.

10. *Very hungry angels.* Watch out for angels who want to invest more than you need. Of all the angels, they expect the highest rates of return and are usually not business owners themselves. They want to get control but seldom do.

11. *High flyers.* These are angels who want only the super-high payoff, an average return of at least 40%. They are usually wealthy businessmen and are often dissatisfied with their investment's performance because they expect too much. They rarely obtain voting control.

12. *Impatient angels.* These angels want a quick payoff on their investment, usually 3 years. They are hard to please and want to get in and out quickly.
13. *Green angels.* They're investors without any personal entrepreneurial experience. They look for deals that are less risky and like more established firms. They have no ambition to get voting control.
14. *Nickel-and-dime angels.* They make very small investments — usually less than $10,000 per company — and are usually more harmful than helpful. They are young, infrequent investors, have low incomes, and are not business owners or managers. The use of nickel-and-dime angels can result in serious undercapitalization and dissatisfied investors.

Leaving angels behind, let's examine several investment situations now.

15. *Kiss of death.* This describes investments that are unlikely to succeed. The following business opportunities have the least chance of attracting adventure capital according to Gaston's studies:
    a. Deals in the transportation, utilities, natural resources, and mining industries.
    b. Deals using exotic investment instruments.
    c. Deals involving liquidations to outside investors.
    d. Deals involving investors who are not business owners or live far from the entrepreneur's firm.
    e. Deals involving investments with government economic development agencies.
    f. Deals with incomplete business plans.
    g. Deals with angels who have four or more other investments.
    h. Deals where the angels want to be full-time active employees.
    i. Deals where all the angels are hard to please, such as Corporate Achievers, High Flyers, Nickel-and-Dimers, and Green Angels.
    j. Deals with very old and/or very young angels.

Here are some other interesting findings from Gaston's research on angels:

Occupation. Close to 70% of all angels are business owners or managers.
Age. Angels are generally about twenty years older than the entrepre-

neurs they finance. Few angels are under 35 or over 65, with the average age being 47.

Gender and race. Close to 84% of all angels are white males.

Education. Over 72% have a college degree.

Income. The average annual income for an angel is $90,000.

Wealth. The average net worth of an angel is $750,000.

Deal acceptance rate. At 20%, this rate is not bad compared to 1% for formal venture capital.

Co-investors. Only one of twelve angels is a lone investor.

The following are reasons Gaston found that most adventure deals are *rejected.* They are listed in order of importance:

Company's inadequate growth potential.

Angel's inadequate personal knowledge of the firm, principals, and key personnel.

Management's lack of experience or talent.

Unrealistic proposed value of firm's equity.

Venture concept needing further development.

Insufficient information provided to angel.

Angel unable to assess technological aspects.

Working partners

Sometimes you can get an investor and a good working partner in one person. An ideal situation is where one partner's skills augment the other's weaknesses. A synergy is created with the partners' achieving what they could never accomplish individually. If you can find the partner with the right chemistry, you will have a good "partnership marriage."

Active partner checklist

Before you sign on that dotted partnership line, you should check out your angel, especially if he or she is going to be an active working partner. Active partners are called working financiers because they supply both money and experience. For an active partnership, there should be a period where you get to know each other better and check each other out, like a courtship. The things you want to know are:

Past performance and track record.

Personal history reflecting any problems that could be fatal to the relationship: chronic illness, gambling, alcoholism, drug abuse, or worse.

Any prior partnerships and how they worked out.

The spouse, who often has the real power; you want to deal with partners, not their spouses.

Lifestyle, high roller or low roller, able to meet personal obligations on his or her own salary.

Compatibility, emotionally and intellectually.

In the courtship, get together socially so that you can let your hair down and really get to know each other as people, not just partners.

Legal aspects of contacting angels

When it comes to the adventure capital market, you should be aware of what you can and can't do.

Contacting intermediaries is not a problem from a legal point of view. These firms are in the business of arranging investments and can judge and evaluate them.

When you contact the angel directly, however, you should know that there are securities laws in this country that you must abide by. Since angels are not in the business of investing in businesses, they need to be protected from unscrupulous entrepreneurs who try to sell them a false picture of their business.

The securities laws are set up to make sure the angel has all the correct information before making the decision to invest in an entrepreneurial opportunity.

Both federal and state laws are applicable here. Federal laws come to bear when you try to contact angels over state lines. State laws govern solicitation within state borders.

In effect, the law says that when you look for any type of passive investor or partner you are offering a security, and all securities must be registered with the state if they are sold within the state and with the federal government if sold interstate. There also are exemptions to these laws.

Federal security laws are administered by the U.S. Securities and Exchange Commission. To find out about them, contact:

U.S. Securities and Exchange Commission
450 Fifth Street N.W.
Washington, D.C. 20549
202-272-7460

You may ask for a useful guide, *Q & A: Small Business and the SEC.* You may also contact the Office of Small Business Policy, at 202-272-2644, for more information on federal securities regulations.

State security laws are called *blue sky laws* because they are designed to prevent entrepreneurs from selling investors "blue sky." Each state is different and should be contacted individually to determine what security laws are applicable.

Seek counsel from an attorney specializing in securities law before using the methods outlined in this chapter. Your lawyer will answer specific questions regarding current state and federal securities regulations and will make sure you abide by them.

Your objective is to be exempt from any regulations that would require you to spend a considerable amount of money on registering your investment as a security. You will have to use your attorney's good judgment on what you spend in order to attract capital.

What the law is trying to do

The laws are trying to accomplish the following:

1. Make sure the investor/angel has the information to analyze the risks and merits of the investment and can bear the economic risk. The angels should be intelligent enough to understand the risks and be able to withstand a complete loss if necessary.
2. Make sure that if there is more than one investor, each one has access to the same information.
3. Make sure the angel will not resell the investment to the general public.

4. Make sure there is not a general advertisement of the investment. The only exception to this rule is to advertise for an active general partner.
5. Make sure that the investor has all the necessary information to make an intelligent decision and that there is no misrepresentation about the project and all interested parties have been adequately warned of all the risks.

Exit strategy for nontraditional investors

Buyout by the entrepreneur or sellout to another company is the only real exit strategy for the investor because the majority of nontraditional ventures rarely go public. Less than one half of one percent of the businesses in this country are public companies. When you set up the investment plan, make sure there is an exit strategy, a way for the entrepreneur to buy back the interest in the company from the investor. Set up a buyout arrangement where the investor can sell his or her interest back to the entrepreneur on some settlement basis. Make sure it is a deal you can live with. It should be tied to your ability to pay off the investor out of your future cash flow. Most investors don't want to be in any one investment for more than three to seven years, so you are offering them something they will probably request anyway.

Ideally, the entrepreneur should structure the payback so that the investor gets paid a certain amount each year — almost like converting equity payments into debt payments. Of course, the entrepreneur will want to profit from a sale if it occurs before the entrepreneur can pay back the investor.

The investment does not have to be cash

Just because the angel/investor does not have cash doesn't mean you can't make a deal. The angel's investment can be in the form of a *guarantee* so that you can get some bank or asset-based financing. Often, with the substantial increase in residential appreciation, many investors use the equity in their homes as collateral so that a lending institution can lend the entrepreneur the capital he needs. Affiliated investors can invest their products or services as a substitute for capital.

Having your main supplier give you credit might be enough to get you off the ground. This is creative guerrilla financing.

Most angels back their equity investments with personal loans to their entrepreneurs. So a good amount of your angel's money could come in the form of debt, not just equity.

There is hope for the entrepreneur

Because of the information in this chapter, you should conclude that there is an angel or choir of angels for every entrepreneur, including you. Still, don't abandon your search for financing.

13

101 Guerrilla Financing Techniques

In addition to all the guerrilla financing sources and methods evaluated up to this point, there are, at the very least, *101 other ways to get money for your business* using creativity, innovation, and finesse. Guerrilla financing is also finesse financing.

These guerrilla financing techniques — call them secrets if you will, since so few people know them — have been proven to solve financing problems that everyone else said *could not be solved*.

The information and case histories in this chapter alone can make you a guerrilla financier!

State-of-the-moment technology

You're going to be exposed to the state-of-the-moment technology developed to finance the unfinanceables. You're going to learn how to do it without credit, collateral, or even cash in true guerrilla fashion. Just about every technique discussed here is being used today by savvy guerrillas.

The techniques are simple, realistic, and logical. Some involve no capital whatsoever. Many of them are *noncash solutions to financial problems*.

These innovative solutions will help you learn how to *think* about solving any financing problem. You will develop the mindset of a guerrilla. You will see how to think creatively about your own financing problems, to find the perfect solution to your situation. By the end of this chapter, you will have thought of several solutions and will be itching to try them. Strong words — but true.

Positive attitude

The main point is *not* to try all 101 techniques but to *open your eyes* to the many opportunities available for you to engage in alternative ways of thinking about money. You must always maintain a can-do, don't-say-no attitude toward raising capital. Never ask, "Is my company financeable?" Instead say, "I'll find a way to *make* it financeable!"

The 101 guerrilla financing techniques are divided into four categories. They are techniques to: (1) start a business, (2) buy a business, (3) expand a business, and (4) mine the lucrative world of investment banking.

The last section applies guerrilla financing to the traditional world of investment banking.

Don't just read the part of this chapter that pertains to your particular situation. For example, if you need capital to buy a business, *don't* just read that section. Read *all* the sections, because many of the techniques can be used for any purpose.

All set? Put on your guerrilla financing uniform, which may be a dark three-piece suit, and get ready for a financing foray, guerrilla style.

Guerrilla financing techniques to start a business

1. Barter financing. Think about what you need the money for and try to barter for it.

A man with little capital wanted to open a comedy club. He needed a location, furniture and fixtures, and a marketing campaign to get customers. He sought restaurateurs who needed business on weekends. One restaurant provided the location, furniture and fixtures, even the customers. The man got his comedy club, and the restaurant got more business on weekends.

A photographer used makeup and other products to make his clients look more attractive. He wanted to raise capital to set up a studio. Eventually he discovered how to set up his studio, rent free, inside hair salons that *already* had the traffic. The hair salons loved the idea because it was something new to offer their clients, and he got his customers at the perfect time — right after they got their hair done. A guerrilla victory.

2. Landlord financing. Your own landlord is probably an excellent source of capital. Imagine yourself owning a building and watching company after company prosper, then reading about the enormous success of several of your renters years later. Landlords are ripe for lending or investing in your business. If your company is exciting enough, they may jump at the chance, knowing that if they don't, they may well have to read about your success in years to come.

The most popular arrangement is to have the landlord pay for some or all of your leasehold improvements, then just add that amount to the rent and amortize it over the life of the lease.

If the landlord really likes your business, he or she may just invest outright in your company or offer you free rent for a period of time for a piece of the business. To raise money for an upscale billiard parlor, with no capital, an entrepreneur convinced his landlord to put in the leasehold improvements for part of the business.

Landlords make excellent angels. All you have to do is to ask. The worst they can say is no.

3. Contract financing. This technique requires the customer or client to prepay for services, using an agreement upon contract. A businessman started an air-conditioning repair business with hardly any capital by selling 1-year maintenance contracts with a 24-hour emergency repair service. His market was small retailers who couldn't afford to lose their air conditioning for too long.

The man learned how to sell these annual contracts and now has more business than he can handle. But as a guerrilla, he is handling it.

4. Other people's credit. If you need capital because you have no credit, why not *rent* someone else's credit? A man sold his business in one city and wanted to start the same business in another city, but he needed more capital to buy inventory. With the permission of the owner of his old store, he was able to use the credit from his old store and buy the inventory, then pay back the new owner within the supplier's terms. You have to get a friend or business acquaintance to do this for you, but using someone else's credit works very well, especially when you need inventory or anything that can be bought for you by someone who already has credit.

5. Concession sales. Selling space to other vendors in your own retail store is an excellent way to raise small amounts of capital. This is called concession sales, which means subleasing part of your space to other

companies. You can collect a fee up front, a royalty, rent, or a combination of all three.

A woman wanted to open a bookstore and coffee shop but did not have enough capital, so she began selling concessions to different companies to raise the capital. She sold the bakery concession to a local bakery, the use of the walls to a local art gallery, the gift concession to a local gift store, and even attracted a local florist to open a flower concession. The bookstore attracted the customers who could then be sold other products when they were in the store. The woman operated all the concessions and collected a percentage of their sales as profit. This is guerrilla financing at its best. Everyone came out well. That's the way it should always be.

6. Future commitments. You can raise money based on commitments from your customers. Obtain letters of intent or commitment letters that certain customers will do business with you. This increases your credibility tremendously and helps reduce the risk in the eyes of the lender or investor. Sometimes a letter of intent to do business with you or even a purchase order is all you need to swing the loan or the investment.

7. Manufacturer's outlet. An entrepreneur wanted to set up a Jet Ski rental business but had very little capital. He contacted a manufacturer for used Jet Skis and promised to rent its brand only. He offered to maintain the skis and to repair any ski when it became necessary. The manufacturer owned the skis, but the entrepreneur got his business off the ground by using the manufacturer as his supplier. The advantage to the manufacturer was that this was an inexpensive way to get its product onto the market for demonstration purposes. If you solve a manufacturer's problem, it will do the same for you.

8. Dealer's outlet. The same man used the facilities of a local retailer of Jet Skis in return for setting up a rental and repair business for the dealer.

9. Buy instead of starting a business. As you know by now, there are many different ways to buy a business. Most sellers finance up to 80% of the price. It is easier to get financing on an existing business than a start-up. So, instead of starting a business, buy a similar business. *Later*, when you've got your feet wet, convert it into what you want it to be. Guerrillas must be patient.

10. Lease space at your competitor's. A recording studio start-up needed money for leasehold improvements. Instead of putting a lot of money into someone else's property, the studio subleased space from a

competitor who had too much room. This avoided the costs of opening a new studio and still got the business going.

11. Work out of your home. Why sign a lease when you can perform most of your work at your home and get all the tax deductions? Few businesses can't be started in a private residence.

12. Incubators. This is a new breeding ground for small businesses and is just getting started. The incubator phenomenon consists of putting a number of small businesses under one roof and providing lots of auxiliary services to support these companies. It has been referred to as a climate-controlled greenhouse, where businesses can be watched over like fragile seedlings. Many state and local governments and universities are sponsoring these incubators, offering free or below-market rent and other free or reduced services. Contact the following:

National Business Incubation Association
One President Street
Athens, Ohio 45701

or write for the *Annual Directory of Business Incubators*:

International Venture Capital Institute
P.O. Box 1333
Stamford, Connecticut 06904

13. Tenant partnerships. Suppose you want to start an advertising agency. You could bring all the necessary subcontractors together under one roof and share facilities, maybe even form a partnership. For example, a printer, graphic house, copywriter, and public relations firm could all split a large suite of offices. Each could stay separate but share certain services and facilities. In effect, you have created your own incubator. You can also share a lot of the equipment, such as the fax, copy machine, and other pricey items.

14. Equity sharing. You can use the principle of equity sharing for any business that requires real estate. Just get investors to put the down payment on the real estate for part of the property. You pay the mortgage and maybe you own the building as "tenants in common." It is easy to attract people to invest in real estate. Just try putting an ad in the Real Estate or Business Opportunity section of your local newspaper.

An equity sharing agreement matches an investor who provides the bulk, if not all, of the down payment with an owner/occupant who picks up the remainder of the down payment and makes all the mortgage payments. Both parties share in the appreciation of the real estate.

The owner/occupant pays all the closing costs, makes minor repairs, and pays the mortgage. Both the owner/investor and the owner/occupant are on the deed to the real estate.

After a specified period of time, the owner/occupant has to refinance the real estate and buy out the investor, or the real estate is sold and the profits split. The success of equity sharing depends on the real estate's appreciating. Investors need appreciation to make the investment worthwhile, and occupants need enough appreciation to refinance and buy out the investor.

A version of this allows the investor to buy the real estate outright, while you operate the business. A day care center convinced investors to put a down payment on a home and own it outright while the day care center just operated its business in the home. The investors got a secured real estate investment with a new tenant, and the day care center got the building it wanted.

Equity sharing is an ideal way to get angels to invest the down payment in any project involving real estate.

15. Staged financing. Staged financing is raising capital for each stage or milestone in the development of your business. It is an ideal technique for new companies. You don't look for capital to finance a company completely, from beginning to end. Instead, you raise just enough money to finance each stage of development. The key to the success of this technique is always to line up enough capital at the beginning stage for all or most of the later stages. This is not an idea to raise only enough funds to get you going for a few months. It is an idea to fund you only enough for you to *prove you can successfully reach certain goals.*

Test market your product

Is it possible to get too much money for a business? Yes. Professional venture firms are notorious for giving start-ups too much money, which is usually squandered on unimportant things. Lean and mean is the guerrilla's motto. Prove your success at each stage, and there will be money waiting for you to fund the next stage. The concept is to test market your product continually at each stage so that you are only investing more based on the results of each market test. You are tying up money for the test market only. In this way, you continually roll out the product based on its success.

The concept of staged financing is to give your product or service a *reality check*. By having you actually market the product or service in the real world, you get instant feedback and can modify your idea accordingly.

The stages of a start-up

Successful start-ups move through clearly defined phases:

- Idea
- Feasibility/Prototype
- Verification/Face the public
- Demonstration/Customer feedback
- Assemble management team
- Commercialization

Staged financing allows the entrepreneur to raise small amounts of money to prove the viability of a product and to continue to raise money at each success benchmark.

Angels don't like to put money into an unproven idea but will invest in a proven idea. This lean and mean approach has been used by countless successful entrepreneurs in the past. It forces you to watch expenses carefully and use only money you need. At the same time, it offers the investors time to invest in stages of success, reducing their risk.

A budding business owner needs over a million dollars to get a video concept off the ground. As a guerrilla, he opts for financing the various stages of the proposed company. First, he raises a small amount to develop the prototype. Then he raises another small amount to test the product to see if anybody will buy it. Eventually he raises enough capital to start manufacturing the product.

There is no limit to the amount of capital you can raise using this method. Investors love this type of financing for start-ups; nobody gets in too deep. Create a plan of attack and follow it stage by stage.

16. Three sources for small unsecured loans. To finance any start-up situation, try these three methods of raising small amounts of unsecured credit. Up to $50,000 has been raised this way through many different lending institutions. The only requirements are that you have fairly good credit and hold a job when applying. Always apply for credit *before* you leave your job to start your business.

Credit unions. Many credit unions offer easy credit to their members in the form of small loans. You could join a credit union for just this purpose. Make sure you learn the length of time you have to be in the credit union before you are allowed to take out a loan.

Credit cards. Credit cards can be a good source of small amounts of capital, providing your personal credit is solid. The best technique is to turn in your credit applications to banks simultaneously so that you can obtain a number of cards with a cash advance privilege. This is called a *multiloan* concept. A cash advance allows you to take out your line of unsecured credit at any time. Approach your banks all in the same week so that on your application you can honestly state that you hold no other cards. By applying for credit at a number of sources simultaneously, you can truthfully disclose that you have no other outstanding loans. What you are looking for is an unsecured line of credit between $1,000 and $5,000 from each bank. If you contact enough banks, you can pick up substantial credit instantly. Don't mention the reason for the use of the funds. Banks usually don't like issuing credit card money for business. But they love deposits made by thriving, growing businesses.

Thrifts. Small consumer loan offices offer small unsecured lines of credit. Treat these loans as you would credit cards and approach these thrift and loan offices all at once. They can be found in the Yellow Pages under "Loans." In every case, be sure you know how you'll pay back the money. Guerrillas pay their bills on time.

17. Pyramid your credit. Here is a technique to increase your credit rating and unsecured borrowing power. Take out a $3,000 30-day loan from one bank and deposit it in another bank in an interest-bearing account. In 25 days, withdraw it from the second bank and pay off the loan to the first bank. Then wait a few weeks and go back to the first bank and ask for a $4,000 30-day loan. You'll probably obtain it because you have proven your credit reliability. Now deposit your $4,000 in the second bank for 25 days and then pay it back. As you keep repeating the process, your credit and borrowing capability grow. It's guerrilla financing in a pure form: no money needed, just imagination and information.

Guerrilla financing techniques to buy a business

18. Seller financing/earnout. How can you easily raise money for a business? Buy one. Why? *Because the seller will usually finance most of the purchase price.* Most owners of small businesses will take back a note for up to 80% of the purchase price.

Sellers usually give a 5-to-10-year note at 10%, terms usually much better than you can get from any financial institution. If the buyer can't make payments, the seller gets the business back. The fact that the seller is willing to wait for his or her money is a good sign that you are not buying a pig in a poke. *You are really buying a business and paying for it out of its own profits.* With guerrilla marketing added to guerrilla financing, you can turn the business into a cash cow.

If the seller lends you the money to buy the business, that is a good indication that the seller is confident you will succeed. Most sellers are anxious to sell and much more flexible regarding terms than any formal lender. Normally, you can get a below-market interest rate, and you do not have to go through all the formal qualification procedures that a lender would require. Make an effort to keep the down payment as small as possible. Any loan payments you make after you start operating the business will come out of business profits, not your own reserves.

These are the reasons that sellers are good sources of money to finance their own business:

- *Sellers offer the best terms.* Sellers will finance more of the purchase price, up to 80% or more, and you can usually get a seller to agree to 5-to-10-year terms.

- *Financing costs less.* Most sellers only ask for 10% interest on their money. Why 10%? It is easy to calculate.

- *You'll need less collateral.* Usually, only the assets of the business are used to support the seller's note. Very rarely do sellers take personal assets as collateral.

- *No credit checks.* Sellers usually don't do a substantial credit check on the buyer.

19. Leveraged buyout. How do you finance the purchase of a business with little or no money down? Use the same tactics the big boys use, a leveraged buyout (LBO): the purchase of a company using its own assets to secure loans that are used to pay the seller.

It all boils down to using the assets of the business you are buying to raise enough cash to buy the business. Think of the business you want to buy. What type of assets does it have? Receivables, equipment, whatever. Think of how to finance those assets. Then arrange their financing *before* you buy the business. Simultaneously, you will get the funding to buy the business, retain the legal ownership of those assets, and either sell them off or finance them. To get the actual cash to buy the business, sometimes you have to arrange a one-day bank loan to make the transaction legal.

Not only are there many ways to finance some of the assets, but you can also sell some of them off to raise the capital. Guerrillas will find a dazzling array of financing options. Again, the sale of the assets has to be set up before you actually buy the business. Many businesses are sold with *excess inventory that can be presold* for extra cash to buy the business. Look carefully at the assets you can sell. For instance, sell the customer lists to other companies before buying the company. Sometimes you have to *sell the patent or trademark* to raise capital. Another way to obtain funds is to *license a foreign company for the rights to sell* in that country. Selling off foreign rights can raise a lot of capital quickly. *Rolling stock* is very easy to presell when buying a company. You could use a *sale and leaseback*, where you sell the asset to a leasing company that rents or leases it back to you. You can use a sale and leaseback with used equipment, too.

Sometimes you can get the supplier to *buy back some of your inventory*. Or maybe you can *sell some of your inventory to your competitors*. Of course, you always have the option of *selling your inventory to your own customers* at a substantial discount.

Look for assets you can sell, rent, license, or borrow against. Always arrange the money-raising transaction *before* the sale and make it conditional upon the closing of the sale. Then coordinate the closing transaction so you can use the money to finance the acquisition. Don't forget to make sure any asset you want to sell or encumber has the right to be sold or encumbered after the sale.

Leveraging your buyout means using *other people's money* to get what you want. Is the risk worth it? Ask Victor Kiam, who bought Remington Electric Shavers, a $25 million company, for a total cash outlay of only $750,000! Victor even has the perfect first name for a guerrilla.

Some assets that are frequently overlooked can be used to raise money: customer lists, trademarks, patents, and copyrights, any excess equipment or inventory, and credits due from suppliers.

You can also borrow from the company's pension plan if it has one.

Here are some leveraging techniques to buy a small business without borrowing or getting investors.

20. Assume liabilities. Get the seller to accept your offer to assume the liabilities as part of the purchase price.

A woman did not have enough cash to buy a laundry business. The seller wanted to get cash to pay off all the debts and keep the rest himself. She convinced the seller to leave all the debts in the business; she assumed them all, which reduced the price to something she could afford.

21. Broker's commission. How do you get some extra cash to buy a business using a business broker? Have the broker leave his commission in as a liability to you. This reduces your price, and the broker takes a note for his commission to be paid over a period of time.

22. Seller assumes the receivables. Problem: how to buy a business with little cash. Solution: arrange for the seller to keep the receivables and reduce the price accordingly. In effect, the seller accepts his own receivables as part payment for his business.

23. Offer less than 100%. Once you have bought the business and assumed the liabilities, a good financing technique is to offer the creditors something less than 100%. The better you are at negotiating, the more money you can create to operate your business. If you understand the creditor's alternative of accepting sometimes only 2% to 10% on the dollar, the concept of debt reduction becomes more realistic and acceptable. Creditors will accept any amount beyond what they think they would receive if the business were liquidated. All you have to do is offer a little more than the creditor thinks he or she would get out of liquidation.

24. Use cash flow for a down payment. Sellers are sometimes willing to wait a few weeks for their down payment. Determine the net cash flow generated by the business over the first several weeks by calculating the difference between cash receipts and what must be paid out. Then structure the deal so that the seller receives the down payment out of the cash flow available once you acquire the business. Sometimes you can work it out so that the company advances its cash flow as part of

the down payment. Some sellers who are anxious to sell don't care where the down payment comes from, even if it is from their own business.

25. The escrow method. With the aid of a good attorney, you can insist that the down payment be held, not cashed, by the escrow officer until certain conditions have been satisfied, such as auditing of books, counting of inventory, and others. During this period you should be able to accumulate enough cash flow from the business to cover your down payment. Some ways to do this are to dump the inventory, sell off the assets quickly, or just defer every possible expense and avoid paying bills until the cash builds up.

26. Option financing or lease purchase. *How do you buy a business with no money down?* Some sellers will allow you to lease their business with an option to buy. This is a new concept, but it is starting to take hold in certain parts of the country. A man wanted to raise money to buy a liquor store. He lived next to a run-down liquor store whose owner had died and whose widow was trying to keep things going. The place was a mess and the widow kept no financial records. The man felt he could turn the store around with little effort but had no money.

In true guerrilla fashion, he offered to buy the store at the seller's price and get a 12-month option, with the right to manage the store during that period and keep all the financial records. The seller accepted, and within 6 months the man made the store very profitable and had enough positive financial information to attract partners to put up capital to exercise the option and buy the store.

What you do in this type of guerrilla financing is use the credit of the seller and operate the business as if the sale has been made. When you exercise the option to buy, there is a good chance that you will have enough rapport with your suppliers to continue obtaining credit for merchandise or products. Another version of this technique is to become a partner with the seller until you are ready to buy.

27. Partners with the seller/lease part of the business. There are times that you can get the seller of a business to *take you in as a partner* until you find the money or the credit to buy the entire business. Make sure you have an option for the rest of the business. One entrepreneur did not have enough net worth to get the approval from a major oil company to purchase a gasoline station. The solution was to buy a *minority piece* of the business, *take over the operations*, and *still use the credit* of the seller. Eventually, the oil company recognized the creditworthiness of the new partner, who then completed the purchase of the entire business.

28. Similar buyers. Often guerrillas have to use guerrilla techniques to find a *partner* to help them buy a business.

- *Franchise buyers.* Problem: you want to buy a franchise, but you don't have enough money. Solution: contact the sales representative for the franchisor and ask for a list of other people like yourself who want to buy the franchise. Contact these people and form a partnership or co-op to buy the franchise. The advantage is, these people have already shown interest in the franchise and are very susceptible to a co-op idea.
- *Other buyers.* Problem: you want to buy a business, but you don't have enough money. Solution: ask the seller for a list of people who wanted to buy the business but can't come up with the cash. Contact these people and form a partnership or co-op to buy the business. Again, many people just don't have enough money to pull a deal off but, banded together, can make it happen. In the future you can always arrange to buy each other out, if necessary.

Guerrilla financing techniques for existing businesses

29. Supply-side financing. Suppliers and vendors can be excellent sources of capital in many ingenious ways.

Trade credit. How much credit suppliers will give you, and how flexible they will be regarding terms, depends on how important your business is to them. Most businesspeople just don't ask for enough credit. You'd be shocked to know what can be done by just asking for better credit terms. All you do is speak to the presidents of the vendor companies and explain how much business you're prepared to do with them if they extend more credit. It works. Generally, vendors will assist you with credit if they see you are having cash flow problems because of rapid growth.

If you are a new business owner, it will be to your advantage to visit your major suppliers in person. Meet with the credit manager and work out the best possible terms. Ideally, the vendor will agree to ship goods to you on credit and will let you sell the goods and collect on them before you have to pay for them. Getting even one extra day's credit before your payments are due means that you will have that day's receipts as extra working capital.

Meet with your suppliers' and vendors' accounts receivable departments and explain your situation *before* a cash flow crunch hits. You will be pleasantly surprised by how much cooperation you will get by being candid with them. Make special credit arrangements with a vendor before you order, not afterward. It is one thing to arrange an extra 30 days' credit before ordering and another to just let the bill go an extra 30 days before paying it. The former builds credit and the latter destroys it. Guerrillas build.

If your cash flow gets tight, ask your larger suppliers to allow you to issue notes to extend their payments. They will charge interest, but it is well worth it. In effect, you will have turned a short-term debt into a long-term debt.

You can be very innovative in supply-side financing. A car nut needed capital to buy three Ferraris that he would then restore and sell. He had buyers lined up, but no money to buy and restore the cars. So he got the sellers of the Ferraris to *finance the restoration themselves for one half of the profits from selling their cars.* The car nut put up no money and took half the profits. Guess he's not really a nut.

A young man needed capital to buy a vending route. The vending machine offered stuffed toys, so he asked his supplier of toys to help finance the purchase of the vending route. The supplier had a stake in the success of his business and got a contract that guaranteed that all the stuffed toys sold by the vending machines would be bought from him.

If several suppliers carry about the same merchandise, you can pit one against the other to see who gives you the best terms and credit. This is called *business.*

Suppliers don't have to put up cash, only use their credit to arrange for a loan or purchase of inventory or equipment.

Even service suppliers, like advertisers, can contribute credit to your business. Companies that are going to do a lot of advertising can sometimes get an advertising agency to work on a results basis. You might offer them a percentage of the new sales generated by their advertising.

All in all, if they want to do business with you, suppliers and vendors can be a great source of cash or credit. Use your imagination, and you will be surprised at how eager they are to help finance your business.

Problem: a man did not have enough capital to swing the purchase of a bar. Solution: he arranged to guarantee a vending company a long-term lease of its machines in return for putting up some of the down payment.

Concentrate on your larger suppliers where your business offers them a large profit potential. Suppliers cannot only offer you credit, but can make loans to or investments in your business to get it off the ground or save it from collapsing.

30. Inventory/supplier financing. Use inventory for improving your cash flow. Keep more inventory in your supplier's hands, not yours. Order in economical quantities. Schedule production to minimize floor inventory. This is called *just-in-time inventory purchasing*: you schedule your purchases to arrive just when you need them. Tailor payments for raw material to coincide with revenues.

31. Customer financing. Customers can also be an excellent source of financing. Try guerrilla techniques using a customer's money or credit.

Offer a membership. A former insurance salesman wanted to open a brew pub. So he created a *brew club*, then sold founding memberships by offering such privileges as discounts on beer and food, a private newsletter, a membership card, special founders' activities, tours, raffles, personalized beer steins, and more.

Selling memberships in advance has succeeded many times in raising capital. A smart way to attract members is to announce that you have already signed up some celebrities as members, for you got the celebrities to become members by offering them free memberships. It works every time. Who wouldn't want to join a club whose members include the local sports and entertainment celebrities? People love to mix with the rich and famous. You will be amazed at how many people will be attracted to your concept.

A former teacher wanted to start a nightclub with little capital. He sold memberships in the club to get enough capital to start the business. Owners got special privileges when the club opened: special late hours, discounts on drinks and food, and reserved tables.

Another guerrilla technique using customer financing was used by a woman in the travel business who wanted to open a school for travel agents. She tested her idea and got it to work, but had no capital to set up a solid business. Instead of obtaining standard financing, she found a way to finance her *customers*, the students. She contacted local government agencies that had people looking for work and explained that she would provide both an education to the agency's people and actual jobs.

She said she could arrange a loan for each student if the agency guaranteed the loan. The agency agreed. Then she contacted a bank and arranged to have the bank finance the school tuition. To make it easier for the bank, she arranged to put up a reserve in the bank for each student the bank financed. With the students practically guaranteed a job, the bank's getting to make high-interest loans plus a cash reserve on each loan, and the government agency's boasting it was helping to create jobs, the travel lady ended up with an endless supply of students — all with the money to enroll in her travel agency school! Everybody won. How's that for guerrilla ingenuity?

Carrying this idea of getting the customer to finance your business further, consider a publisher of mystery novels with a problem of selling very few copies but a need for money to pay off old bills and expand. The publisher was forced to look at the business from a different angle. All kinds of authors were continually approaching it to publish their books. The publisher changed its business from *paying* authors to publish to *charging* authors to publish. No new capital was needed because *the authors paid to get their books published.* Even if only a few hundred copies were sold, the authors could tell their friends that their book was published by a legitimate publishing company. Call it guerrilla publishing.

Remember, customers don't have to put up cash but can just cosign for loans, leases, and other obligations.

32. Advance payments/anticipation. Another method for getting money from your customer is to ask for money before shipment. This is called *anticipation.* Your customer pays before shipment, sometimes in return for a substantial discount in price.

A business owner had to find a way to finance a drapery business, so he contacted a number of interior designers to ask for a cash advance in exchange for a discount on all future work.

The examples of this concept are endless. One of the best examples of customers advancing funds is American Express, whose millions of cardholders pay a hefty membership fee each year in advance. Millions more purchase traveler's checks that they hold on to and don't use. American Express loves these people, absolutely adores them. Wouldn't you?

33. Private flooring of inventory. When banks put up the money to finance durable good inventories such as cars, refrigerators, and TVs, it is called *flooring.* The bank owns the inventory until it is sold "off the floor." You can accomplish the same type of financing, using private investors instead of a bank. For example, any business selling used cars can finance its inventory with titles of ownership. You finance cars bought at auction by using private investors. The private investors are given the titles to the cars as collateral plus half of the profits on the sale of the used car. It's a great investment because investors can double

or triple their money in a few months and are collateralized by the cars bought *below* wholesale. You can get an unlimited supply of investors to buy these used cars just by advertising in the newspaper.

This concept was also used by a dealer of baseball cards, who used private investors to finance his inventory of cards, which he bought and sold in case lots.

34. Royalties.

Do you want to make money or own a business?

Pause in your exploration of guerrilla financing techniques to gain insight into the problems encountered with inventors. There is a lot of work involved in running a business. Every inventor must choose between *making money* or *managing and building a business*. Some people think that owning a business means they will automatically make money, which, as you know, is not necessarily true. On the other hand, if you license or sell your invention for a royalty, at least you know that there are no costs involved. Depending on the sales of your invention, you simply receive regular royalty checks every month. Most royalty deals involve a sale of the rights plus a royalty. So you get a fee up front *plus* royalties. The truth is, not everybody has the skills to be a successful entrepreneur. An inventor has a better chance of making money by licensing the invention than by starting a company to make and sell the invention. Guerrilla financing experts recommend that inventors license unless they show the ability and skills to manage a business and have a good reason that licensing is not appropriate.

Royalty checks can pay for a lot of new inventions. This is really a case of letting other people do the work at which they excel. When deciding whether to license or build your own business, know that it is easier to have someone make and sell who is equipped to make and sell. Many businesses are already equipped to manufacture and sell your product. They have the marketing and sales staff to get your product to market quickly. Forget business. Just invent!

35. Licensing. Distributor licensing is a popular way to sell partial rights to your product or service. Some people sell territory rights by licensing distributors. You can also have another company market or make your product or service for a fee. Usually you are selling an exclusive product or territorial right. By licensing specific product lines to be made or sold by somebody else, you are reducing your costs.

Overseas licensing is also an excellent way to raise capital. Licensing overseas companies to manufacture or distribute your product or service is a way to set up an overseas distributorship and raise needed capital at the same time. Some companies sell the territory and then charge a royalty on everything sold! Not bad when you can get it, and guerrillas can get it if they try.

A couple developed a new game and needed capital to market it. Instead of reinventing the wheel by creating their own manufacturing and distribution company, they licensed it to a company that does all that. Now the couple relaxes and collects royalties. Sounds like fun.

36. Franchising. Why not become a franchisor to raise capital? It is an excellent way. All you need to start a franchise is to set up one prototype of your operation. Systemize the operation, put it in a manual, and set up a system to train other people to do what you do. There are going to be legal expenses, but you can get those back almost immediately by: up-front franchise fees, royalties, per store opening fees, sales of supplies, and selling master territories.

You can get income from all these sources and methods.

Some companies sell master territories, such as entire states, for huge up-front fees and then require the master territory holder to sell the franchises in its state. In this case, the franchisor assumes *none* of the cost of selling the actual franchise; that is left to the master territory holders. For any franchising, see a franchise attorney. Franchising is profitable, and nearly risk free these days (1.2% failure rate), but it abounds with red tape.

37. Timesharing. Turning idle equipment, excess space, or anything you are not using all the time into dollars is what this concept is all about. When you can't use equipment fully, tap into a timesharing arrangement. Rent it out when it is not working for you. You can even get some people to pay the rental payments in advance for a discount. You can rent computer time or printing time. You can sublease unused space or timeshare the same space.

A restaurant timeshares its entire premises in the evening. During the day, it is used as a delicatessen, and at night, with a few changes, another owner uses the space as a restaurant. Talk about efficient use of facilities!

If you need capital and the only thing you own is your equipment, rent it to other entrepreneurs or have them use your facilities at night or at off-hours. Heavy equipment that can be operated 24 hours a day is ideal for timesharing. It's a guerrilla sin to keep potential capital idle.

38. Sublease. Want to buy a building for your business but can't come up with the down payment or meet the mortgage payments? Sublease part of the building and ask for several months' rent in advance. You can even timeshare your property. A man subleased his parking lot

to a parking company during the day and used it for his own restaurant at night.

Another enterprising soul opened a nightclub and leased the space during the day to a dance studio and for rock band rehearsals in order to get more capital. In other words, use your own facilities on a 24-hour basis if possible.

39. Advertising space. If you own property that many people see daily, you can raise capital by renting space for advertising and display. Contact a local advertising agency or rent the space yourself. Check with your local authorities first.

A trucking enterprise sold the rights to advertise on the sides and backs of their trucks to an advertising agency. Sometimes the side of your building can be rented or sold to an outdoor advertising agency.

40. Preselling/paid subscriptions/advance bookings. You can sell just about anything in advance or get advance subscriptions. Problem: how to get the funds to start a magazine. Solution: paid subscriptions to get enough money to print small quantities of the magazine. This is classic staged financing. Test and finance each stage for consumer acceptance and roll out the product as you get acceptable consumer response. That way, you are not wasting a lot of money on something that might not sell. There is no end to the preselling concept of raising capital. Both authors of this book used it to finance their first books!

41. Direct response/preselling. After selling advertising space in a book, an author obtained *more* money to publish by mailing a direct response brochure selling the book. The cash he received from these subscriptions was used for the final graphics and printing necessary to deliver the books. Nobody complained that it took two months for their books to arrive. If you want to try this, you must give the buyer an honest date of when you can deliver your product. As long as a delivery time is stated in the direct mail piece, you are okay. If you put no time limit for delivery on mail order products, you must deliver within six weeks.

There is no end to the products or services you can sell for capital to get your company off the ground. How about selling enrollments for a school you want to start? In effect, you can take orders for anything and take quite a bit of time to ship. Just be sure to be totally honest.

42. Coupon preselling. You can practically sell anything using *coupons*. For example, a balloonist had his balloon company sell balloon rides during the off-season by selling half-price coupons to be used during the regular season. He had the use of the money for six months before the customer used the service. People bought balloon ride cou-

pons as gifts during the winter to be used in the summer. Any type of gift coupon is a form of preselling.

43. Prepaid subscriptions. Think of all the companies that use this method of financing: Book-of-the-Month, Fruit-of-the-Month, Tape-of-the-Month, CD-of-the-Month, plus all direct mail order offers of special editions, such as those used by the Franklin Mint, which sells collectibles using direct marketing.

44. Deposits. This is one more form of selling in advance. Ask for a deposit or down payment with an order.

45. Improved collection procedures. It's amazing how many firms don't follow simple proven guidelines to improve their collections and consequently their cash flow. Here are a few guerrilla suggestions:

Bill customers quickly.

Set a definite written policy for handling past-due accounts. Set payment due dates before billing. Your customers should understand your credit policies before you ship goods to them. The more formal your credit policy is, the clearer it is to your customers that you mean business.

Establish penalties for late payment and make them real penalties. Actually charge your customers when they are late.

Contact past-due accounts by telephone immediately. Don't wait. Get on the phone and start calling as soon as the account is overdue. It's not fun, but it works and it's fair.

Set up your collection procedures according to the customer's size, amount outstanding, prior collection history, length of time the account has remained unpaid, and customer's relationship to your business. Longtime customers deserve special treatment.

Determine how you will handle bad debts, disputes with customers, chronic past-due accounts. Decide about contacting a collection agency or attorney for further action.

Delegate responsibilities. Determine who will implement the collection program and be responsible for its success.

46. Shoestring economics. This is a catchall for the wheeler-dealer types, for you must have this type of personality to use these methods effectively. If you have to force yourself to do these things, don't do them. Some people are natural wheeler-dealers and are masters at solving their financing problems using the following techniques. Only a few are listed to give you the main idea:

Leaning very heavily on suppliers for credit.

Buying all equipment and fixtures at foreclosure sales, or from classified ad bargains.

Using seconds as inventory, buying out bankruptcies, closeouts, and excess inventory.

Selling consignment merchandise.

Bartering for your services.

In reality, it is a bargain-for-everything attitude to save every single nickel. This is a very difficult method of operation, but it is how to get what you want by spending very little money.

47. Rent it. Why buy or lease when you can rent just about anything you need from equipment to furniture? You can literally rent everything you need to start a business. Many people think they require large amounts of capital for equipment that can easily be rented until their company builds up enough cash flow to buy or lease the equipment. Renting is *not* leasing. Renting is usually done on a monthly basis. When renting, find out if the monthly payments can be applied to the purchase price if you decide to buy it later on.

48. Subcontractors. Let someone else do it, make it, deliver it, even sell it.

Problem: a design firm has a new idea for closets, but no money to expand. Solution: subcontract all the work. All the construction and carpentry, including installation, was subcontracted out and the design firm just concentrated on marketing. This can be done with any business. It is a much more efficient way to operate until you have the money or expertise to produce things yourself. Some subcontractors eventually join your business or you buy their business.

This concept has become so popular that there now is a name for entrepreneurs who use it extensively: *minimalists.* The minimalist entrepreneurs pare their operations to the bone by subcontracting just about everything to outside specialists. They farm out virtually anything they can. They leverage themselves by associations with clusters of related businesses and support services. Little money is needed in this kind of business. The independent contractors they hire will naturally build a profit into their prices, which comes out of the entrepreneur's profit. The result is that it costs more to run a business this way and you may sacrifice some quality control, but you can start a business with minimal capital. To gain quality control, many entrepreneurs offer their outside suppliers an equity stake in their business to make sure they do a good job. The minimalist's strategy leads to lower costs up front. Offering equity to suppliers improves long-term control by linking the subcontractors' fortunes to their own.

49. Competitors. Getting money, products, or services from your competitors can work under certain circumstances. For instance, a

man needed work for his backhoe machine, so he went to his competitors and offered them his services. He would be their subcontractor. This can work with any piece of equipment you may have that is not being used 100%: rolling stock, trucks, anything that can be used for your competition where you get paid for your work. Renting out your equipment is a temporary solution until your own business picks up.

A Californian had a new idea for a drive-in video store but needed money for videocassettes. He obtained inventory from a local video store that would be his partner. It was a way for the local store to expand, and the Californian could sell the old videos through his new partner's store. In effect, he was using his competitor's credit to buy inventory.

This is one technique where you really have to be creative to find a way for your competitors to help you by helping them. But creativity is a guerrilla byword.

50. Charity. They say you can't get something for nothing, but that's not true. A firm had a children's home for the disabled and needed furniture and fixtures. It solicited charitable contributions for furniture, toys, and food. Not only did it end up getting the furniture and other items, but it also got volunteer personal services such as gardening and maintenance. Even the local sheriff got prisoners to work off their time at the home, doing leasehold improvement work.

51. Replacement/substitution. To lower the costs of a business, replace or substitute a major purchase with a different, less costly purchase.

A person wanted to open a hot dog business in a mall's retail space. Rather than looking for the money to pay for all the leasehold improvements needed to launch the enterprise, he purchased a much less expensive portable hot dog cart that could operate anywhere in the mall. Later, if his hot dog business did well, he could then consider renting a retail space.

The point is to look for another way to do what you want, *without* having to spend a lot of money.

52. Shows/showrooms. Instead of tying up money in a retail store, test the concept out of motel rooms, other people's show space, showrooms, or even flea markets. One way is to put on your own show and invite complementary businesses. For example, if you want to sell apparel, put on a fashion show with compatible businesses. An excellent example of cooperation within a market niche is all the companies that exhibit in a bridal show. You can create a mobile retail store without the permanent rent of a fixed location.

53. Piggyback through other companies. Sell your products in complementary mail order catalogues. Find a way to use what other companies have instead of spending money yourself. The example of the comedy club's using the facilities of the restaurant is a good example of this technique.

54. Multilevel/party plan marketing. This approach gets other people to sell your products for you, eliminating the money necessary to train your own sales force and sometimes eliminating the cost of your own facilities. Selling without stores, directly to consumers at their workplace or home, is a way to get started with very little cash. Other people buy your products and resell them door-to-door or at meetings or parties.

55. Become a management company. If you can't get the financing to expand your business, get more business by setting up a management company offering services for your competitors. The problem is getting money to expand a cleaning and janitorial business. The solution is to become a management company for an association of cleaning people. The members of your association will use you to get business, bill, and collect revenues.

56. Prepayment inducements. Offer your customers inducements to pay in advance for your product or services. You can offer free delivery, free installation, free service, free gifts. People love anything for free.

57. Newsletters and seminars. An interesting way to raise capital is by selling your own personal expertise. What do you know that would be valuable to other people? Help others learn what you know and make some extra cash at the same time. Getting subscriptions to a newsletter is a form of up-front financing. The *Guerrilla Marketing Newsletter* (call 800-748-6444) is living proof of this technique, and this sentence is living proof of guerrilla marketing.

58. Facilities management. Here, you agree to manage a certain facility for another company, or even the government, at a price equal to or less than what it is already paying. Doing someone's payroll or operating a cafeteria is a prime example. The customer is providing the capital, the people, and the operation on a silver platter for the entrepreneur to run.

59. Selling off your assets. Why not sell off some of your unused assets for fresh working capital?

Accounts receivable. Discount or sell off notes or accounts receivable. See the ads in the classified section under Money Available for people who buy notes.

Inventory. You can sell inventory without hurting your own customers. Depending on your type of inventory, you can now hire companies that do nothing but sell off your inventory to people other than your own customers. Their job is to go out and find unusual customers for your merchandise, then offer it at the right price.

Here are some tips if you want to raise money from your inventory yourself:

Sell it to employees or friends.
Hold an open house on weekends (factory or warehouse sale).
Marry unwanted products to fast-moving goods in one package.
Negotiate a buyback provision with your suppliers. If they won't pay
   you back for the leftovers, try for a credit against future orders.

Disposable fixtures and equipment. Not only can you sell off equipment, you can do a sale and leaseback.
Trademarks and patents and copyrights.
Distributor territories.

Selling off assets is also a good way to buy a business with little or no money down because you can pay back your down payment in a matter of weeks. A good technique for using this to buy a business is called the *simultaneous selloff.* You locate a buyer in a similar business who agrees to buy the excess inventory from you at the time of the sale.

60. Direct response financing. This is a way to get capital by selling the product or service through direct mail, radio, TV, newspapers, or magazines. In this approach, you get the money first and have time to deliver. It is called *up-front financing.* You apply the revenue from the direct response program to produce and deliver your products. You are using your customers' money to finance your business.

61. Free advice. Many entrepreneurs spend a fortune on all kinds of services for their companies when they could have received the same advice free. Here are some ideas on how to get good free advice about your business.

Suppliers. They will bend over backwards to help a business succeed. Get their advice free.

Associations. This is a fine source of information on how to run your business. Most businesspeople miss this source. The best part is that each association is giving you specialized information about your own industry.

Government. Take advantage of your tax dollars and contact the thousands of government agencies set up to help small businesses.

Manufacturers. If you are a retailer, many manufacturers help with displays, research, advertising dollars, and marketing materials. All you have to do is ask.

Freelance consultants. Find one who will accept payment based on results. Marketing, advertising, and public relations specialists can be found in every city. Look for people who have the courage of their convictions to work this way.

MBA candidates. Graduate students can be used to work on your project as *interns* for pennies or less. Talk to the dean of your local business college.

62. Purchase order financing. This is commonly referred to as work-in-process financing or financing based on invoices, back orders, purchase orders, or production schedules. Money is dispersed per order. Sometimes a company just arranges for a bank line of credit to the entrepreneur, to be taken down as needed to deliver orders.

63. Internal capital. There are many things to do to get capital from your own business. You might call it a cash management system or a cash generating system:

Shorten credit terms to accelerate cash flow.

Raise discounts for early payment of invoices.

Tighten credit policies so that marginal, slow-paying customers are required to pay in cash.

Use more aggressive collection practices.

Accelerate billing procedures so that invoices are mailed at the same time as shipments are sent.

Review inventories for excessive stock, and accelerate inventory turnovers by tight merchandise controls.

Pay bills at the last possible date, and use discounts only if it is cheaper than retaining the cash for your own business.

Increase prices or gross margins.

Increase C.O.D. orders, offer a discount, and reduce receivables.

Sell off equipment, inventory, and other assets.

Establish minimum orders or service fees on orders below your minimum.

Settle customer disputes immediately.

Contact late-paying customers by phone first.

Sell gift certificates.

Provide salespeople with incentives for collections. Give all salespeople an aging of accounts receivable.

Improve your credit checks.

Open all mail immediately, and deposit checks the same day they are received.

Take out bad debt insurance.

Use the fifty free marketing weapons described in *Guerrilla Marketing Attack*.

64. Per inquiry sales. A per inquiry sale on TV, radio, and in some magazines is when you pay not for the advertising but only a percentage of the sales you generate. Certain forms of communication will offer free air time or print space to use unsold air time or display space. You really have to shop around to find the radio and TV stations and magazines that will do this. Many will.

65. Cooperatives, trade associations, networks. Groups of companies get together to buy in larger quantities in order to get better prices from suppliers. Cooperative efforts can be applied to other areas, such as marketing, shared advertising, cooperative printing, and mailings. Some cooperatives have formed their own banks, where members pool their own money to back loans to other members for specific purposes. By putting all their money together in one bank, a cooperative or association then has clout with that bank. Talk to your own industry association about this new idea or form your own.

66. Cooperative advertising. A glider company needed money for advertising. As part of the glider ride, the company arranged a stay at a local hotel and a meal at a nearby restaurant. The concept was to make the whole experience an exciting weekend package, with the hotel and restaurant contributing toward the cost of the ad for the glider ride.

67. Reduce accounts payable. With each vendor, work out an agreement to delay payments or spread them out. A long payout over one year can be secured by a note, will reduce your accounts payable on your balance sheet, and go under long-term obligations. This improves your working capital position from any lender's or investor's eyes. Remember, once you have made an agreement with a supplier or vendor, stick to it! Guerrillas keep their promises.

If you are not going to continue doing business with some suppliers, offer to settle their invoices at less than 100% on the dollar. You can negotiate payables if you try.

68. Create a school or clinic. Create a school to teach people something about your product or service. For example, a wine importer taught wine appreciation. You can use hotel seminar rooms as your facilities. You can also get your students to do some of your work for you as part of the course.

Another example of this concept is a chiropractor who developed a machine that would absolutely make money for other chiropractors, but he needed to raise money to sell it. So he set up a clinic of chiropractors, all using his machine. He soon made enough money from his clinic to sell the machines around the country.

69. Interns. Most colleges today will provide you with students *free of charge* or for a minimum wage. Set up an intern program where students earn college credits by working at your place of business. How can you beat cheap, well-educated labor? Talk to the dean of your local college about how to set this up. Interns *need* you to get going with their careers.

70. Pawnbrokers. Certain business and personal assets can be pawned for cash. People forget that every town has a pawnshop that does just that.

71. Movie credits. Want an innovative way to attract angels to invest in a film? Give credit to all the angels who buy an interest in the movie. How much they put in influences the form of their credit. The benefits or credits may include the following (guerrillas are going to love this):

Amount Invested	Benefits
$ 1,000	Invitation to premiere
$ 5,000	Premiere cocktail party
$ 10,000	Premiere dinner
$ 25,000	Screen credit: "Special Thanks to . . ."
$ 50,000	Appear in movie as an extra
$100,000	Screen credit: "Associate Producer." Friends can be extras
$250,000	Main title and print ad credit: "Executive Producer" and complete access to set

Every angel also gets all the benefits of the other angels below their category. That's show biz, guerrilla style.

72. Restructure financial statements. Many business owners redo their financial statements to show a more favorable picture to the financial community. This is perfectly legal. For instance, a company was showing a loss because it wasn't capitalizing research and development costs but expensing them. It was being turned down by bank after bank. But after it worked on its statements, it was easy to get financing because the new statements showed a substantial profit. The problem is that *accountants are not necessarily familiar with what financial sources are looking for and are only preparing statements for tax purposes.* That's fine for saving on taxes, but not for raising capital. Guerrillas get ac-

countants who know what financing is all about or advisers to help them with their financial statements.

73. Discounting notes and mortgages. Many firms have personal or business assets that can readily be converted into cash. *Just about any secured IOU can be discounted.* Notes receivable and mortgages can be sold off for a discount. To find a buyer, look in the classified section of your newspaper under Money Available for firms that buy mortgages. Or place an ad under Money or Capital Wanted. Some hard money lenders will buy notes backed by real estate or other assets, such as equipment or businesses.

74. Sale and leaseback of your own equipment. Selling off your own equipment to a leasing company and then renting or leasing it back is very common. Look into it.

Guerrilla investment banking techniques

These techniques are mostly used for larger deals of $250,000 and up. The descriptions may sound a little like financial mumbo-jumbo, but worry not, many investment bankers will teach you how to use these concepts. They will give you a glimpse into the world of guerrilla investment banking.

75. Revenue-sharing notes. This new concept is being applied successfully to small businesses. It is a way to attract investors/angels without giving up almost any equity in your business. It uses a new kind of financing instrument for small businesses called a *revenue-sharing note, revenue participation note,* or *participating revenue certificate.* Instead of sharing the revenues *after* expenses, the buyer of the note (the investor) gets a share of the revenue off the top, before any expenses have been deducted. This makes it a very attractive instrument to offer an angel who is uneasy about waiting around for a company to make a profit. Here's how it works and why it is such a popular method to finance a small business.

Problem: A company wants to sell stock to an investor but doesn't want to give away a big chunk of the company. The investor, on the other hand, does not like the insecurity of just owning stock and waiting for the profits to be produced.

Solution: The company offers the investor a revenue-sharing note or bond. This is an unsecured note to pay the principal back over a period of years or months. You can determine how and when the principal payments are paid back to give you time to use the funds. Sometimes you can wait 6 to 12 months before starting to pay back the principal.

The investor/angel likes this because now he or she is a full-fledged creditor, not a last-in-line stockholder, and if anything goes wrong he or she gets paid before any of the owners. Also, the investor gets paid off the top, not the bottom, of the profit and loss statement.

To provide an incentive for the investor to lend the company money, the company agrees to pay the investor a percentage of the gross sales for as long as the investor's note is outstanding. This percentage is over and above any principal payments. Most of these notes collect an average of about 1% of the revenues. This should cost the company nothing because almost any business can raise its prices by 1%. The company continues to pay the 1% as long as the note's principal payments are outstanding. Obviously, the company has a great incentive to pay off the note as soon as possible to eliminate the revenue expense. As an added kicker for the investor, you might want to issue warrants or options to buy 5% to 10% of the stock of the company. This way, the investor does not have to buy any stock if he or she doesn't want to, and the company is now selling stock, not giving it away.

This lucrative method of raising capital for both the company and the investors can offer the investors double or triple their money in 12 to 18 months or more, depending upon the revenues.

An added attraction: the angel does not have to worry about an exit strategy to get his or her money out since that is worked out at the beginning.

Check with your lawyer before attempting this type of financing. Some states might consider the note as carrying usurious interest. The revenue aspect of the agreement is not usury interest because it is based on *future income* or something that will happen in the future. To comply with some state usury laws, an existing company might want to use a revenue note to fund a particular new product line it is marketing.

76. Product-preferred stock. This is a preferred stock that gets its income stream in the form of profits from other aspects of the business, such as royalties on the sales of specific products. This is another new and creative way to sell a security. It is like a revenue-sharing note, but it is preferred stock.

An entrepreneur had to get money for his mail order business. Instead of getting investors to buy into the company, he arranged for investors to use the product-preferred stock concept (which can also be used in limited partnerships) — to invest not in the company but in new customer lists. Each investor ended up owning a number of names and received money each time those names bought any merchandise. If the company was ever sold, then the mailing list of customers would be valued and the investor given part of the value of those names.

77. Zero coupon bonds. This is a way to raise capital from angels by guaranteeing their principal investment. Zero coupon bonds are annuities that pay the bond back in one lump payment at the end of the maturity of the bond, so the bonds have no principal or interest payments until the final payment.

Say you need $600,000 for your business. You could form a limited partnership and sell ten limited partnerships at $100,000 each, guaranteeing your limited partners that they will get their money back in 10 years. How do you do that? You take the $1 million you have raised from the limited partners and buy a $1 million zero coupon bond for only $400,000. In 10 years, the $400,000 will be worth $1 million. The rest of the $600,000 is yours to put into your business. It's wild, but true.

Besides guaranteeing the investors' money back in 10 years, you can also give them a percentage of your company for the investment. So the investors are getting a piece of the action plus a guarantee for their money. This is a dandy deal for all parties and a good way to raise large amounts of capital. Savvy people do it every day.

78. Private placements. Through a private placement, you can offer stock in a corporation or units in a limited partnership to a relatively small number of private investors. And you don't have to meet the expensive registration statement requirements set by the Securities and Exchange Commission. Because private placements don't have to comply with such complex regulations, there is much less paperwork and they are much faster and cheaper to complete. They are usually known as Regulation D offerings because they fall under Regulation D of the Securities and Exchange Act. Also, they are sometimes referred to as "exempt offerings" because they are exempt from most of the procedural hurdles that apply to major public offerings.

These special offerings are termed private placements because they are usually offered to a few private investors, not to the general public. The investors are not primarily concerned about the liquidity of their investment, because private placement stock or units are usually not easy to resell to other investors. The most common type of private placement is the limited partnership.

79. Limited partnerships. A limited partnership offers an exciting way for a business to raise money. A typical limited partnership involves one general partner, the business owner or management team, and a number of limited partners, or investors/angels. The investors are called limited partners because their role as partners in the business is very passive and limited. In fact, the general partner usually holds full authority for all business decisions and operations.

Entrepreneurs are attracted to raising money from limited partners because these partners, by law, cannot tell them how to run their businesses. Limited partnerships are not new. For years they were the primary financing vehicle for real estate and oil and gas ventures, where they were used as tax shelters for investors. Recent changes in the tax law, however, have practically eliminated the tax shelter value of limited partnerships.

Now limited partnerships are finding a strong new appeal as financing vehicles for business opportunities. Most limited partners are looking for a high rate of return on their investment and are willing to accept more risk in exchange. Usually collateral is not an issue for them in a business opportunity. Limited partnerships are relatively inexpensive to underwrite, as registered securities go, and can be sold in a few months. They can be used to raise money to start, buy, or operate any business enterprise.

Limited partners like the concept because they are limited in their liabilities and don't have to come up with any more money, no matter what happens to the investment. The entrepreneur likes limited partners because they cannot tell him how to operate his business. Not a bad arrangement! It's a win-win situation for all concerned.

The popularity of limited partnerships has created a myth that they are a magic way to raise capital. Not true. They are just a legal form of ownership. Even though you form a limited partnership with you, the owner of the business, as the general partner, you must still find limited partners to whom to sell the investment. The owner can sell the units (the denomination of a limited partnership as compared to stock in a corporation) without any licenses. You must register your partnership with the state and, if you are soliciting partners outside the state, with the federal government. Contact your attorney to set up a limited partnership.

Limited partnerships are not for every deal, but are effective *when you know who your partners are going to be*. A physical therapist wanted to raise capital for an indoor pool facility. Her customers would come from doctors who would recommend the facility to their patients. This was an ideal situation for a limited partnership because it could be sold to the doctors who would benefit the most from the facility.

This is a good example of when to put together a limited partnership because you know who the ideal investor is *before* you invest the money to create the partnership. The problem with a limited partnership is when it is created *without* any idea of how or where or to whom to sell the units.

Do not go through the expense of creating a limited partnership agreement until you have a very good idea of who your limited partners will be.

It is not expensive to form a limited partnership; you can even form a public limited partnership and advertise for partners.

80. Master limited partnerships. Commonly called "roll-ups," the assets of a number of limited partnerships can be pooled together into a new partnership and the old partners given a stake in a new master limited partnership. The new partnership offers the old investors a way to cash their weak investments into a stronger investment. A master limited partnership can be a publicly traded company. This is a way for a limited partnership that is not going anywhere to take a limited loss and sell out to a much stronger partner.

A man was a syndicator of real estate partnerships but couldn't borrow more money on each partnership. By combining all the partnerships into one big master partnership, he was able to raise fresh capital. New partners were brought in for a piece of the pie and old partners took slightly less, but the total package was now well financed.

81. Research and development partnerships. These are specific limited partnerships where the angels invest in a losing situation because the company usually has no sales but is in the development stage. The partnership owns the rights to the results of the research and usually ends by selling these rights when they become valuable. This becomes the exit strategy. The investors use the losses as writeoffs to reduce their income taxes. When the company becomes profitable, the investors receive income, usually as a percentage of sales. Because of the changes in the tax laws, these types of partnerships are not as popular as they used to be.

82. Last sale commitment. Use this technique if you are contacting angels or limited partners because it eliminates their fear of being the first to invest. With the approval of your attorney, tell each investor that he or she does not have to come up with any cash until you have

raised a majority of the funds. Tell them you will come back when you have a majority of your capital committed. When you get a majority committed, go back and collect the cash.

83. Third-party guarantee. A lot of angels would like to invest or lend to your project but don't have the cash or are not liquid enough. A good solution is for the angel to *guarantee a loan* from a lending institution. This is called a third-party guarantee. You get money from a bank that receives a guarantee from the third party, who is the investor. Look for investors who have strong personal balance sheets, which means they have a high net worth made up of real estate, stock, bonds, or other valuable assets.

84. Third-party collateral. Stronger than just a guarantee is the situation where angels allow a lien against their real estate. Millions of people own real estate that has gone up in value. They cannot afford to sell or refinance it. Their equity in their real estate could be *your* collateral for a loan or investment. They don't have to put up any cash, only allow their real estate to be used as collateral. Your company makes the mortgage payments.

85. Buying collateral/credit enhancements. Another very popular method of financing is to literally *buy the collateral* necessary to secure the loan. There are many different ways to do it, but it all comes down to borrowing much more than you need, usually three times as much, and using the extra two thirds to buy bonds or some type of collateral, guaranteeing the principal payments of the financing. Only the interest is at risk. These deals are usually handled by boutique investment bankers throughout the country and are called credit enhancements.

86. Overseas or offshore capital. Foreign financial sources are getting into business opportunity financing in a big way in the United States. They're getting into it in many different ways, but the most popular seems to be through a third-party guarantee, where they put up enough money to buy collateral to protect their own investment. Even though the deals they get into could be very risky, they usually want only to get interest on their money, not equity. Their rates are competitive, and they take risks that no stateside financing firm would dare to take. They will even lend money to start-ups!

87. Offshore underwriting. This is another way to get foreign capital. It consists of having an offshore merchant bank or underwriter sell stock in your company to foreign investors or angels. In these situations you have to be wary of the firms you deal with; the security laws in other countries are not as protective as they are in the United States.

88. Reverse mergers into shells. This is a fairly new phenomenon. You become a public company instantly by being bought by a public shell. A shell is a public company that may or may not have assets, but it is a conduit to get your company public. After the merger, you can usually sell more stock to the public very inexpensively to raise more capital.

These mergers may take place in a blind pool or a shell. The shell may have been an old public company that sold off its assets and left only its corporate public "shell." The shell company usually adopts the operating company's name, headquarters, and management. Hence the name "reverse" merger.

89. The shell. This is not to be confused with the old shell game. The shell can be either a company that ceased operations or a blind pool. The operating company usually will get stock and cash. To raise additional capital, the new combination of shell and operating company ordinarily does a follow-up public offering or gets existing shareholders to put up additional money by converting warrants into stock.

Both the reverse merger and blind pool are ways to go public for a fraction of the cost of an initial public offering, and they can be done much more quickly. It allows weak companies to go public regardless of stock market conditions.

90. Blind pool. A version of this shell concept is the blind pool, a company created specifically to find and acquire operating companies. It accepts money from people who do not know or specify the investments to be acquired. The managers of the blind pool invest the capital raised in small businesses.

91. The spinoff. A private company becomes a public company via a spinoff by issuing shares of its common stock to an existing public company. The public company then registers these shares with the SEC, and, upon registration, the shares are distributed as a dividend to the shareholders of the public company. The dividends of the stock of the once-private company are considered a "spinoff" of the private company's shares. This is also quick and inexpensive compared to an IPO (initial public offering). Weak companies or even start-ups can go public this way without the normal due diligence. Generally, only 10% of the stock of the private company's shares are distributed as a spinoff, preserving the corporate ownership.

If all these private placements sound like gobbledegook, don't worry; investment bankers arrange for all these types of financings.

92. London and Canadian stock exchanges. A way to raise public

capital for about half of what it costs in the United States is to "go public" on the London or Canadian stock exchange. There are a lot of pitfalls, and it is best to contact your brokerage firm for information on going public this way. But as a guerrilla, check it out.

93. Penny stock market. The penny stock market has had its ups and downs, but it is still a viable way to sell a new public issue. It is still somewhat expensive to go public, even with a penny stock, although many good companies raise money this way. Contact your brokerage firm to find out who is underwriting penny stocks.

94. Corporate venturing or partnering. Corporate venture investments, joint ventures, technology transfer, and strategic alliances are all part of corporate venturing. The idea is to use the capital, credit, management, and facilities of major companies to get the things you need for your own company. Corporate venturing takes many forms, through both direct corporate investments and joint collaborative efforts. One of the significant features of most corporate venturing relationships is that the large and small companies are considered equals, with important benefits accruing to each. While the larger company may or may not eventually acquire the smaller, it is not a condition of the arrangement. Outside any specific areas of collaboration, the smaller company remains independent to pursue its own business goals and objectives.

Corporate partnering is ideal when you have a product or technology that is so difficult to understand that it would take an interpreter to explain it to an angel or lending institution. On the other hand, the appropriate corporation, in the same or related field, will have the staff to understand the technology. In effect, in selling your concept for financing you should market to people who understand what you are talking about.

95. Corporate venture capital. Large corporations have set up traditional venture capital subsidiaries with a twist: the companies they invest in must have something to do with the corporation's industry or help the corporation in some way now or in the future. It is also appropriate where the product, market, or technology is related to the parent corporation's operations or where the business provides an opportunity for diversification. Corporate venture capital is often made in conjunction with other business arrangements, such as license or royalty agreements, research contracts, or volume purchase agreements.

96. Joint ventures. This involves two companies going into a market together, each one complementing the other. Both companies want

to collaborate on a specific project or series of projects that capitalize on their relative strengths. The joint venture is usually done under a separate legal organization, such as a new partnership or corporation. There may be certain aspects of your business that appeal to major companies so that they would want to be associated with you.

97. Strategic alliances. Two companies come together on a project to help each other, but these collaborations do not involve setting up a new legal entity. Strategic alliances are usually used for research contracts, marketing, or licensing agreements. Under a research contract, your company performs research for the sponsoring corporation in exchange for financing. Under a marketing or licensing agreement, your company receives either up-front or future payment financing for giving the right, exclusive or nonexclusive, to another company to produce or sell your product as its own.

The advantages of using the capital and other resources of another business are enormous. More and more small businesses are forming a partnership or alliance with a larger, better-capitalized business to get their product or service to the market. This is good business. Large companies are relying on the innovation of small companies to develop new technology and are either investing in those companies directly or sharing their facilities or other resources for a piece of the action. Strategic alliances are sensible, enabling the small business to enter the market for much less money and much faster. It is much less risky to use a corporate partner to help you finance your business. Guerrillas delight in using this approach. They don't have to give up any control and still get the capital and other resources they need to grow.

98. Technology transfer. This is where corporations or governments want to buy rights to manufacture, market, and/or distribute your product or technology outside the country. Technology transfer agreements allow you to penetrate foreign markets easily and profitably.

A company had a piece of equipment with twenty moving parts but was having difficulty with its equipment. It went to a major company to fix the equipment's technology. The result was that the big company, because of its resources, was able to reduce the equipment to five moving parts, saving substantial production costs. It turned out that the major company was using a government grant that required it to help little companies. Check out what a major company can do for you. Even giants can be guerrillas.

99. Employee stock option plan (ESOP). You can raise money from your own employees to buy shares in your own company. Do this by borrowing money to purchase the stock. Many guerrilla financing

sources are anxious to make these types of loans because they pay taxes on only 50% of the interest income. Use an aggressive bank as your lending source. Your accountant or lawyer can also help you set up an ESOP.

100. Merger. There is always the option of merging your company with another that has what you need, such as products, services, or expertise. But be careful not to get in over your head. Many mega-conglomerates have merged into oblivion.

Maybe, with these techniques, you can create your own guerrilla conglomerate.

101. The mastermind concept. Two heads are better than one, and three are even more valuable. Brainstorm creative ways to raise capital. Motivated people can work out innovative solutions of all kinds. Napoleon Hill called this "the mastermind concept," and it has worked exceptionally well for thousands of companies in the United States.

Only scratched the surface?

You have reached the 101 mark, but you have really only scratched the surface in applying creativity and innovation to the world of finance. You get the point by now. Using a mixture of common sense and innovative ideas, there is nothing you can't do.

If you need financing, try some of these techniques. If one won't work, another will. Ask any guerrilla.

14
How to Write an Effective Business Plan

In order to raise any capital, you must be able to put in writing who you are, where you are, where you are going, and how you are going to get there. This is called a written presentation.

One of the most difficult aspects of raising money for many would-be business owners is to get their story in writing. We live in a visual age, in which most people learn to communicate orally and visually. But when it comes to raising capital, talk will only take you part of the way to your goal.

Learn to put your ideas into writing. Writing effectively may determine the difference between your success and failure in raising capital. Communication is the key. The financial source will base 50% of its decision to lend to or invest in a project on the presentations it receives, both oral and written. More important, *the presentations constitute the first 50%.* If your oral presentation is poor, you may never get to offer your written presentation. Likewise, if your written presentation is poor, you may never have the opportunity to present your project in person. Learning how to communicate effectively, in person and in writing, is necessary if you want to raise money. This chapter will cover both types of written presentations: the short financing plan and the long business plan. The next chapter will show you how to present your story over the phone for the appointment and in the face-to-face meeting.

Whether you make your oral or written presentation first is not significant, because guerrilla financiers don't even attempt to use their oral presentation without having already written their financing or business plan.

Putting things in writing crystallizes your thoughts and makes them all seem logical. Once you have written your plan, the oral presentation comes much easier. Many people find it impossible to communicate effectively in person about any project or business without first taking the time to develop a written plan.

Under no circumstances should you contact any type of financial source before you develop and complete your written presentation.

What is a well-written plan?

A well-written plan is a document that contains all the information necessary for the financing source to make a decision without even talking to the entrepreneur. Such a plan should stand by itself without the entrepreneur's being present.

It is unlikely that you will have to submit a written presentation without being there at some point. But if you can write a plan that can stand on its own, you will have created an excellent written presentation and will have a good chance of getting your money.

Not just another chapter on how to write a business plan

There are plenty of good books on how to prepare your written presentation, be it a business plan, financing plan, or loan package. Because of the amount of information you need to know to prepare an effective plan, either purchase a book on the subject or have someone or a company help you.

The intent of this chapter is to make you aware of the different kinds of plans you can write and to help you decide which one is appropriate for your particular project. Without learning the difference between a complete business plan and a financing plan, you can waste a lot of time preparing a detailed business plan when all you need is a short financing plan. Once you have decided what type of written presentation you need, it is important to know what to concentrate on, what to emphasize, and what to watch out for. This chapter will help you determine whether a full business plan is necessary and will also give you an overview of writing an effective plan.

The financing plan vs. the business plan

One of the first things you must do is determine whether you need to prepare a *financing plan* or a *complete business plan*. A business plan takes more time and effort, so there is no sense in spending all that time and effort if it is not necessary.

What is a financing plan?

The *financing plan* can be used to raise debt or equity or both. The financial community sometimes calls it a loan package, but this book calls it a financing plan because loan packages are only for debt financing, not for any equity financing.

Use the following criteria to determine when to write a financing plan:

Local market. Financing plans are most often used to raise capital for businesses with *local or regional* markets, whereas business plans are used to raise money for companies with *national or international* markets.

If your business is in a single location or retail store and you are looking for $200,000 to bring on a partner, you probably do not need a full business plan. If you have a retail business that you intend to develop statewide or nationwide and need $200,000 in equity money, you probably will need a complete business plan.

Debt financing. If you are only looking for a loan and do not want equity financing at all, a financing plan is all that's necessary.

Small amounts of capital. Business plans are very similar to financing plans, except that much more detail is required. Financing plans should not be used to raise equity capital unless it is for a small business with only a local market looking for less than about $250,000.

Financing plans don't require a marketing plan. A *big difference between a financing plan and a business plan* is in the marketing section. Every plan, no matter what type, has to have some discussion about the market the company is selling to. The financing plan needs only a brief marketing section — maybe a page or two — while up to 30% of a business plan might be devoted to the marketing plan. A marketing plan is a key part of a business plan and will be discussed in detail later.

Going business. Financing plans are usually more appropriate for businesses that have been in business for at least 2 or 3 years. Financing plans emphasize the *past*; business plans usually emphasize the *future*. Most start-ups will need business plans unless the enterprise has a very local market.

What is a business plan?

Business plans tell the story of your business or business-to-be. They are usually created for projects over about $250,000 where the business has a national or statewide market and the bulk of the financing is equity financing. You could go for a $1 million loan and need only a financing plan. But if you need $250,000 in equity financing and are a potential national or statewide company, you will probably need a complete business plan.

Don't always let the amount you are looking for influence what type of plan you prepare. If you want to start a national company and need only $100,000, then by all means, do that business plan.

A business plan includes a detailed analysis of your market, management, and organization, an evaluation of the competition, a list of the anticipated problems and their solutions, realistic projections of the capital required, and how and why the plan is expected to work.

A good way to decide whether to write a financing or a business plan is to look at the management. If you need a skilled management team to run your business, you most likely need a business plan. This means a true management team, not an employee team. A management team means that you need, or will need, at least a chief executive officer (CEO), a chief financial officer (CFO), a chief operating officer (COO), a chief marketing officer (CMO), and possibly more. If the company can be managed by one person, you don't need a business plan.

Who should write the plan?

By sticking closely to what you learn in this chapter, you could write your own plan, especially if you're good at written communication. But very few entrepreneurs have the necessary skills to write an effective plan, so consider having it written — in final draft form — by a pro. One of the main things you will learn from this chapter is the complexity of writing a truly effective plan.

Still, if the entrepreneur is not included in the strategy or creation of a plan, it loses much of its effectiveness. After all, one of the reasons for writing the plan in the first place is to crystallize the entrepreneur's thinking about the business.

Plans are marketing tools

A plan really has one purpose: to raise money. Sure, it can be turned into an operations manual, and it does help you focus on what is important about your business. The truth is, no matter what you put in writing, the minute you get the money you're looking for, the information and strategy in the plan will change, sometimes dramatically.

Plans are tools to sell your story to financial sources and should be recognized as such. The plan is a guerrilla marketing weapon created to sell your story to a lender or investor. You will need all the help you can get to make that tool sell for you. You may decide to use it for other purposes as well, but your job is to keep your eye on the ball. *And the ball in this case is getting money.*

Take a few moments now to learn how to write a financing and business plan that will sell your proposal or business to the financial community, be it lender or investor.

Rules to follow

There are rules that both financing and business plans should follow. There are no exceptions to these rules. If you sincerely want to raise capital, you must follow them religiously.

1. *Make it neat.* Appearance is critical. Use a laser or letter-quality printer on white paper. With the current easy availability of laser printing, no plan or proposal should come out of an ordinary typewriter or dot-matrix computer printer. Clean white paper is the only color paper to use. Sloppiness of any kind will reflect negatively on the way you do business.

2. *Make it grammatically correct.* Have a friend who is an English

student or teacher read your draft and correct any spelling, typing, or grammatical errors. Just because you have the ideas doesn't mean you can communicate them correctly. You don't have to be a scholar to write a business or financing plan, but you had better have one proof-read it before you submit it to any financing source.

3. *Make it honest.* Don't exaggerate or lie. Tell it exactly as it is, not as you would like it to be. This does not eliminate making optimistic projections, which are necessary. Realize that with all the fancy terminology, *the plan is still only a marketing tool.* Outright exaggeration and truth-stretching come back to haunt you. A miserable life experience is to lie to get the money, then have to tell your lender or investor the truth when the facts inevitably become known.

Facts can be stated favorably, without bending the truth. Don't ignore a previous mistake or failure, such as bankruptcy or default. Be completely candid. Financial sources are looking for integrity and honesty. Everyone admires a person who can overcome mistakes or rise above adversity.

If you have had ups and downs, explain why they occurred and will not happen again. If you went through a rough period, explain what you are doing to correct the factors responsible for it.

Make-believe has no place in professional business or financing plans. You must be prepared to back up everything you say. If you have to fib to get the money, maybe you should rethink your project altogether.

4. *Write in laymen's language.* Communicate in clear English, not technical jargon. Some 80% of all plans and proposals have too much jargon, which only someone in the exact field can understand. With the exception of some traditional venture capitalists and their staff of technical experts to read the plans, *no one* with money, lender or investor, wants to wade through technical language. Most jargon does not impress financial sources as much as short simple words that communicate effectively.

Breaking the next rule may be why only 5% of all financing and business plans are funded.

5. *Don't overemphasize your product or service.* Many business owners know a great deal about their products and services and can talk or write for hours about them. But the product or service is just *part* of a business. A business involves many resources: people, money, products, and services. You can't have one without the other. No financial source wants a course on your product line. *Don't sell the product, sell the company.*

Do you think Ray Kroc, the founder of McDonald's, was selling hamburgers? No way. He was selling cleanliness, economy, atmosphere, consistency, speed, and convenience. He was selling the *business*, not the *product*.

Keep the description of your product and service short and to the point. Concentrate on the benefits your customer gets from using your product or service.

The financial resource's point of view

Forever remember that people who make decisions about lending or investing money think differently than you do. They look at your business project from a unique and narrow perspective. If you are not on *their* wavelength, you are not going to sell them. *The number one reason any type of financing or business plan fails to communicate is that it is written from the entrepreneur's point of view, which is not the lender's or investor's point of view.*

Why financial figures are important

Financial sources are mainly numbers people. The numbers must be correct, add up, and make sense. Some financial sources want to hear more about your figures than about your product or market. They focus on your bottom line. How much does the business have after paying all cash expenses and a salary for the owner(s)? This is called cash flow and determines the health of a business.

If you have been in business for a few years, the figures tell the story of how you have used your product or service to make money. The figures tell how well you have done in the past and how well you might expect to do in the future. Figures, as far as the financial community is concerned, don't lie.

If you are thinking that a good accountant can do wonders with figures, you're right. A company's profit performance and balance sheet can be made to look substantially better or worse by using different accounting techniques. But lenders and investors were not born last week, and they will not examine your figures with untrained eyes.

They verify the information you present. They will compare your business finances with your personal finances. They will study your business and personal tax returns. In fact, it is best to explain up front any tax-avoidance procedures your accountant is using so that the financial source can interpret your statements correctly.

Tax returns can tell a lot about your business. Financial lenders especially like to see profits on a business tax return. They feel if you are making enough money to show a profit and pay taxes, you are making enough money to repay their loan or produce a good return on their investment.

What financial figures require concentration?

Nonguerrilla entrepreneurs enthusiastically talk of their sales revenue but only casually refer to profits. Sales tell a financial source how well your *suppliers* are doing, but the profit line at the bottom shows the money available for loan repayment or investor return. *The bottom line is the most important figure.*

For start-up companies or businesses in their early years, the *cash flow break-even point* is the most critical figure to financial sources; that is the point at which the company's revenue will support all its expenses.

Keep this distinction in mind: *lenders* will be more interested in *historical figures* as proof of your ability to repay a loan; *investors* will be more interested in your *projections* of the returns they can expect.

Figures disclose management's decisions

Is there anything more important than figures? There sure is — *management*. In business, management makes the world go around. But good figures are just a direct result of management's correct decisions. Bad figures are a direct result of management's poor decisions. Except for start-ups, the financial community can judge the management of a company by its figures.

Read both sections

Even though you may now have made up your mind about which type of plan (financing or business) you will need, read about both plans. Much information about each plan is useful for both.

The format

There is no magic formula or format. But following an outline or checklist helps ensure that your plan will be comprehensive. It will not be "wrong" because it fails to follow some special equation. There are not as many definitive guidelines to follow as there are significant items to cover.

The financing plan

The financing plan is an abbreviated business plan. It should include:

1. Cover letter
2. Cover
3. Table of contents
4. Amount requested
5. Purpose of financing
6. Use of funds
7. Description of collateral or source of repayment (if seeking any debt financing)
8. History of business
9. Description of business and market
10. Financial history of business
11. Financial projections and assumptions
12. Schedule of major assets and liabilities
13. Management/ownership
14. Financial status of owners
15. References
16. Supporting documentation

Get to know these components a little better to improve your chances of getting your money.

Cover letter

This should be a personal letter directed to a specific person by name and title. It should outline on one page why you are sending the financing plan to him or her, why the financing opportunity is a good deal, and how you plan to follow up the solicitation. If you know what the reader is looking for, point out where in the plan it can be found. Sign your letter with a fountain pen and blue ink.

Try *not* to make your cover letter look like part of a mass mailing. Adapt it to the particular financing source. Mention something you may know about the source that would tie in your company with what it wants — which is usually more money.

Cover

The cover is the title page and contains:

1. Contact name
2. Company name, address, and phone number.
3. Legal structure. Is it a sole proprietorship, partnership, or corporation? Show the date the company started in business or the date of partnership or incorporation.
4. Disclaimer. This basically says that the writer of the financing plan is not responsible for any errors or omissions and that the plan should not be considered an offering of any security. Contact your attorney for what to say as a disclaimer. Up ahead, read some sample disclaimers.

Table of contents

This should be prepared last, after all the sections have been completed. Use major headings only.

Amount requested. A financing plan gets right to the point by stating how much money it is requesting. Give an exact figure, not a range.

Reason for the request. This gives the purpose of the financing and describes how the money will be used to improve the value of the business. Quantify and justify the amount you need.

Describe the impact the financing will have on the business. Answer the question, *Why are you looking for financing?*

Sources want to know how the new financing will improve the profit performance and net worth of the company.

Use of funds. Describe how, where, and when, if possible, the money is to be spent. Say exactly what you will use it for. Be specific. If you are buying equipment, list each piece. If you are paying off a debt, list the debt to be paid off. If it is for marketing, tell how it will be spent: for creative media, production, direct mail, sales commissions, and all the rest.

Explain how you intend to improve your cash position or pay off bills. Be precise, stating the exact amount of each bill. Name each item of equipment and state exactly why you need it and what it will cost. Explain any benefits the equipment will offer to productivity, costs, and so on. State the number of inventory items to be purchased, the category of the goods, and the cost. Describe the real estate and the reasons for the purchase.

Finally, name each creditor and the amount to be paid. Be precise with your descriptions and your accounting.

Source of repayment/collateral. If you are seeking debt financing, your source of repayment is cash flow. Mention this in your plan and refer to the section on financial projections.

Most debt financing sources want a secondary source of repayment, which is another term for collateral, such as real estate, equipment, or just about anything of value. If you have something of value, mention it here in the plan and then refer to another section where it is listed, which may be under Major Business Assets, Personal Assets or Assets to Be Acquired from Funding.

History of business. When you write about the history of the business, start with when you began or bought the business and bring the reader up to date with a list of the important events that have occurred.

Talk about the company, its founders, and management team. Indicate when it was formed and what it has done up to this point. Explain any trends that have occurred over the years. List the objectives of the company.

Description of business and market. Next, describe your business and its products and services. Describe the market and how you compare to your competition. Describe the unique features of your products and services.

Include the market opportunity for what the business will do in the future. Include information on the size and growth rate of the market. State the percentage of the market that the business holds or intends to capture. Comment briefly on industrywide trends and expansion plans. Explain the marketing strategy of the company. A timetable for the sequence of events is not necessary but is a special bonus for prospects.

Describe any proprietary technology, trade secrets, or unique capabilities of the management or company that give it a competitive edge.

Explain the exact nature of the operation. Describe what the company does and how it operates, including its method of distribution.

If you are a new business or entering a new market, get supporting data about your ability to produce business. If possible, list the names of potential customers. Try to show commitment letters or letters of intent to buy, any indication of an interest in doing business with you. You must show evidence that you can obtain or expand sales.

Include a brief market survey showing a favorable trend toward your market.

If you are in a volatile industry, it is important to explain the nature of the business and how you are prepared to handle any changes that may occur. You may want to show data indicating industry trends and explain how you expect to react to contingencies.

Financial history of the business

The financial historical section of the plan should include the financial statements and tax returns of the company for the past 3 years; if possible, interim financial statements should also be included, statements showing your operations since your annual or fiscal statement.

Explain in detail any discrepancies between the tax returns and your financial statements. Financial sources understand that what you report to the IRS may be different from what you report to yourself or your partners or stockholders. But these sources are not mind readers. Always explain your accounting system and what you are trying to accomplish.

This section should also include a financial summary of the business, especially sales, profits, and return on investment. Always include a brief explanation of the figures.

Financial ratios

If you can, show the ratio of profits to sales. You may want to show a strong cash position by showing the ratio of current assets to current liabilities. You should not show every financial ratio in your plan. Different lenders and investors look for different financial ratios. The financial source will calculate its own ratios if it needs more information. Your accountant can help you with this section.

Financial projections

This is where you state the impact of the financing on the business statements. The cash flow projections and a break-even analysis are all that is really necessary. Pro forma profits and loss and balance sheets are helpful but, again, not necessary. Follow the same procedures used for business plans, up ahead.

Assumptions

Assumptions are the hard facts and figures that support your forecast estimates. They are not hunches. *Assumptions are one of the most important parts of the financing plan.* They should be spelled out in detail. Financial estimates about what will happen in the future are useless without knowing the assumptions to support those figures.

You can't do projections without assumptions. Make sure your assumptions are defensible. The financial source will surely question how you arrived at your figures.

If possible, summarize sales and profit projections and outline the key factors underlying them. Explain any trends and how they support or relate to the projections. Break-even charts are good visual aids.

Projections should always be done on a monthly basis, at least for the first year. State your anticipated revenues, collections, and expenses. You must be able to show you can pay your bills and yourself and still have enough income to service debt or show an adequate return to an investor. Don't understate or overstate your case. Just put what you think will really happen in the future and back up your figures with facts or assumptions.

Be sure you cover the following in your cash flow assumptions: (1) the terms of sale of your products or services; and (2) the historical payment schedules for receivables and payables.

Just because you make a sale today does not mean you will receive any cash today. That depends on when your client or customer pays you. Conversely, just because you ordered or received merchandise from your supplier does not mean you have to pay that bill right away. Both these factors should be considered when creating your cash flow and should be addressed in your assumptions.

When going for debt financing, your cash flow projections should indicate an ability to repay the loan. There has to be adequate cash available for repayment.

Break your sales into units

How do you make assumptions for revenue? You start with revenue and break it down into units sold. Then you add the price of each unit times the number of units sold and finally the total dollar income collected. This should be spelled out in the financing plan.

It is crucial to turn your revenues into units sold so that they can be measured. You may have to do this with each product or product line. Don't go crazy and break down every item in your business, but do show major categories. For example, a hardware store may break down revenues into hardware, giftware, outdoor/patio and garden.

Even if you are a service business, break down your services into units. If you are a hair salon, break your sales into categories: haircuts, perms, manicures. Then the calculation of the price per unit in each category times the number of units you will sell per month will yield your monthly sales estimate.

Schedule of major assets

Include the cost and market value of major tangibles, equipment, and fixed assets. Put any liens right next to the asset listed.

Also include an accounts receivable aging. List everything your customers owe you. This tells the financial source how quickly your customers pay and indicates the creditworthiness of your clientele. Financial sources also want to know the distribution of your receivables. Do you have a few big clients, on whom you rely for most of your business, or many small ones? If sales are dominated by a few large customers, the loss of their business could create a tremendous problem for you. A large number of smaller accounts, on the other hand, spreads your risk around, making you less vulnerable to the loss of one particular customer.

If your assets are going to be an important part of the collateral for a financing, you may want to have them appraised. Any type of equipment can be appraised, even leases. If your lease has a long time left, it may be worth using as collateral. A valuable lease on a building was taken over as a result of the merger of two banks. The bank that took over the lease of the old bank learned that the lease had 40 years left to go; when it was appraised, it turned out to be worth over $1 million! The seller had no idea of its value.

A person wanted to buy a Wendy's franchise but lacked the funds. As a guerrilla, he paid for an appraisal of the lease and discovered that it was more valuable than the franchise. He was able to fund the franchise using the lease as collateral.

If your inventory is a substantial part of your assets, you should include an inventory schedule in the financing plan.

If any of the owners' personal real estate is being used as collateral, that should be listed here, giving the date of purchase of the real estate, the cost, the cost of improvements, the market value, and any liens on the property.

Schedule of major liabilities

Include debt schedules of all long-term obligations, including balance owed, interest, monthly payments.

Include an aging of your accounts payable. This will let the financial source know your current obligations and how delinquent you might be. Don't let delinquency intimidate you or make you defensive. If you didn't need the money, you wouldn't be preparing a financing plan.

Management/ownership

You must describe who is running the show and give their experience and skills. Dissect the organization of the company and say who does what.

For each owner with a 20% or greater ownership interest, include the following information: name, address, phone number, percentage of ownership, management position if active, annual compensation, and résumé.

The résumé should include employment background, education, special experience, skills, areas of expertise, and accomplishments.

Financial status of owners

Personal statements and tax returns of all the owners with a 20% or greater interest in the business should be included.

Financial sources want to know where the owners' income has been coming from. Don't feel offended or intimidated by this apparent intrusion into personal finances. The owner or owners are the driving force behind a company. They are the brains and brawn. Whether it is a bank or a private investor putting money into the business, the entrepreneur is, in effect, a partner with that source. It is only right for one partner to want to know about another.

Credit reports on the owners are a must. The owners should each order one on themselves.

Personal guarantee

If you are seeking any type of debt financing, most likely you will be required at least to personally guarantee the loan. Your willingness to put yourself on the line indicates that you are prepared to stand behind your company. If you don't have that much confidence in your own business, why should the financial source?

Collectibles

Some of the personal assets of the owners may be used as valuable collateral for a loan. Collectibles can be used as collateral for some lending institutions. For example, the following and more have been used as collateral for a loan: antiques, paintings, silverware, Oriental rugs, jewelry, china, and classic cars. The list could go on forever. Think of the things people collect: stamps, coins, baseball memorabilia, rare books, fine wine.

References

What third-party endorsements do you have? Personal, bank, attorney, accountant, trade, and customer references are all possibilities. Don't forget to include their name, address, and phone number.

List a few of your major customers and suppliers as references. The financial source may want to check how long you have been doing business with them and what type of business relationship you have created.

Always alert your references that they might be called by a financial source. That way they will not be caught off guard when they are contacted; this is common courtesy and can only enhance your goodwill.

Supporting documentation

Include brochures and company sales materials, advertising, articles, leases, contracts, appraisals — anything significant. This is a catchall for items left out of other categories.

If one of your major assets is real estate or if the money will be used to purchase or refinance real estate, or if any real estate is being used as collateral for the financing, include a copy of the appraisal, purchase agreement, or escrow instructions, or get a letter from a Realtor stating the estimated value of the property. This is called a *drive-through appraisal*. In real estate matters, a formal appraisal is the best verification of value, but a letter from a Realtor is the next best and may be sufficient for the initial approval. Most lenders and investors will perform some due diligence and most likely do their own appraisal to verify the accuracy of your information anyway.

If the money will be used for construction or leasehold improvements, include a copy of the contractor's bid and a description of the work to be done.

If one of your major assets is equipment or if the money will be used to buy equipment, include a description of it and a breakdown of its costs. Equipment, like every other asset, should be valued at its quick or forced sale value. What can you get for it on the open market within 30 days? Get a letter from an equipment dealer to support your valuation.

If the money you are seeking will be used to refinance a note or obligation, include a copy of the note or obligation.

If equipment or real estate is a significant asset that will be used as collateral for the financing, take a picture and include it in the financing plan.

Include a copy of your lease in any financing plan. Be prepared to answer questions about what you will do when it expires.

Any important purchase orders or contracts showing future sales should also be included. Letters of intent from customers are good verification of your sales projections.

Points to remember when preparing a financing plan

1. Be thorough, and pay attention to documenting your information. The more thoroughly prepared and documented your presentation, the more a lender or investor will perceive that you fully understand what you want to accomplish and how you plan to do it.
2. If you are pursuing equity financing, place a heavy emphasis on management capabilities in your company and on the marketing opportunities ahead. Remember, equity investors are looking for growth and profit opportunity as well as evidence that your company can take advantage of that opportunity.

3. Be reasonable in your projections. Try to incorporate standard industry ratios in your analysis and presentations. These ratios are published by Robert Morris Associates, Financial Research Associates, and Dun and Bradstreet. You should be able to find them in your library.
4. Don't hide relevant information. Acknowledge past failures as well as successes. If you are in a financial bind, explain how you are going to get out of it. If you are candid, financial people will sense your integrity.
5. If you are applying for a loan to purchase an asset, keep in mind that the debt you intend to assume must be justified by the contribution the asset will make to your business. The strongest justification you can present would be to show that the asset will be the key factor in generating the funds necessary to repay the loan — by increasing sales, reducing costs, improving efficiency, and generating profits.

What not to include in a financing plan

Do not specify the terms you are seeking from investors or lenders. Indicate only the amount of money you are requesting. Omit any reference to such items as interest rate, maturity of loan, amortization, or equity percentage you are willing to offer. These matters should be left for the lender(s) or investor(s) to present to you in their offer. It is not your role to try to structure their offer, especially at the beginning of the financing process. If they are interested in your proposal, they will work out an agreement and present it to you. If you suggest terms in your plan, you may be your own worst enemy. Suppose you suggest a loan interest rate of 12% in your plan and the lender was willing to offer you 11%. Suppose you indicate in your plan that you will give up 40% equity for a certain amount of money. How do you know that the investors would not have been willing to take just 20% for the same investment?

You cannot know what terms a lender or investor will offer, so do not suggest any in your plan. Let the financing sources present their terms *after reading your plan.* You can negotiate from there. Generally, the *first* person who mentions a number in a negotiation is the eventual loser.

What extra benefits will come from preparing a plan

You will find that all the research, work, and strategy to prepare your plan will require you to analyze carefully how much money you really need, exactly what you need it for, and how much you can expect to benefit from it. It will force you to examine your business in great detail: past, present, and future. You will finish with a much clearer picture of the parts that make up your business and of your business as a whole.

The business plan

Now comes the big one, the business plan. There is no ideal model plan that you can buy and just fill in the blanks. If you use a book or software product on how to write a business plan, remember that yours should be designed to fit your business. Developing an entire business plan for a company is like building a business. It is a process of making decisions, chronicling market evaluations, mobilizing people, developing product lines and services, and creating a formula for consistent profits.

Most entrepreneurs can do all that by themselves, but most need help to prepare both the financing and business plans. The object of this chapter is for you to understand the complexity of the task of correctly writing a financing or business plan and for you to be aware of the entire process.

Therefore, there is no sample plan to copy. But, as with the financing plan, there is a guide that tells you the rules that successful plans have followed and the pitfalls that the unfunded business proposals have fallen into.

Strategy comes first

Before you do any writing, do a lot of thinking about why your business deserves the money and what it will be like when it has the money. After all, you are going to a third party and saying, "Give me some money and I will show you what I can do with it." That is what a business plan is all about, showing investors why they should invest in your business.

What must a business plan be to succeed?

Here is what experts, who read plans all day, say a business plan should be:

1. It must be arranged appropriately, with an executive summary, table of contents, and its chapters in the right order.
2. It must be the right length and have the right appearance — not too long and not too short, not too fancy and not too plain.
3. It must give a sense of what the founders and the company expect to accomplish 3 to 7 years into the future.
4. It must explain in quantitative and qualitative terms the benefit to the user of the company's product or service.
5. It must present hard evidence of the marketability of the product or service.
6. It must justify financially the means chosen to sell the product or service.
7. It must explain and justify the level of product development that has been achieved and describe in appropriate detail the manufacturing process and associated costs.
8. It must portray management as a team of experienced people with complementary business skills.
9. It must contain believable financial projections, with the key data explained and documented under assumptions.
10. It must be easily and concisely explainable in a well-orchestrated oral presentation.

See your company through the eyes of an investor

While entrepreneurs are full of optimism — a valuable and necessary trait — investors are full of skepticism. Investors know the score; they know there are very few real winners. They have to weigh the risk of losing their money against the opportunity of a substantial gain and all that comes in between. They seek to maximize opportunity and minimize risk — not an easy thing to accomplish. One way is to seek only companies with an exceptional growth rate and high profit margin.

Remember one thing more: investors, like everyone else today, have a very short attention span. You must get their attention and keep it. Most investors, formal and informal, are inundated with proposals: *yours must stand out as a winner.*

How to turn investors on

Here are some important points that turn investors on:

1. *Evidence of customer acceptance.* How can you demonstrate that someone will buy your product or service? Do you have any actual sales? Do you have purchase orders or commitment letters? What feedback do you have to confirm your belief in the market for your product or service?
2. *Evidence of focus.* Every business has many opportunities, but the most successful businesses have focused on one or two only. You can't do too many things well at once.
3. *Proprietary position.* Investors understand that patents, trademarks, copyrights, and trade secrets don't guarantee success, but they do reduce risk by limiting the competition somewhat. Investors look for what is special about your product or service; what makes it unique? You will hear that over and over again as the second most important thing to investors.
4. *Management.* Investors want to know about management's ability to make the company a success. Everyone knows that management is the key to every company's success. When it comes to the type of business financing that requires a full business plan, management, from the investor's perspective, is everything. A good idea with poor management will most likely lose, but a poor idea with good management could easily win.
5. *Return on investment.* Investors want to know why this company will make a lot of money.

How to turn investors off

1. *Product orientation.* Excessive infatuation with the company's product or service is a turnoff. The emphasis should be on the market, on the needs of your potential customers. Don't devote too much space to describing your product or service. Concentrate on who will buy it and how it will be sold.
2. *Projections that deviate excessively from industry norms.* Each industry has a range of accepted or standard financial norms. Don't get too far away from those norms in your projections. That is a quick way to create the old "red flag." Deviations from industry norms suggest that the entrepreneur hasn't done his or her homework or is being unduly optimistic.
3. *Unrealistic growth projections.* This is probably the most common characteristic of unsophisticated management. Don't be unrealistic. It doesn't inspire confidence.

Outline of a well-written, effective business plan

You already know what should be in a financing plan. The following is an outline of what should be in a business plan. You don't need to follow it literally, but you should cover most of the points mentioned.

1. Cover letter
2. Cover page
3. Table of contents
4. Executive summary
5. Description of the company and history
6. Description of the product or service
7. Marketing plan
8. Management team
9. Organization and personnel
10. Operations
11. Funds required and their use
12. Financial data

13. Risks
14. Research and development
15. Legal/insurance
16. Appendices

You'll notice many similarities to a financing plan. Indeed, many items are exactly the same. That's why they are repeated here.

Cover letter

This should be a personal letter directed to a specific individual by name and title. It should outline in one page why you are sending the business plan to the person, why the investment opportunity is a good deal, and how you plan to follow up the solicitation. If you know what the investor is looking for, point out where it can be found in the plan.

Customize the letter to the particular financing source. Mention something you may know about the source that would tie in your company with what it is looking for in an investment.

Cover page

This should include the following:

1. Company logo (if available)
2. Company name, address, and phone number
3. Contact person name, phone number, and position in company
4. Disclaimer

Table of contents

The table of contents should list the titles and page numbers of each of the main sections and subsections of the business plan. It should be done last, before preparing the executive summary.

Executive summary: plan overview

The most important part of a plan is the overview or executive summary.
It may be your first, last, and only chance to get the attention of the
investor. *Only 10% of all business plans get read beyond the summary.*
Think of your summary as a two-to-three-minute commercial to grab
the reader's interest. Better still, think of it as an advertisement in a
singles' magazine where you hope to entice someone to "fall in love"
with your company.

The executive summary is simply a sales pitch for your company,
your idea, you, and your team. It should be polished with dynamic
words that sell your concept.

It must be appealing and convincing and capture the reader's attention enough to make him or her read the remainder of the plan. Although it appears as the first part of your plan, it should be the last part
you write because it summarizes everything. Only when you finish
your plan will you have a good idea of what should be in the summary.

When you have finished writing it, make sure it is an exciting description of an opportunity that should not be missed. But don't overdo
the pitch; superlatives scare investors.

An effective summary should be brief, emphasize the key points, and
yet sell at the same time. Maybe that is why 90% of all plans are never
read past the summary. The following are the points that should be
covered. Your first attempt will probably be much too long. That's all
right. Then you'll cut, cut, and cut until your summary is down to the
essence of what you are trying to accomplish. For the sake of brevity,
you may end up with only one sentence for each topic covered.

The executive summary should cover:

1. A *brief outline and description of the company*: its stage of development (its current status: start-up, development, turnaround), a
   thumbnail sketch of its history, its products, services, and technology if appropriate.
2. *The market segment you are attempting to reach* and how you plan
   to reach it. Describe what is happening to create a need for the
   company's product or service. What are the benefits of the product
   or service to its customers?
3. *The unique features of the product or service.* What is proprietary?
   Why will the product or service succeed over all the others? Dis-

cuss the competition briefly in order to show the niche you occupy in the industry.

4. *The overall strategy and direction* of the company.
5. *An overall financial glimpse of the company.* Include a history and forecast of sales and earnings.
6. *The company's objectives* and how it proposes to reach them.
7. *A brief management team profile* of backgrounds and responsibilities plus an explanation of why the team is best able to run the company. Focus on the actual achievements management has accomplished to date.
8. *How much money the business requires to achieve its objectives* and how it intends to use the proceeds. When describing how the funds will be used, avoid broad terms like "working capital" or "to pay expenses." Be a bit more specific: to pay salaries, build inventory, buy equipment. Always give an exact amount, never a range. State whether you are looking for debt or equity funding or both.
9. *The collateral offered*, if debt funding is needed.
10. *How and when the investors* will benefit from their investment.

Last thing you write

The executive summary should be the last thing you write and should be only two or three pages long. It must summarize the essence of your business.

Should you send out just the executive summary?

Not usually. Today, investors want either the full plan or what is now called a concept paper. Guerrillas hand or send out the whole plan, not an executive summary, overview, or concept paper. If the investor is looking at a complete business plan, he or she has all the necessary material on hand to make a decision and make it quickly. If you get turned down, you can always ask the investor to mail the plan back to you.

What is a concept paper?

A concept paper is a summary of a business plan. It is a very abbreviated business plan with an emphasis on showing an investor how the company will succeed. It has been called a mini–business plan or financial proposal and is a promotional document meant to sell the idea to an investor. It is longer than the executive summary, but shorter than a full business plan. Usually, it is ten to fifteen pages and contains the most important points from the business plan, including projections. Often it is the first thing to be mailed to an investor.

If you are going to the effort of creating a full business plan, why write a concept paper? In order to do a concept paper, you need practically all the information in the business plan.

If there is *not* enough time to create a full plan, a concept paper may get you sufficient interest for a face-to-face meeting. But even after the meeting, and even if the investors are interested, most would want to see a complete plan before they would actually fund the project or business.

Description of the company and history

This section describes the company, its origins, and its expectations. It covers the company's overall objectives.

Describe how your company got to where it is and where it intends to go as a result of the financing. Everything in between is a matter of telling the investor what the company must do to reach its goals and be a success. Here is a chance to emphasize your strengths and competitive edge.

Description of the product or service

Entrepreneurs tend to see a business plan as a description of a product or service. Since they know the subject so well and are so enamored of it, they often wax eloquently in describing it. When writing this section, be brief. Investors want to know what makes the product more desirable to a customer than what's already on the market. Is it better, faster, cheaper?

As you describe the product or service, don't get too technical. Explain the proprietary nature of the product and its life cycle.

You can describe the technology behind your major product and/or service and its applications, but again, don't get too technical. Try to show the special aspect of your product or service that will help sell it successfully. Explain what new element your product brings to the marketplace and what unrecognized need it fulfills. Explain why the window of opportunity for your company is now open or opening.

What problems does your product or service solve? What needs does it satisfy? Compare competitors' products and services. How do you intend to compete?

Some of this information can be incorporated into your marketing plan.

The marketing plan

The marketing plan is a plan within a plan. A good place to begin is the seven-sentence marketing strategy mapped out in the book *Guerrilla Marketing*. Explain your marketing strategy and what it is based on. Explain why consumers will buy from you, at what price, and how you intend to make a profit.

In the marketing plan, you must define and quantify the benefits your customer gets from buying your product or service. You must establish the size of your market and the potential customer interest in your market. Also, your competition must be evaluated and assessed. Investors are more attracted to markets and sales potentials than the technical features and/or the attractiveness of your product or service.

In other words, you must be customer-oriented or "market-driven." Explain the benefits your product or service has to your customer, how your customer will profit or gain from your product or service. Explain why your customers will buy your product or service over those of your competitors. The following should be in the marketing plan:

1. Description of the market. Who are the customers and why will they buy your product or service?

Explain what perceived need you fill in your target market. What is your market niche? How do you position your product or service? Your positioning strategy must be elaborated in detail.

Most investors consider every business to be market-driven. So an expression of a deep knowledge and understanding of your market is essential. Do you know all the factors that will affect your sales? Describe in detail the background of your industry, including its size, chief characteristics, trends, and major customers. Project any changes inside or outside your industry that will affect your business.

Don't forget to describe your customers in detail, including their demographics and psychographics. Remember, *businesses* don't buy products or services, *people* do. You must understand all about those decision makers.

2. Customer benefits. What are the benefits of the product or service to the customer?

In talking about benefits, you must relate them to the customer and to the competitors' products or services. These are some of the ways to do that.

Your product or service is better than the competition's because it is: (1) cheaper, (2) better quality, (3) more efficient, (4) convenient to use, (5) has fewer rejects or breakdowns, (6) reduces the customer's labor costs, (7) lowers the customer's inventory costs, (8) improves the customer's productivity, (9) improves the customer's performance, (10) saves the customer money or time or both, (11) entertains the customer, (12) improves the customer's appearance or health, (13) solves problems, and (14) generates profits.

Try to document these claims.

3. Market share. What are your assumptions about your market share? When explaining market share, instead of just stating what percentage of the market you intend to capture, employ a bottom-up approach based on sales projections, using specific customers. A common mistake made by most people in discussing market share is assuming they can predict sales by gathering some general numbers on the size of the market, then projecting market share from there. The old statement "we only want 1% of the market" does not cut it anymore. You must explain in detail just how you arrive at your market share. Document your assumptions with marketing research.

4. Competition. Who is your competition? Compare their products to yours, and outline your strategies to sell more than they do. Explain how difficult it is to compete with you.

Don't underestimate, ignore, or downplay the competition. Everybody has competition, and if you say you don't, investors will feel skittish and believe you are ignorant of the market or don't comprehend the weakness of what you are trying to accomplish.

5. The sales strategy. This is one of the most critical parts of the marketing plan. You can have the greatest technology in the world, but if you can't figure out how to get it into the customers' hands, you've got nothing! The world will *not* beat a path to your door if you have a better mousetrap! You have to *sell the world* on buying your mousetrap — your product or your service.

If you can think of marketing as strategy and selling as tactics, you have a good idea of what you should put into your plan. How are you going to get your customers to buy your product or service? You must describe the nuts and bolts of your selling process. What is your distribution process? How will you service and support your product or service?

Explain the selling process step by step, from distribution to sales to servicing of sales. What is your sales strategy? How is the company going to approach its customers and capitalize on its potential? Go into detail on how the product is sold and/or distributed.

How will you advertise and promote your product or service? If possible, get a reaction to your product from potential or actual customers.

Go over your distribution methods, geographical penetration, roll-out schedule, and locations.

Discuss the pricing structure you've developed to make your product or service competitive yet generate enough profit. How you arrived at the price shows the investors the degree of information you have about your market and customer.

Identify prospective customers, your selling strategy, the size of and compensation techniques for your sales force, your selling cycle, and the milestones you want to reach.

Forecast sales by units and dollars.

6. Proprietary protection and uniqueness. Explain what makes your company stand out from the rest. The degree of uniqueness is considered a major strength in the venture community.

Explain the range of protection against competition, including patent or copyright protection. What is your strategy to create barriers for others in your market beyond patent or copyright protection? Describe any available technology that is superior or equal to yours. What creative technology or research are you doing to provide future sales?

In the final analysis, what most investors are looking for is a pent-up market with unlimited demand. Combine this with capable management and you can get the money you need.

Management team

The most carefully read part of a business plan is the management team section. The type of investor or lender who reads business plans, versus financing plans, considers management the most important issue. *People* have priority over products and markets. Risk or venture money will bet on management skills before any product or service. Without a well-qualified management team, the chance of getting any venture capital is very difficult.

First of all, the day of the one-man band is over. You definitely need a *team* of people to succeed. Besides listing all the skills and experience of each team member, you should highlight the experience and skills likeliest to contribute to the success of the company. Emphasize how each team member's individual specialty will complement the others'.

Investors look for a well-rounded management team with compatible members. Explain their experience, track record, education, other outstanding jobs and accomplishments. *Always focus on how the credentials of the team meet the company's needs.* Investors tend to concentrate on entrepreneurial skills. Working for a major company may *not* qualify a person to work for an entrepreneurial company. Intelligence, experience, and the temperament to carry the business through the critical years, as well as enthusiasm, energy, and a competitive spirit, are desirable attributes. Stress how they all relate to the success requirements of your business. After all, what good are world-class skills if they are not needed in your particular venture?

If you feel your management team is weak, describe the kind of person you *will hire* as soon as you get the money. Or find that person and say that he or she will join the company as soon as the money is available. The point is, you must have the key positions in management either filled or to be filled upon funding. What is your strategy for hiring and compensating the people you still need?

In this section, also list the owners, legal structure, and the Board of Directors and their qualifications.

Organization/personnel

What is the organizational structure? A description of the labor force and employees should be in this section, including number of people, union or nonunion, white collar, blue collar — anything that's pertinent. Talk about how you intend to attract and keep good employees. Talk about anticipated human resource requirements.

Operations

How is the product or service being developed or tested? How will it be produced and serviced? What type of quality control does the company have?

Cover your major suppliers and subcontractors in this section, or make a separate section for suppliers and subcontractors if they play a major part in your operation.

A description of equipment, property, and facilities should also be in this section.

The operations of the company should be evaluated, stressing such points as the amount of research and development that has to go into the product or service, how much engineering, how much testing, and what kind of quality control is needed. Finally, state exactly how you are going to make your product or service and how expensive or inexpensive it will be.

For manufacturers only. Explain your operations. How much will you subcontract and why? Describe the nature and setup of your facilities, including plant and office space, storage, land, and all the rest.

Cover such subjects as distance to customers, vendors, worker training, access to skilled labor, inventory management, quality and production controls, and, if appropriate, the bidding process you plan to use or are using.

Cover any effects of zoning or any local, state, or federal laws affecting your facility.

In the financial section, explain from a financial point of view standard production costs at different volume levels and how overhead, labor, material costs, and the cost of parts will affect production costs. Outline the capital requirements, how costs are recovered, and the time period. Investors want to know what it takes in time, materials, and labor to manufacture a product.

Funds required and their use

Detail the use of the required funding and its impact on the company. Include long-range funding strategies and their influence on the company.

Staged financing should be covered when describing the financial requirements of your business. Adjust your planning to allow for funding at various stages of growth rather than all up front. Construct your plans against certain milestones or targets you have to meet to get more funding.

Financial data

All the operations of the business are summarized in financial statements, projections, and summaries. All the data must have assumptions to back them up. All figures must be justifiable. Summaries are preferable to page after page of computer spreadsheets.

Pay particular attention to cash flow projections that indicate how well your financing is timed.

Financial data should include the following: current financial position, payables and receivables, cost control, break-even analysis, financial ratios, and financial projections.

Projections. Don't get "Lotus-itis" when doing projections. That is, don't get carried away with many different versions of what will happen in the future. Put all you have into just one version and be prepared to defend it. Do your projections on a monthly, not a quarterly, basis because investors want to examine the figures from month to month.

Worst- and best-case scenarios. Don't project your worst- and best-case scenarios in your plan. You can go through the process yourself when preparing the plan, but it is too confusing when it is put in a plan. The investor does not know which set of projections to believe.

Assumptions. No one will accept your figures at face value. You must explain how you arrived at them; you must explain your assumptions.

Management is the most important ingredient in a business plan; *uniqueness* is the second most important ingredient; your *assumptions* are number three.

The assumptions leading to your financial material should be well documented, geared to industrial standards and accepted accounting methods. It is incumbent on the entrepreneur to persuade the investor that the projections are real and achievable.

Assumptions and projections are *the hardest part* of a business plan to create. Why? Because it is so difficult to predict what will happen in the future. Entrepreneurs often wonder how they can be expected to know what their sales and costs will be over the next 5 years.

They are missing the point. The point is not that anyone is going to believe that these figures will be accurate predictions, but that the entrepreneur has gone through the thought process. Most investors will take your figures with a grain of salt anyway. In fact, most take the sales and profits you have put in your plan and *halve* them and *double* the expenses!

But the strategy and planning that went into the projections will enable you to create the assumptions behind them. Your assumptions explain your thought process, and that is what the investor is looking for. Do all the figures make sense? Does the logic behind the figures seem valid?

Beware of manipulating the figures. Stick to normal, industry-accepted accounting procedures. Don't go to extremes; don't overstate or understate your case. Be as realistic as you can.

Attention to detail. The smallest details in your assumptions must be thought out. For example, providing for a monthly telephone bill of just $25 may indicate a lack of careful analysis; providing for a bill of $5,000 may suggest that cost controls aren't sufficient.

Risks. What are the risks involved in this project and why do the rewards outweigh them? What can go wrong? How can the investor lose his or her money? Anticipate any major problems or challenges that might arise and how the management team will solve them.

Research and development

What are you doing or going to do to keep your market? If research and development is a large part of the budget, you should describe precisely what you intend to accomplish with the money.

Don't make the mistake of comparing the technology you will put on the market in the future with what your competition *has now.* Instead, compare what you *will have* by the time you are in the market with what others *will have.*

Legal/insurance

This section should include the legal form of the business, a breakdown of ownership, and a discussion of any pending or existing litigation. Include any significant government regulations that will affect the company. If the cost of insurance is important or there is a major risk in the business, that should be covered in the plan.

Appendices

The last part of the plan should contain any back-up or supporting documents you feel are necessary for the rest of the plan. Here's a sample of what may be included:

- Pictures of products or facilities
- Company literature and sales material
- Newspaper and magazine clippings
- Market survey
- Production flow chart
- Patent description
- Significant contracts/purchase orders
- Price list
- Sample advertisement or press release
- Historical financial statements
- Table of start-up costs
- Fixed asset acquisition schedule
- Break-even analysis
- Management résumés
- Management tax returns
- Management financial statements
- Letters of intent
- References

There you have it — all the main topics that should be covered in a business plan. You will find that writing a complete business plan is difficult and time-consuming, but it should be a labor of love. It's your baby; it's your business. If you don't love it, don't write it.

Preparing a business plan versus a financing plan is a lengthy, detailed, and difficult process. Do not take it lightly. The amount of effort you expend in preparing the plan will reduce the problems you encounter in attracting needed resources, people as well as money.

Exit strategy

Contrary to popular opinion, the entrepreneur should not put any exit strategy into a business plan. Talk about guesstimates! Five-year projections are hard enough, let alone deciding how the investors will get their money out 5 to 10 years in advance.

It is anybody's guess how any investor will get his or her money out of an investment. If you define your exit strategy in writing your plan, it might be the opposite of what an investor is expecting and kill the deal. Instead, just tell the investor that the exit strategy is negotiable.

Get someone to proofread it

Obviously, it must be proofread for mistakes. But more important, it should be read by someone who is related in some way to the investment/venture community. The more of these investors who read it, the better. Ask them to keep in mind the following questions when they go over it: Did it grab their attention? Did it prove your company to be a tremendous investment opportunity? Was it easy to understand? How can it be improved?

Don't say the following

Do not describe in your business plan what type of investment vehicle you prefer or what portion of your company is being offered for sale. This information is too premature to go into a business plan being read by strangers. The form of the investment and what the investment will purchase can and should only be discussed in person. You know what not to include in a financing plan. The same applies to a business plan.

Legal aspects of what should be included in a financing or business plan

A financing or business plan is by no means an offering of a security of any kind, and there are no legal limits to what you can put in it. It is assumed that the person reviewing your plan, even an informal investor or angel, is somewhat sophisticated.

On the other hand, do not include fraudulent or misleading information. You want to fully disclose any material item that a lender or investor would want to know *before* lending or investing in your business. It always pays to tell the truth.

Nondisclosure agreements

A nondisclosure agreement provides that the investor will maintain confidentiality with regard to the business situation presented in the plan.

Many experts do not like nondisclosure statements in business plans. Use them only in rare situations where the plan discloses some idea that could be damaging if found out by the competition. Few if any people in the formal or informal venture community are interested in stealing ideas from business plans. Still, the decision regarding a nondisclosure agreement is up to you and your legal counsel.

Notice of disclaimer

In case of mistakes or misinterpretations in your plan, you should put something of a disclaimer on the cover page of both the financing and business plans. The following is a sample disclaimer. Check with your attorney before deciding what to say in yours.

Sample Disclaimer

The information contained in this plan is confidential and proprietary and is intended only for the persons to whom it is transmitted by the company. Any reproduction of this plan, in whole or in part, or the divulgence of any of its contents, without the prior written consent of the company, is prohibited. Receipt or possession of this document does not convey any rights to disclose its contents, in whole or in part, to any third party, or to develop, manufacture, use, or sell anything described herein.

This plan does not constitute an offer to sell any securities. Any such solicitation will be undertaken only under appropriate documents and pursuant to all applicable securities laws.

The information set forth herein is believed by the company to be reliable. It must be recognized, however, that projections and predictions about the company's future performance are necessarily subject to a high degree of uncertainty, and no warranty of such projections is expressed or implied hereby.

How to package your plan

Remember that an investor's first impression is critical:

1. Paper. White.
2. Type. A laser printer is a must today.
3. Margins. There should be one-inch margins on all sides.
4. Graphics. Use if essential to make an important point.
5. Pictures. Use as appropriate.
6. Binding. Use bindings that allow the pages to be turned easily and lie flat when left open.

Should you get professional help to prepare your plan?

Most entrepreneurs need help in preparing effective plans. A cooperative effort combines the expertise of both the entrepreneur and the plan writer.

How to find these writers is problematic. Financing and business plan writers are not listed in the Yellow Pages.

Ask your accountant or a consultant. Don't just think that someone who is a writer will do an effective job. It takes someone who specializes in writing financing and business plans to do the best job. For professional help, see the last page of this book, which describes the services of the Capital Institute. On the other hand, perhaps that pro can now be *you*.

15

How to Get an Appointment to Present Your Plan

Now that you have your financing or business plan, it's time to contact financing sources. You now have a good idea of whom to contact, but let's review them.

Debt sources

If the type of assets you have personally or in your business favor debt or secured sources, you should be contacting one or more of the following:

1. Purchase order sources   Chapter 5
2. Receivable sources   Chapter 5
3. Inventory sources   Chapters 5, 8 and 10
4. Equipment sources   Chapters 6, 8 and 10
5. Real estate sources   Chapters 7, 8, 9, 10 and 12
6. Working capital sources   Chapters 5 through 12

Most likely you will be presenting a financing plan to the above sources.

Equity sources

If you feel you will be looking for equity or unsecured capital sources, your choices are:

1. Traditional venture capital   Chapter 11
2. Adventure capital   Chapters 12 and 13
3. Guerrilla financing capital   Chapter 13

You will present either a financing or business plan to the equity sources.

Guerrillas know just how to make an appointment with a financing source to present a financing proposal, then how to present that proposal in a face-to-face meeting. You absolutely must know how to arrange for, then make, an oral presentation because, no matter how good your plan is, if you can't get anyone to read it or if you can't present it in person, you are not going to raise the money you need.

The oral presentation

Getting the appointment and presenting your proposal to potential sources are major skills required in guerrilla financing. The oral presentation is actually two presentations: the telephone appointment presentation and the oral interview.

The face-to-face presentation is an *interview*, not just an oral presentation. A formal presentation to a large group, where only a few questions are asked, is rare. Often, the face-to-face meeting is a two-way street, with questions asked and answers given. Everything you know about an employment interview will apply to an oral financing request interview.

Selling yourself and your project is the name of the game. Read a good book on employment interviews before meeting your first source. We recommend *The Ultimate Interview* by John Caple (Doubleday, 1991).

The oral interview can take two forms: an individual or a group interview. Both require a written plan and a professional presentation.

The professional presentation

A professional presentation consists of the following:

1. Telephone appointment presentation
2. Oral interview, both individual and group
3. Written presentation

Even though the written presentation is listed third, it has to be produced first. There is no way an entrepreneur can effectively make an oral presentation without going through the time and effort to put the concept on paper.

At the same time, if you can't get an appointment, you won't get a chance to give your oral presentation.

Telephone appointment presentation

Now that you know which source or sources to contact for your particular needs and situation and you have prepared your financing or business plan, you are ready to make your telephone appointment presentation.

Whether you are presenting a financing or a business plan, you have to get the lenders or investors to meet you in person. Most of the time you try to make an appointment over the telephone. What you say on the phone determines your chances of getting that appointment.

You don't want to eliminate any potential sources because you aren't prepared for the questions asked in the telephone conversation. *You must be prepared before you pick up that phone!*

Do not call anyone about an appointment until you have completed your financing or business plan. You may be anxious to talk to people and think you have an answer to any question that might arise in the conversation. *This is not true! Not only do you not know the answers, you don't know the questions. Not until you make the effort to write a plan will you have any feel for what will be asked.*

To mail or not to mail the plan first

This is a touchy question because some sources want to see the plan first and others want to see you first. When you make the telephone presentation, you will find out if the source wants to see you first or would rather read the plan first. Or neither.

Some experts say it is better to have the sources read your plan first, while others say it is better to meet the sources before they read your plan.

Guerrillas go along with the wishes of the sources. If the source offers you a choice, arrange the meeting first. Even though your plan might be excellent, your ability to think on your feet in front of a source may give you that extra edge to say something to pique the source's interest. The mail deprives you of the chance to do that.

If you have to mail the plan first, give the sources about a week before following up with a phone call. A busy financing source needs at least that much time to read and analyze the information in your plan before you call for an answer.

If you are going for traditional venture financing, you usually have to be very persuasive over the phone to get an appointment without having sent a plan first. Adventure capitalists, on the other hand, make their decisions more on feelings and intuitions from conversations with you, and they can often be persuaded to meet first.

Either way, nothing is going to happen until you actually *meet the source*. So your prime objective is to get that personal meeting or interview.

What to do *before* you make the phone call

Before you speak to any source, obtain:

1. Information about the financing source.
2. The name of the appropriate person to contact at that source.
3. Information about that specific person.

Learn about the company you are calling

If you are talking to a banker, learn about the bank before calling. Most banks are publicly held, so you can get an annual report and study it to understand how they operate. If you are contacting a traditional venture capital company, you can study its requirements in the directories listed in Chapter 11. If at all possible, try to get some background on the company you are contacting before you make that call.

Identify the person to contact

The second objective is to determine the appropriate person to contact at each source. You can do that just by calling and asking who handles your type of business. Talk to the receptionist or secretary to get information. Try to find out something about the person you are contacting. What is his or her position? How long has this person been with the company? If you are calling a factor, for example, you can ask, "Who is handling factoring for manufacturing companies?" You can also say that you don't want to speak to the person yet, but just wanted to learn a little about him or her before calling directly. It is astonishing how much information you can get if you are cordial and polite. Of course, there will be times that you just don't know who you will be talking to, but always try to learn in advance who will be reviewing your application for funding.

What to do if you can't get to speak to anyone

Many times, especially when contacting traditional venture capitalists, you will not be allowed to speak to any decision makers until you have submitted your plan. Then you just have to find out who would be the appropriate person to review your plan, mail it to him or her, and then follow up with your appointment phone presentation.

What to say first

When you get the right person on the phone, be cordial, polite, businesslike, brief, and to the point. *Tell him or her why you are calling, briefly what the business is all about, how much money is needed, and what you plan to do with it.* This guerrilla approach is a no-nonsense start. Get to the facts. Explain the key ingredients: management team, market, niche, and benefits. Emphasize your strong points. Be optimistic.

Keep your eye on the objective of the call

Your goal is to make an appointment with as little discussion about your business as possible. *Just get an appointment; don't try to sell the listener to lend or invest over the phone.* This first call is only to get an appointment for a personal oral interview. The listener will decide if more information is needed before making an appointment.

Financial sources, as you can imagine, are being contacted all the time by people looking for money. They most likely will try to qualify you on the phone to see if it is appropriate for them to make an appointment with you. Your objective is to *listen* to what they have to say, answer any questions they may have, and go for the appointment. As you answer questions, always keep your responses short and to the point.

Few financing sources can make a decision over the phone just by asking a few questions. Understand that you have different objectives from the person you are calling. You want to set up a meeting. The potential investor wants to qualify you to see if he or she is interested.

Most of the time, sources, not callers, have the upper hand. The sources dictate what will be discussed over the phone. They do not want to waste their time seeing people they don't think will meet their criteria. You may not be able to control the conversation, but you can follow some basic rules.

Don't say too much

Think ahead of time of two major points you want to make in the conversation. These points should be the most important reasons the person on the other end of the line should meet with you. For example, if you are calling a bank, you can mention that (1) you had $3 million in sales last year and (2) you are thinking of changing banks and would like to talk. Don't even mention that the only reason you will change banks is to get a loan. That will be discussed at the appointment. If you are talking to a factor, you can mention that (1) you have many receivables and (2) they consist of some of the top companies in the area. That should interest the factor enough to set an appointment. Give just enough data over the phone to get interest.

Major points that are interesting to some sources are:

Debt sources: strength of collateral, financial condition of the company, credit of the company and owners, and cash flow to repay the loan.

Equity sources: potential of the business, uniqueness of the product or service, and return to the investors.

Always have your financing or business plan with you when you call. It may be necessary for you to look up answers to some of the questions that arise.

General questions sources may ask over the phone

1. "What kind of business are you in?"
2. "How did you get my name?"
3. "How much money do you need?"
4. "What do you need it for?"
5. "How do you intend to pay it back?"

Debt source questions

1. "What collateral do you offer?"
2. "When did you buy the real estate?"
3. "What was the cost of the real estate?"
4. "What are the total liens on the property?"

Equity source questions

1. "What is unique about your product or service?"
2. "Do you have any patents on your product?"

You must be prepared to answer these questions over the phone.

Actually, the questions can range from who, what, where, and when to how. Can you imagine your chance of getting an appointment if you aren't totally prepared?

Common mistakes made on the phone

These are things *not* to do while phoning:

1. Don't get involved in long discussions that are not relevant to the subject, such as explaining how you got into a situation in which you need financing in the first place.
2. Don't tell the potential source what terms you want for the money.
3. Don't allow yourself to be unprepared to answer relevant questions.
4. Don't try to sell the financing; just go for an appointment.
5. Don't use technical words that the listener might not understand.
6. Don't assume the listener knows a lot about you, your business, or your industry.
7. Don't leave out explanations of what has happened or expect the listener to read your mind.
8. Don't give too long an answer. Sources want short answers that stick to the point.
9. Don't volunteer information. You never know what reaction it will have on the listener. Listeners will decide if they have enough information to meet with you. End by asking, "When can I see you to explain my project in more detail?"

Phone attitude

Smile when you dial. This telemarketing tactic forces the tone of your voice to be friendly. Not only *what you say but how you say it* is important in making an effective telephone call. The only way the listener can judge you and the deal is by your phone attitude, the tone and pitch of your voice, how fast you speak, and the information you're imparting. Attitude is based on *confidence*. Confidence is based on preparedness. If you are not prepared, you will not be confident in your answers, your attitude will not be positive, and all this will come across in the sound of your voice.

Killer mistakes made over the phone

The following is a list of comments made by people in telephone conversations who *never* got their appointment.

- "I'll have to look that up."
- "Let me check that out and get back to you."
- "My accountant does all the books; I'll have to ask him."
- "I don't know exactly how much money I need."
- "How much money can I get from you?"
- "What is your minimum?"
- "We have to have the money within a few weeks."
- "You'll have to sign a nondisclosure agreement before you can see the plan or we can talk."
- "We really have no competition."
- "You have to move fast if you want to get in on this financing."

Do these people sound prepared? Absolutely not. They are saying things that sound as if they don't know what they need, what they are doing, or what is involved in raising capital. Raising capital is a *process*; no one wants to be rushed or intimidated.

Why be so businesslike over the phone?

When it comes to raising money, friendship, gift giving, personal favors, rewards for good intentions, and upstanding citizenship go out the door. Business financing is strictly a business transaction, and you've got to act accordingly.

Lenders and investors will be talking to you because they want to make money, period. Their business is one that produces money, and their main concern in evaluating you as a potential customer is, in the case of lenders, your ability to pay them back, or, in the case of investors, your ability to generate an attractive profit for them. In order for them to decide to meet with you, not only do the figures have to be right, but, more important, they must believe you have confidence in what you are doing.

If they hear any hesitation or uncertainty in your voice, they will view you as a bad risk and probably not want to meet with you. They are not going to be concerned with who turned you down before, how badly you need the money, how much you think you deserve it for working hard, or how good a citizen you are. To them, money is the commodity they sell, and they will evaluate you simply to determine if you will be a good customer — one who will pay a good price and be reliable in repaying the loan or in generating a profit on their investment. Guerrillas sound professional and exude a strong belief in themselves and their business projects.

The oral interview

Once you have made the appointment for an oral interview, there are things you should be aware of before you go.

What to wear to the meeting

Naturally, you should be well groomed, neat, clean, and have had a recent haircut or have had your hair done.

The decision to lend or invest in your business can be made on the most ridiculous emotional basis. You don't want to do *anything* that would detract from the lender's or investor's opinion of your plan.

Unless you are in the fashion business, a business financing meeting is *not* a time to express your personal taste in fashion. People with money are usually very conservative and you should dress conservatively. Look dignified. Appearance still goes a long way toward creating a favorable impression. In the back of the lender's or investor's mind is a nagging concern that the entrepreneur may lack the judgment to handle and spend the money wisely. You want to convey the image of a self-confident, self-reliant, dependable, and successful person. Most likely, there is no way of knowing the fashion preferences of the people you will be meeting, so just dress conservatively and you will fit in.

Get a well-fitting guerrilla business uniform: men should wear conservative dark suits — blue or gray, not sport coats. Wear a conservative tie and a white shirt. Believe it or not, white shirts denote honesty. Wear dark socks and dark shoes. Women should wear a tailored business suit with a white blouse. They should not wear anything sexy that could distract from the point of the meeting.

Anything that distracts the source's attention from the conversation is off limits to a guerrilla.

Your objective is to get them to concentrate on the merits of financing your business, not on the merits of your personal fashion preference.

Jewelry should be plain and understated. Heavy, flashy gold or silver jewelry, necklaces, bracelets, and rings (except wedding bands) should not be worn. Neither should bright clothing.

What to bring to the interview

Bring your plan and a sample of your product, if possible. Besides that, bring anything you think might be useful in explaining your story. You may not need it, but at least you'll have it handy if you do.

Study your plan

Financial sources will be impressed if you know what you are talking about. So *study your plan from top to bottom before the meeting.* You must understand every word in it. Be able to explain every part of the plan, including the projections. Sometimes, when an entrepreneur has a third party do the projections, he or she is not familiar enough with the reasoning that went into the assumptions to explain them adequately. If your sources feel you don't understand the reasoning behind your projections, they will lose confidence in you. So be familiar with the numbers. Your financing success may depend on it.

There is nothing wrong with referring to your plan when answering questions at a face-to-face meeting. But if you have to constantly refer to your plan in order to answer questions, the source may have doubts about your ability to understand and run your business.

How to make a good impression

When presenting yourself and your project to a lender or investor in person, keep in mind:

1. *First impressions are crucial.* Enter the meeting with confidence, a glowing smile, and an extended hand. Make eye contact. The financial source will attempt to read your personality. He or she will be analyzing your character and judging and evaluating your ability as an entrepreneur. The initial meeting is critical. Your voice, tone, and confidence are extremely important. Your clothes, personal appearance, and conduct in person all reflect on your ability to conduct a profitable business. From the instant you make that first telephone call, you will be sized up inside and out, from head to toe. Anytime you are communicating with a source, be on those toes!
2. *Be businesslike and prepared.* Do your homework, such as getting information about the people you are going to meet and reviewing your plan. Expect questions.
3. *Be honest.* Always tell your story truthfully. There may be certain pieces of your story that are not ideal from a financing standpoint, but that is true of every business in need of money. If you hide one important fact, it is guaranteed that the lender or investor will discover it sooner or later. When that happens, your credibility will be destroyed, along with any chance of getting financing.
4. *Talk in specifics, but don't use technical jargon unless it is genuinely helpful and you are certain that it will be understood by all the people in the room.* As a matter of course, don't assume that the people you are speaking to understand what you are saying. To make sure they understand, periodically ask questions such as, "Do you understand that?" or "Does that make sense?" This will check how effectively you are communicating.
5. *Your talk should be energizing but not detailed or long-winded.*
6. *Be aware of the impact of body language and actual words when you are selling your proposal.* Sit forward and straight if possible. Never lean back and become too relaxed. It is all right to stand up and walk around the room, especially to emphasize an important point. Look and act like a leader. Watch the lender's or investor's body language. If the lender's or investor's arms are folded or crossed, your message is most likely *not* being received well; your

listener's mind is closed to your proposal. If the arms unfold, it shows a quickening of interest. There are many such signs to watch for; you may want to get a book on the subject of body language.

7. *Don't forget to listen.* When you listen, you pick up valuable clues; when you talk, you tip your hand.

8. *Put yourself in the lender's or investor's position.* Consider his or her point of view as if you were lending or investing in your own company for the first time.

9. *Be prepared to walk; don't take the first offer.* Don't let yourself become emotionally committed to any one source until you have talked to as many as you can.

10. *Always end your discussions on a friendly note.* Just because you can't meet a lender's or investor's qualifications now doesn't mean you can't in the future. Always leave the door open to come back.

Meeting attitude

Your attitude in the telephone presentation should continue in the face-to-face meeting. You want to win someone's confidence, and you want to show your own confidence. You must adopt a positive mental attitude to impress any lender or investor favorably.

Meeting with financial sources is not the time to be shy or modest. You must project a quiet confidence about yourself and put forth the image of an achiever.

The real question you must ask yourself before you walk into that meeting room is, "Do I believe in what I am doing?" If you are not entirely confident about your ability to live up to your commitments, you should rethink your request and not enter that room.

A few minor misgivings are natural and should not deter you from approaching the financing source, but don't rationalize yourself into a bad deal. Avoid going into a deal that does not make economic sense. Be prepared to recognize the facts as they exist, not as you want them to be. Do not let emotion interfere with sound business judgment.

You may even want to discuss some of your misgivings with the source. You should both be aware of all the risks and uncertainties involved. A good financing is where both parties go into the deal with their eyes wide open.

How to get prepared for tough questions

Think of all the horrible and revealing questions the source might ask, and work out an answer well before the meeting. If you throw out some of the really good points, is it still a good idea? At what point will it not be a good idea?

The interview

You have made the appointment and are going to meet the potential financing source at last. Maybe the source has already read your plan and maybe not. If the source has not asked to read the plan, you will have to go into greater detail at the meeting. Most debt sources prefer to meet you first and have you bring along your financing plan, whereas most equity sources prefer to read your business plan before setting up a meeting.

What to say first

Exchange your opening pleasantries quickly. Try to get down to business right away. This will show the source that you respect his or her time. Financial sources are busy and want to get right to the point.

Don't think you are going to make a friend. That might or might not happen, but it has nothing to do with the financing. Be genuine but, unless your friendliness is real and mutual, stay with a businesslike relationship.

The best approach is to get to the facts. *Tell them what the business is all about, how much money is needed, and what you plan to do with it.* The basic qualities most sources look for are energy and the will to succeed with your plan. Remember, you are not only selling your business project, but also yourself and your management team.

You might start by giving a brief summary of the important points and have the source ask you questions. If you are seeing a financing source cold, without the source's having read your summary, you are obligated to cover the important points in greater detail.

Don't overdo it

Don't overdo self-confidence to the point where you seem phony, cocky, or overzealous. Your confidence should not be forced. Humility with dignity and integrity is appropriate. Emphasize strong points, but don't make it seem as though there are no risks involved. Explain the pitfalls and show that you are prepared for contingencies.

What *not* to say in an interview

Remember what you read about the telephone interview? The same is true for the personal interview. In addition, you should avoid the following:

1. Do not discuss grandiose plans, additional products and services, other opportunities, or mergers that may occur in the future. Such topics will sidetrack the source and probably scare him or her away.
2. Avoid explaining why you are in business or want to go into or buy a business for a reason other than money. The lender or investor is interested in making money, not solving personal, country, or world objectives. The exception would be if your product or service did have an impact on the environment, world health, or peace.
3. Don't tell the source you will make money by doing anything that would be considered dishonest.
4. Don't avoid hard questions with vague answers. Give a direct answer to a direct question. If you can't answer or don't know, just say so.
5. Don't hide past problems like poor credit, bankruptcy, or lawsuits. Reveal the good, bad, and the ugly. The source will eventually find them out anyway.
6. Don't downgrade the risks. If you are asked what can go wrong or how your plan can fail, tell them. Don't ever say, "Nothing can go wrong."
7. Never bring a lawyer to the initial meetings unless requested to do so by the source. Your legal counsel should only get involved during the negotiation period.

8. Don't press for an immediate decision.
9. Don't say your management team makes all the decisions jointly or in committee. You can't run a business by committee; someone has to be the decision maker.
10. Try not to use the word *problem* in phrases such as we have cash flow problems, labor problems, our main problem, or the like. Financial sources have enough problems with the companies they lend to or invested in. They are looking for companies with solutions, not more problems. Also, avoid slang or other street language.

Financing phobia

This is when the entrepreneur cannot adequately express himself at the face-to-face meeting. It becomes evident that he or she is very nervous or uneasy, implying a certain lack of strength. Entrepreneurs, in order to survive, *must* be strong. Fear of meeting the financing source is usually caused by a lack of preparation. If you are adequately prepared, you should feel confident enough to make a favorable impression.

One of the hardest things to do when meeting a financing source is to act as if you are equals. The idea is to meet on equal terms; don't shrink as though your life were in someone else's hands. The financing source knows you need the money or you wouldn't be there.

Just be straightforward and present yourself as the person who can accomplish the goals set forth in your plan. In truth, you probably *are* equals.

Two types of interviews

The *group* interview is presented to more than one person and includes visual aids, such as a slide presentation. The *individual* interview is a one-on-one presentation without visual aids other than pictures in the plan. The group oral presentation usually involves the sense of seeing as well as the sense of hearing.

Rarely is a group presentation necessary for a financing plan.

But, when it comes to a group presentation of a business plan:

1. Usually there is more than one investor to talk to. When you are talking to more than one person, visual aids, such as slides or flip charts, are an ideal way to get a point across.
2. More money is involved. Business plans are usually created for larger deals, which take more convincing. Visual aids help get the important points across.
3. Business plans are usually created for higher-risk deals than financing plans, although this is not always true. The higher the risk, the more wary the investor is, and the more persuasion is necessary to make the sale.

The difference between individual and group presentations

The only difference is the use of visual aids in the presentation. Such aids include movies, computer graphics, videotapes, slides, flip charts, charts and graphics, overhead projections, and handouts.

The advantages of visual aids

We live in a visual culture. Anything that uses the visual medium adds 68% effectiveness to the presentation. The more senses you can appeal to, the more effective you will be in getting your point across. It is easy to make a slide when you make charts and graphs on computers. Actually, it is easier than ever to prepare visual aids of all kinds.

Special things to do in any presentation

1. Appoint a master of ceremonies, preferably the chief executive officer, to run the presentation, introduce the management team, field the questions, decide which questions to answer directly and which to parcel out to other members of the management team.
   Always allow everyone on your management team to participate

in the presentation. This gives your audience the ability to size up your people working as a team.

2. Don't use your visual aids right away. Build some rapport with the audience first. This is especially true if the visual part of the presentation requires turning the lights down. Don't start out by putting your audience to sleep.

3. Concentrate on maintaining eye contact. Don't talk to walls or hairdos. Speak to the audience. Address the members of the audience by name as often as possible to keep them involved. Gesturing is good to emphasize key points. Animate your delivery.

4. When using visual aids, be sure that the words are clear and simple with large letters that are easy to read. Don't use typed pages, and don't put too much detail into your slides and overheads. Don't show difficult financial tables. Instead of displaying the complete tables of projections, show only bulleted summaries of key points. Always use a pointer when using a visual aid.

5. Emphasize the key points of your plan. You don't have to cover the entire plan. If you are going for debt financing, emphasize your collateral and ability to service the debt. If you are going for equity financing, emphasize the market, management, and the investment opportunity.

6. Don't spend too much time describing your product or service, what it does or how it works. Concentrate on the state of your market, how your product or service benefits your customers, and how you plan to attract your customers.

7. Take time to have all the members of the management team introduce themselves and briefly explain their background and their aspect of the business. If only the chief executive officer speaks at this interview, the audience tends to think the management is really a one-man show. Venture and adventure capitalists want to invest in companies run by management teams, not by individuals, no matter how talented.

8. Demonstrate the product or service if possible. This enables people to understand the product or service without having to endure a long and complicated explanation.

   Even if you have to use a model, something visual that can be seen and touched adds to the effectiveness of your presentation. Try to demonstrate your product as early in the presentation as possible to secure audience interest. (Make sure the product works before the demonstration!)

9. Rehearse, rehearse, and rehearse. Rehearsals help smooth over or eliminate the rough spots and make the management or presentation team feel confident about their abilities. Choreograph everything.

10. If you are using your own facilities for the presentation, make sure they are neat and clean.

11. Have sufficient refreshments for the audience. Anything alcoholic is not a good idea.

12. You are going to have to sell your business idea and make it come alive. Paint the picture so that the source can actually visualize it. Answer the one big question: Why will you succeed?

13. Selling management is really selling yourself. Financial sources bet on people, so sell yourself and your capabilities. Here is your chance to blow your own horn and convince the source you know what you are talking about.

14. While answering questions, call on people who have raised their hands and recognize them with an open hand, never a pointed finger.

15. Learn the art of rephrasing questions. Here's why:

    It lets both the questioner and the responder understand the question.

    It lets the speaker establish concurrence with the inquirer by nodding and saying in effect, "I understand you."

    It lets the speaker regain control of the floor.

    It buys valuable thinking time.

    It lets the whole audience in on the question.

    It lets the speaker turn a hostile question into a neutral question by removing the negativity. Example, "Why do you charge so damn much?" could be restated, "Your question is, 'How did we arrive at the pricing'?"

    Rephrasing. It is done for the above reasons and is *not* designed to avoid or distort any question. Keep in mind that you are a businessperson, not a politician.

What the experts say about good presentations

People who listen to plans every day say:

1. Always plan your presentation from beginning to end very carefully. Rehearse your presentation and get critiques from people both inside and outside your firm.
2. Keep in mind that the object of your presentation is to make your plan, quite literally, come alive!
3. In a face-to-face interview, financial sources carefully scrutinize the entrepreneur's:

   Attractiveness
   Appearance
   Dress
   Behavior
   Conversation
   Preparedness
   Clear and coherent explanation of the project
   Quickness in responding to questions
   Flexibility in accepting advice
   Receptivity to constructive criticism
   Ability to confront issues and avoid negative responses

4. However much investors or lenders like the written plan, they won't back entrepreneurs who can't stand up and articulate where the company has been, where it is now, and where it is headed.

What to do after the interview

First, *don't be too impatient*. Wait a few days before calling the financial source. The source may request more information. Get it as soon as possible. Don't let too much time lapse between any communication with a financing source. Even favorable impressions don't last forever.

Sometimes venture capitalists and lenders want to meet the key managers on a more informal basis, and they may invite the management team to dinner or some other social engagement. Don't decline such an invitation. It is not strictly social. The financial source is continuing its investigation by trying to get to know the entrepreneur on a more informal basis and possibly to check out the entrepreneur's spouse. The source may be wondering how powerful the spouse is and whether he or she will meddle in the business.

What to do at each subsequent meeting

Reinforce the positive relationship you have established. The second and third meetings will not come about if the source is not interested.

What if the source says no?

Call and find out what happened. Always, *always* ask why. You can change your plan. You can change your strategy. You can change your projections or whatever is necessary. Maybe you can't change this source's mind. But you can make those changes before you contact the *next* source. Take advantage of the wisdom of each source to find out why he or she doesn't want to lend to or invest in your business. By learning from your mistakes, you can make appropriate changes the next time around.

Use the experience productively. Successful entrepreneurs use such negative experiences as opportunities. So don't fight any arguments; learn from them.

The reason you were turned down may have nothing to do with the merit of your request. The source could be out of capital or just not allowed to lend or invest in your type of business, or the chemistry between you may not have been right.

After it is all over, analyze yourself. See if you can spot a flaw. Ask yourself candidly if you displayed a lack of confidence in yourself or if you seemed too cocky or sounded too pushy at the meeting. Did you give the financing source any reason to mistrust you? Were you impolite? It is perhaps impossible to identify the real reasons, but you may spot something you said that can be corrected before the next phone call.

When it gets down to parting with any kind of money, most decisions are made on feelings and intuition. In the face-to-face meeting with a source, it is impossible to predict what it will take to excite that particular source about your project. You learn from your mistakes and keep contacting more sources.

Prepare yourself for rejection. Let it make you stronger, not weaker. To handle rejection, you must be strongly motivated to achieve your goals. Your drive, ambition, and desire to succeed should keep you talking to more and more sources until you find one that says *yes*.

In the end, if you can't get the appointment or your presentation was not effective, ask for a referral. You just may find the perfect source.

What if they *all* say no

For some reason you are not a good risk. If you can't succeed with any of the guerrilla sources in this book, it may be a signal. If you are already in business, you've got to roll up your sleeves and get to work improving your operations with the resources at your disposal before you go for more money. If you are starting up, the rejections are telling you that your idea may not be economically feasible.

If everybody turns you down, try some of the guerrilla financing techniques described in Chapter 13.

Should you negotiate at any of these meetings?

If the financing sources start talking terms, it means they have a definite interest, and the negotiations are starting. If they want to "cut the deal," structure the terms, at the first meeting, it is a very powerful indication of interest in your project. Sometimes an investor or lender will send up a trial balloon and talk terms early in the game to see your reaction. Use common sense, but don't be surprised if you go from presentation to negotiation within a few minutes! It can happen, especially if you have followed the advice in this book.

Now it's time to learn how to negotiate a good deal.

16
How to Negotiate the Best Terms

You've met a source who is interested in funding your dream. Terms are starting to be discussed. Congratulations on coming this far. But don't blow this opportunity through ignorance of the final phase of the process of raising capital — *negotiation*.

You will find that buying money is really no different from buying any other commodity. You want the best deal, and to get it, you have to negotiate.

If you are desperate and will accept any deal on any terms, you don't have to negotiate. But there is always room for a better deal.

Practically everything in a financing agreement is negotiable; don't let any lender or investor tell you otherwise. Most lenders and investors ask for a lot at first, but after smart negotiating they will accept much less.

You've got to know the differences between a good deal and a bad deal. You must be aware of the pitfalls. And you've got to recognize a deal that isn't economically feasible. Why accept money if the cost will put you out of business?

It's time to learn the techniques for negotiating debt financing and equity financing. Although you now know what type of financing you are looking for, this doesn't mean that you should learn the negotiating techniques for just one type. Learn about both; there is information in both areas that can help you.

Bring your lawyer at the right time

Use your legal counsel to help you with the negotiations. Many lawyers are excellent negotiators. Don't enter a *final* negotiating meeting without one. Though this chapter will cover some important points to keep in mind when negotiating terms, it cannot cover them all, so *bring your lawyer to the negotiating table!*

Some financing sources like to see if entrepreneurs can hold their own in negotiations *without* lawyers being present because a lot of the entrepreneur's work will include negotiating with suppliers, vendors, and customers. If the entrepreneur starts the negotiations *with* a lawyer in tow, the financing source may see this as a sign of weakness and too much dependence on outside counsel.

Nonetheless, be sure to bring your lawyer in at the *end* of the negotiations. At the beginning of the negotiations, use your lawyer as an outside consultant by discussing the negotiations after the meetings. Many lawyers tend to be quite combative and argumentative. This may help at the end of the negotiations, to get those final points you want, but could kill the deal at the beginning of the negotiations.

Debt financing

The three most important things to consider in any debt financing or loan are *interest, maturity,* and *collateral.*

Interest

Once you have been told what interest rate the source wants to charge, check it against a number of other sources to determine the range of interest rates being charged in the market for your type of financing. Every type of debt financing has a range of typical interest rates — from strong deals with low interest rates to weak deals with high interest rates. The better the deal, the better the rate or the lower the interest. The weaker or riskier the deal, the higher the rate of interest. To determine the competitiveness of the rate you have been offered, compare it with the norm or average rate of that type of financing. If you are going for a receivable loan, check other receivable lenders for their range of rates. Even if you know in advance that they won't accept you for some reason, they will still quote the range of rates they offer. The same is true for inventory, equipment, and real estate financing sources. They will all give you a range of rates, depending on the strength of the deal.

Since rates constantly change, you must check this out as soon as you are offered an interest rate. By checking with a number of similar financing sources, you will determine the market rate and be able to compare it to the deal you are being offered.

Spend a few minutes to calculate how much each fraction of a percentage costs over the length or maturity of the loan. You will be surprised at how much money you can save by negotiating a rate lower by one percentage point, or even by a *fraction* of a point.

The longer the term of the loan, the more important the interest rate. A one-point difference on a 5-year loan is very different than on a 15-year loan. Check it out. Use an accountant if necessary.

Know your effective interest rate

The effective interest rate is the real interest or cost of money you will be paying. To get the effective interest rate, add all the other fees you will have to pay to the original interest rate. For example, if the lender requires you to maintain a specific amount of money in a non-interest-bearing bank account (a compensating balance), this increases your effective interest rate. For example, if you borrowed $500,000 at 12% interest but are required to maintain a $50,000 compensating balance, you will pay interest each year of $60,000 on available funds of only $450,000 — an effective interest rate of 13.3%.

Don't forget to add loan origination, commitment, and other fees to the costs of your interest rate. For instance, if you pay a 1% (one point) origination fee for a 2-year loan, even though this is a one-time fee, you have actually increased your annual effective interest rate by 1/2% each year.

Watch out for "sliding interest rate" deals, where your effective interest rate can increase dramatically. This is when the lender's interest rate can change at a different pace if the prime or base rate changes. Look out for any contract that states that if the base rate goes up 1/4%, your interest rate goes up by 3/8%.

Fixed or variable rates: which is better?

Fixed interest rates do not change for the duration of the repayment schedule, but variable or floating rates do change. If the basis rate or prime rate is at an all-time high, you may be better off with a variable rate in anticipation of a drop in rates. If the basis rate is at an all-time low, go for a fixed rate so that you can keep that low rate for the duration of the loan. Sometimes you have no choice in the matter. Your accountant can help you here.

The basis rate is the rate that the variable rate is geared or compared to. As it goes up or down, so does the effective rate.

Maturity

Maturity is the length of the loan. Always negotiate the longest maturity possible because the longer the maturity, the lower your monthly payments will be. Even if you think you can afford higher monthly payments, go for a longer maturity.

You may wonder about the wisdom of seeking a long maturity in a business loan, especially with the prevailing theory in home financing of saving interest payments by reducing the length of the mortgage.

Business loans involve an entirely different set of circumstances from home mortgages. It is like comparing apples to oranges. Reducing the cost of your mortgage might be a grand idea, but reducing the length of your business loan is *not* a good idea.

In a business loan, you must always compare the cost of your money, interest expense, to how much that money can earn for you in your business. In simple terms, if you can earn more on borrowed money by putting it to work in your business than it costs you in interest, it is best to keep that money as long as you can and not pay it back quickly.

Suppose, for example, that you are trying to decide whether to take a 15- or a 25-year loan on your commercial building. Suppose also that by taking the 25-year loan, your monthly payments are lower by $1,000. In this situation, you must evaluate how you can use an extra $1,000 per month in your business to make more money compared to paying it back to the lender. With that $1,000, you may be able to get a better discount from your suppliers by paying invoices sooner. You may be able to increase sales and profits by spending more on marketing. The point is, by going for the longest maturity, you will get the lowest monthly payments, which will give you that extra margin of cash flow to use as you wish in your business. If for some reason you don't need that extra cash, then go for a shorter term. You can always pay off the loan or pay the loan before its maturity date, but watch out for any penalties for paying off the loan early.

You should not only negotiate for the longest term, but also try to get the principal payments deferred as long as possible. An interest-only loan for a few years will give you still more cash flow. The point is to generate as much cash as possible for your company; at least make sure that your loan repayment schedule coincides with your cash flow projections. In fact, your expected cash flow should be considerably higher than your monthly payments so that you have a margin to anticipate for seasonal and unexpected fluctuations.

As with real estate financing, the amortization period might be different from your maturity. Either way, go for the lowest monthly payment.

Don't be afraid of debt

Debt is simply other people's money. If you can make money by using other people's money, there is no reason to worry about the fact that you owe money. Debt represents a way to leverage a small amount of capital that you and/or your investors put into the business. Aggressive entrepreneurs try to find ways to borrow as much of the capital as they need. If you are not making money on the money you borrow, don't borrow it. To find out, *simply compare the cost of the money you borrowed to the profit you are making on that money by using it in your business.*

In fact, you should always evaluate the wisdom of borrowing before taking on new debt by comparing what you expect the loan to cost to what you project you can make from it. For example, if your profits show a 25% return on invested capital, it is wise to borrow money at 12%. But if your return on invested capital is only 12%, you will be losing money by borrowing at 12% or more.

Only if the money you borrow will cost *less* than your return on capital or will *increase* your return on capital *is it profitable to borrow money*. Every guerrilla knows this.

Collateral

When offering collateral or your personal guarantee, think twice; you could lose everything. Start the negotiations by trying not to offer any collateral and go from there. In most cases, the lenders will want to secure their loan with everything the business has and wants to buy, plus everything the owners have. The purpose of the negotiation is to come to some common ground between risking everything to risking some things.

If you have to offer collateral, try to negotiate the terms for its release before the loan is paid. Why should a lender be allowed to hold on to a piece of real estate for the entire length of the loan if the borrower can meet criteria showing the increasing economic strength of the company? Some lending institutions will allow collateral to be released if the borrower's net income and net worth increase to certain agreed-upon levels. It's worth checking out.

Amount

Guerrillas always ask for more money than they think they will need. Time and time again, companies that didn't borrow enough the first time soon need more capital.

Use common sense. No matter how hard you try to estimate your needs accurately, you will rarely estimate the right amount. The worst thing that can happen by borrowing *more* than you think you need is that you'll pay a little extra interest. On the other hand, the worst that can happen by *not borrowing enough* is that you'll lose your business.

Of course, you don't want to overdo it. Just ask for about 15% to 20% more than you think you need, but make sure you can realistically handle the cost of the extra money.

Financial covenants

These are certain standards of performance that the lender demands the borrower keep during the course of the loan. If you do not meet these standards, there is a chance that the lender will put you in default or "call the loan," that is, ask that the loan be paid in full immediately.

These covenants are usually expressed in financial ratios that the borrower must meet. Some common examples are:

1. *Minimum working capital.* Usually expressed as your current ratio (ratio of current assets to current liabilities). The more assets you have to cover all your immediate requirements, the stronger your financial condition.
2. *Maximum leverage.* Ratio of debt to equity. Lenders don't want the entrepreneur to continually borrow more and more money without having the net worth of the business increase proportionately.
3. *Quick ratio.* Ratio of cash and receivables to current liabilities. This ratio tells the lender the company's ability to meet its current debts.

These are just some of the ratios that may be in your financing agreement. The point is to be sure the covenants provide an adequate margin so that any drop in performance does not put you in default.

The use of subordination to get commitments from debt sources

A good negotiating technique to get a lender to make the loan is to arrange for some of the other creditors to subordinate their loans to the new lender. In subordination, the new lender improves the possibility of being repaid in event of a default. This is not easy to accomplish, but it can be an important factor in swinging a deal. All shareholder loans are usually subordinated to new debt sources.

If the lender requests debt to be considered as equity for purposes of meeting your financial ratio tests, you should also get the lender to agree on conditions under which the subordination may be lifted.

Financial restrictions

Most lenders will want certain restrictions on any payout of funds. An example is the amounts that can be paid in dividends, owners' salaries, the repayment of loans to owners, bonuses, and the sale of major assets. All these requests must be approved by the lender.

Should your agreement provide annual limits on payouts, try to get the limit set on a cumulative basis so that any amounts not used in one year can be added to the next year's limit.

Financial reporting

Try to get the borrower to ask only for compiled or reviewed annual statements. Audited statements are extremely expensive and time-consuming.

Prepayment penalties

These are financial penalties imposed by the lender to discourage companies from refinancing when the interest rates drop. Try for no prepayment penalties. This will give you more flexibility in deciding what to do down the road.

If the lender insists on a prepayment penalty clause, be sure the penalty does not apply in cases where the lender demands early payment because of default. Also, try to get the lender to agree not to charge a penalty if you pay the loan off to eliminate any financial restrictions, such as no dividend payments.

Clean-up provisions

Lines of credit usually require you to pay off the loan in full once a year for 30 days. With the seasonal nature of your business, make sure you can comply with this provision.

Cross-default clause

Watch out for this clause. It means that if you default on any of your other loans, you are also in default on those with such a clause. You could be in technical default just because you did not pay a very small loan.

How to handle restrictions

A major negotiating objective is to try to minimize any restrictions, covenants, and clauses to the point that they do not hinder the company's operations. Try to identify those items in your financing agreement that are of serious concern to you and concentrate on those; don't nitpick on all the details.

Even though the interest rate is low, if the agreement has many restrictive covenants, it may not be a good deal.

What isn't negotiable in debt financing

Personal guarantees and life insurance on the principal business owners are usually not negotiable.

In the final analysis, when deciding whether to accept an offer or not, take into account all the terms involved: effective interest, maturity, amount, collateral, restrictions, covenants, and clauses.

What to do if you can't agree on terms

Obtain a clear understanding from the source on the reasons why. Ask the source to explain the assumptions behind the reasoning and to offer suggestions for improving the situation. If the suggestions involve conditions that can be remedied, then do so and make the deal.

If you feel the lender's judgment is questionable and you don't want to change your position, you can modify your proposal to respond to some of the reasonable criticisms. If you still can't agree, just continue to search for other debt sources.

If the reason for the denial involves factors that can't be remedied, such as factors inherent in the business or its current financial situation, pursue alternative guerrilla financing sources.

Equity

A crucial point to negotiate in any discussion of equity financing is what percentage of the company the investors get for their money.

Giving away part of your business is rarely a pleasant experience, but it is often a necessary means to a greater end. Remember, one of the great advantages in equity financing is that you are usually not obligated to pay back the investor unless you make a profit.

If the investors structure their investment as some sort of debt, with options or warrants, or just convertible debt, make sure they get less of your company than an investor who gets just equity. In other words, if you encounter investors who want equity plus their money back, make sure you negotiate a smaller percentage ownership than they would receive if their money were to stay in the business.

In the rare case of having to offer collateral to investors to make the deal, again, reduce their share of the company.

How much should you give up to investors?

It is hard to give advice on this subject, for it is a very touchy area. It usually depends on three factors: (1) the amount of capital or collateral the owners put into the business; (2) the upside opportunity; and (3) the downside risks involved. These will be covered later in this chapter. For now, just consider the greatest fear the entrepreneur has when looking for equity financing: *giving up control*. If for some reason the negotiations come down to the point where you have to give up control to get the money, use *the guerrilla formula* for giving up control.

The guerrilla formula

Create a performance schedule that allows you to buy back control based on your ability to meet that schedule. The schedule can be created from your own projections, assuming you believe you can meet them.

The reason most investors want control is that they are afraid you may mess things up, and they want a way to control you and their investment. Agree with them and say if you do mess things up, they deserve a way to protect their money, but if you meet your projections, you deserve to keep control. Any logical person should agree with that formula.

Most investors don't want the responsibility of taking over control of a business. What they really want is a way to protect their investment, and you can't blame them. The guerrilla formula solves the problem. The entrepreneur gets to keep or buy back control based purely on performance. No one can know what the future will bring, but if the investors are willing to risk their capital, the entrepreneur should, under certain circumstances, be willing to risk giving control. Using this formula, the entrepreneur has a strong motivation to do whatever is necessary to meet the objectives of the business plan and also regain control.

Be flexible

Don't be rigid on the amount of ownership you are willing to give up for an investment. Remember, negotiations mean give and take. Both parties have needs, and each is seeking a solution. In a good financing, there is always some common ground you can work on until any deadlocks are solved. Keep the dialogue going until you reach your settlement.

Everything is negotiable. It is *your* persuasive power against *theirs*. You want the highest value and they want the lowest. Somewhere in between is the answer. The worst that can happen is that one of you walks away — and maybe that was for the best anyway.

How to value a business

How much the entrepreneur is willing to give up depends on how the venture and adventure capitalists value your business. Chapter 3 showed you how to value all the assets in your business.

If you are already in business and want to know the value of the company, just put it up for sale and you will quickly have the market tell you its worth. In fact, most business brokers or merger and acquisition firms can estimate what your business can sell for. Once you have a dollar figure, if you want to sell off 25% or 50% you have a good idea of what price to negotiate for.

Factors in evaluating the founder's equity in start-ups

If you are a start-up, the story is quite different.

When venture and adventure capitalists determine the ownership of a new business, they consider these factors:

1. *Entrepreneur's investment.* How much is the entrepreneur investing in the business compared to the total amount that is being asked of the investors? Investors believe if the entrepreneur is investing very little, he or she should expect to receive less equity in the entire deal. The venture community realizes that the entrepreneur is putting time and effort into the company, but if no actual capital goes in from the entrepreneur, what prevents him or her from walking away from the deal without suffering an economic loss? If the entrepreneur can borrow on a house or can get some capital from a friendly source, the venture community will expect less equity in the deal. The entrepreneur's capital can come in the form of collateral, such as equipment, real estate, and other hard assets. With some collateral, the downside risk for the venture capitalist will have been curbed to some degree.

Therefore, the more you can provide in the form of capital or collateral, the greater the opportunity you have to own more of your own company. There is no ratio formula for the amount of money you put in your own business to the amount of equity you will receive in your own deal. It is *all* negotiable.

2. *The entrepreneur's blood, sweat, and tears.* You are probably wondering why, after all the hard work, research, time, and effort you have put into your idea, these factors are not considered when deciding how much ownership you end up with. The investment community will take those sweat equity factors into consideration, but, and it is a big but, when it comes down to the bottom line in a start-up, owners who put very little of their own money into a situation usually start out with very little ownership. This does not mean that they can't negotiate a buyout agreement, in which their share of the profits can be used to buy back more ownership eventually.

However, you may be the exception, and there are *lots* of exceptions. Entrepreneurs come to the negotiating table with very little or even no capital of their own and raise the money they need while still retaining the majority of the ownership. This usually happens when the idea behind the new business has a superb chance of success and the project has all the other factors the investment community likes to see in a start-up: national potential, proprietary position, and excellent management.

One last thing regarding sweat equity: keep in mind that the money of most investors, especially informal investors, came from their own sweat.

3. *Upside potential.* How much money you can make for your investors and the probability of success will also determine the valuation of a company. If you can double the venture capitalist's money in 5 years, that would be only a 15% annual return. But if you could *triple* the investor's money in 5 years, that would be a 25% return, which is the minimum return on capital most investors are looking for. On the other hand, if you could give the investors *ten times* their investment in 5 years, they would be making 58% compounded annual return on their money. You would have what the venture community considers a winner.

4. *Downside risk.* The higher the downside risk and the lower the liquidation value of a company, the more the investors will have to receive in equity ownership to compensate for the risk.

You may ask why an investor would invest in a risky deal in the first place. The answer is that no one actually thinks the risk is that great when they invest. No one intentionally invests in a bad deal; all investments look promising when they are made. But some will turn out to be winners, some losers, and some just mediocre. A mediocre investment is where the investor does not lose money but, on the other hand, does not make much of a return. A winner would bring in a 58% return and a mediocre investment would bring in about 15%. But the investors' greatest fear is *loss* of capital. When they lose their capital they cannot continue to invest, and the less they invest, the less chance they have to find a winner. Be sensitive to this risk-and-reward analysis of the investment community in your negotiations.

What professional venture capitalists look for in evaluating a start-up

Besides looking for the factors already discussed in assessing the makeup of the ownership pie in a start-up, professional venture capitalists also look at the need for additional funds and an exit strategy to get their money out. The more additional funds are necessary, the more ownership they will want because each successive requirement for capital will cause the dilution of ownership by the existing stockholders. Also, professional venture capitalists must look for a way to get out of a deal to satisfy their own funding sources, who themselves want to keep their money fairly liquid.

The golden rule

You have heard that "he who has the gold makes the rules." In equity investing, this does not always work because each party is so dependent on the other. Each party has something to bring to the table. The entrepreneur has his company and his plan of how to make it happen. The investor has money, experience, and contacts. Each party has a position to protect, and each must give good value to the party to make the relationship work.

Investors know that no matter how much stock they control, if management wants to hurt them, it can do so before the investors even find out. Restated, if an entrepreneur wants to cheat the venture capitalists, he or she has ample opportunity to do so while running the business. This is true no matter what percentage of ownership the investors have.

Investors therefore must trust the management team and be considered partners in the true sense of the word.

Don't burn your bridges in the negotiations

During negotiations, always take the long-term view and conduct yourself in a manner that is conducive to a long-term relationship. You may want to go back to the same investors for more money down the road, so try to negotiate a deal that you both can live with.

Most venture and adventure capitalists never try to browbeat the entrepreneur into a position he or she does not want. Keep in mind that if you use an overbearing or hard negotiating technique, you may win the battle but lose the war. Both parties must learn how to live with each other *after* the negotiations are over, and any technique that injures the other party may impair the relationship throughout the duration of the investment. If either side has to push too hard, it's a bad deal.

When to accept an equity deal

You must feel satisfied with the deal you have negotiated or walk away from it. Otherwise it will only end in a great deal of misery for you both. A bad deal for one side will probably contribute to the failure of the enterprise.

Loss of control

Do not believe that loss of control is automatically a bad deal. Even if you don't use the guerrilla formula, most investors do not want to run your business, no matter how much of your company they own. They may have something to say in the management of your company. But as long as you meet your objectives, you should have no fear of their controlling interest.

Third-party opinions

Discuss the investor's final offer with as many people as possible, such as your consultant, lawyer, accountant, banker, and anybody else you think can evaluate the offer. You may be pleasantly surprised that the offer and deal you have structured is the best you can expect in the current marketplace.

Turn all discussions into a commitment letter/ letter of intent/term sheet

Every financing agreement, debt or equity, is first spelled out for both parties in writing using a term sheet, commitment letter, or letter of intent setting forth the proposed terms and conditions of the loan or investment. Putting what you have decided in writing gives both sides time to reconsider all the factors laid out in the negotiations.

These papers are not legal documents, but are intended to convey in writing the terms and conditions agreed upon. The final financing agreement will add all the necessary documentation to which lawyers attend.

These types of documents are usually subject to the due diligence that is necessary to check out the entrepreneur.

Due diligence

In equity as well as in some debt deals, the lenders or investors want to check out the entrepreneur's assumptions, analyze the industry study, verify the representations in the business plan, and check management's credit and background. The entrepreneur may think all investors are paranoid, but, remember, they take a much greater risk than debt sources. Good investors are suspicious by nature. Because of the risk they take, they usually assume the entrepreneur is a crook and then work their way back toward his or her honesty. Don't take this the wrong way; it is their nature of "checking out the deal." Be prepared for a complete background check on all the management — the key to any equity deal. Investors will be quite thorough in their investigation.

Don't argue over minor points

If you have agreed upon the major points, let the lawyers do their job and you stay out of it, if possible. But make sure you read over and understand the final financial documents before you sign.

Don't "bolt for the finish line"

Don't accept the first financing offer presented to you. It may be tempting, but be patient and don't lose sight of the realities of the situation. Once you know where to look for financing sources and how to persuade them to lend or invest, you should find plenty of sources from which to select. Ideally, you can compare the agreements of several financing sources to choose the best one for your situation. Sources don't like their agreements to be seen by other sources. Therefore, never show one source another source's agreement. That is the quickest way there is to turn your name into mud in the financial community.

If you have followed the instructions on how to choose the right source and create an effective financing or business plan, you should have the luxury of showing it to a number of sources and getting the best deal.

You will be surprised at the large differences in the terms offered by the variety of sources. Based on the odds, it is unlikely that the first offer you get will be the best one.

17
Parting Advice to Guerrillas

By now, you have learned that getting turned down for a financing request is not the *end* but the *beginning* of the search for money.

The sources for money are all around you. Besides the financial institutions covered, private capital can come from your friends, suppliers, customers, and even neighbors.

You have been given a lot of information about the entire process of financing a business. You have learned that raising money is a multi-step process and you must go through it one step at a time. You have learned each step of that process.

This last chapter gives you an overview of the process. It also imparts thoughts on a key concept that has helped many entrepreneurs achieve their financing and business goals: *partnerism*.

Five steps to raising capital

Take a moment to review the five steps to successful financing:

1. Identify all the assets of your business, including your own assets, and place them in the appropriate categories of funding. The first step is to study your own situation to determine the credit potential of each asset you own or will own with the money you are looking for. Identify the many intangible assets that are often overlooked by the accounting profession. Then identify all the liabilities that will reduce the value of these assets in order to arrive at a true value of your business. This value can be considered your borrowing power or investment worth, or how much capital you can borrow or attract at this point. Every business has some sort of value and financing power.

2. Identify all the financing sources that are appropriate for your

situation. Much of this book has been devoted to this step to make sure that you know *all* the choices of financing sources available to you so that you can exploit each asset for its maximum financing power. You now know how and where to find these sources of capital.

3. Deliver the most effective written and oral presentation of your concept. You know your business, but communicating that information in a favorable way to the outside world takes considerable skill and effort. Put your ideas in writing and communicate them effectively to the appropriate sources.

4. Use guerrilla financing techniques. If necessary, as you have seen, there is a whole world of techniques if you're a guerrilla.

5. Negotiate the best possible terms. You now know the do's, the don'ts, and the key areas on which to focus.

The entire process

When you combine your knowledge of your guerrilla assets and liabilities and guerrilla financing sources with all the guerrilla financing techniques, you should be able to finance *any* type of business situation.

That is the entire process. If you try to skip *any* step, you won't get the best deal for yourself or your company. It's like shortchanging yourself. The reason that so many people can't raise money is that they don't follow these guidelines.

You will find that raising money is not one step; it is a *continuous process* of many different steps. In fact, even after you get money for your company, you will probably need more in the future, and the process starts over again.

Time and effort

By now you know that the process requires time and effort. It is not going to be easy, and there aren't any shortcuts. Nothing worthwhile is easy. And that goes for raising money. There is no easy solution or quick miracle to raising capital.

Go for management first and capital second

To attract capital, attract *management*. If you can get the right management first, the capital will follow. Even if your management team is just advisers at first and not full-time, the mere fact that they are associated with you lends support to your idea.

If you have assembled a good, strong, experienced management team, financial sources will ask, "What are these people up to? It must be something good to get that much talent together in one company."

If raising money is a process of persuasion, the first group you must persuade is *your own staff*! If you have a hard time attracting anyone to the management team, maybe the people who are rejecting your management positions are telling you that your idea is not good or that you should rethink it. Guerrillas know if they can't find a team first, they won't find the capital. If you can't convince another person to join your team, how are you going to convince a financial source to lend or invest in your business?

Your journey

The information you have been given in this book will set you apart from 99% of all the entrepreneurs in this country. You have taken a journey into the world of small business finance, a journey that very few people have taken. You can now benefit from the experience of others who have tried to raise capital. What are you going to do with this information?

Are you going to use it to actually go out and raise capital? Or are you going to pay lip service to it and not even make an attempt?

Give guerrilla financing a try. The techniques you have learned in this book will get you the money you want, but *you* have to make the attempt. It *will* work, and you will be amazed at how effective these guerrilla techniques are.

You now have the tools to get the job done. Use them correctly and there's no situation you can't finance.

Good old perseverance

How you handle rejection will be a measure of how successful you will be in raising capital and operating a business.

Suppose you have tried some of the sources and techniques in this book and you have not succeeded. What do you do? You *keep trying*. If you are turned down by one source, you have other sources and techniques to try until you find the one that works for your situation. One couple went to seventy-three banks before they found one to loan them the money.

Sources are like snowflakes: no two are alike. Persistence and perseverance are the keys to raising capital. To continue your search in spite of all the difficulties, to refuse to give up — *that* is the real secret of guerrilla financing. Keep trying new sources and techniques until you find one that works for you. The real question is, How much staying power do you have to keep on trying?

If anyone tells you it can't be done, think about the ways you are trying and going to try, the ways it *can* be done and *has* been done.

This country has given you the opportunity to succeed. If money is the only thing holding you back from success, you now have the secrets to get that money.

If you use the technology of guerrilla financing, you will reach your financing goals. It is *not* a sin to be rejected by a financing source; it *is* a sin to give up trying.

How long will the process of raising money take?

There is no answer, since every business situation is different. It depends on how long it takes for you to go through the five steps in the process. It could take weeks, but it usually takes months or sometimes years.

The funding process is a real process and it takes a very precious commodity — *time*. It is harmful to rush a financing. It should be planned well in advance. *Do not wait until the last minute to look for capital.* Make a time line for raising money that includes the time you think it will take to go through all five steps. Very few companies get what they want by rushing the process of raising capital. Even if they do get their money, they usually get a very poor deal because they waited until the last minute to get started. After all, it takes nine months to make a human baby. This is your baby. So be prepared for a long-term commitment to the project. *If you will need money any time in the future, start working on it right now!*

What are you willing to pay?

What will the money cost? Again, there is no pat answer; each situation is unique and different. Raising money for just about any business or project usually comes down to two factors: what you want to *pay* for your money and/or what you are willing to *give up* for your money. If it is debt financing, it comes down to how much debt you are comfortable with or how much you can afford, and whether you want to take the risk of losing your collateral. If it is equity financing, it comes down to your comfort with your new partners and how much of the business you want to give them for their money.

It is not easy to pay more interest than you want to pay. It is not easy to give up more of the company than you want to. But there are ways to get the money to do the things you want for your business. Capital is the glue that keeps your business going. You need enough to make it succeed. Every guerrilla knows that.

Your attitude toward the financing

When all is said and done, your attitude toward the financing will have a dramatic impact on its success. If you are not happy with the terms of your financing agreement, your chances of delivering what you promise have been diminished. On the other hand, if you feel the financing source has given you a fair deal, you both have an excellent chance to reach each other's goals.

Whether your source is a bank or a private investor, it is, in effect, your partner. The financial fortunes of both parties are tied to your success. It is no longer you alone against the world. You must have the right positive attitude toward your partner to make it work. That brings up *partnerism*, which is the key to success in the 1990s for any entrepreneur.

Just don't be afraid to borrow money. Walt Disney once said, "I must be successful, I owe seven million dollars!"

The new key to success: partnerism

The day of the rugged, swashbuckling, individualistic, self-made entrepreneur is over. The myth of the independent individual who has a specialized knowledge and unique psychological makeup to go his or her own way is not consistent with the reality of dependence on all the forces that make a successful business. The 1990s will be a period of cooperation; that is especially true for entrepreneurs. The secret to successful entrepreneurship in the 1990s is in creating the network of contacts and colleagues to help build your business. It will be a cooperative endeavor, not just an individual inspiration. The loner has bought himself just a job; the team player has bought himself a business.

Partnerism is combining all the necessary resources to make a business successful. It takes a lot of resources to make a business: people, money, equipment, inventory, technology, and more. They all add value to the business, and that increases its financing power.

When you are looking for money from strangers, you will be getting a partner, whether it is a bank or a private investor. Both have an investment in the success of your business. You will have to report to both. Is this so bad? Absolutely not. Every businessperson should have someone to report to. It is these checks and balances that have produced the most successful form of government in the history of mankind, and the same is true in business. Even if you own 100% of your company, this concept of partnerism is still relevant.

You must consider everyone you deal with on a business basis as your partner: your employees and associates, your suppliers and vendors, your customers, your financial sources, your bank, your landlord, and the outside support services you hire. They are all your partners. All these sources have an interest in *wanting* you to succeed. They all add value to your company. And they all should be treated and thought of as partners. You may not know it, but you are even partners with your *competitors* in the same industry. There will be times when you will join together in associations to help each other.

The entrepreneur is in an alliance with all those people, and it will be the success of the alliance that makes the entrepreneur successful.

Take the concept of management. No one wants to invest or lend to just one person. They want a team that works together to build a business. It takes a team effort to put together all the necessary pieces to make a business work in today's world.

And, of course, this holds true for whatever financing sources you choose. Whichever they may be, those sources *want* you to succeed and have a stake in your business. Your job is to treat them as such. Keep them informed. Take their key people to lunch. Learn about their business. Get to know them personally. Do all the things you would do with a formal equity partner. Treat everyone you deal with as if they were your partners and you dramatically increase your chances of success.

The search for money never ends

Choose your partners carefully, not because you will be with them for life, but on the contrary, because you will have partners come and go throughout your business life.

In your search for money, you will be talking to debt and equity sources throughout the life of your business. As your business has its ups and downs, different financial sources will come and go. There will be times when you need receivable financing, equipment financing, real estate financing, or government-backed financing. There may be times you will need some sort of venture money. And there will even be times when you need to apply the guerrilla techniques covered in this book. You might invent some new ones yourself! The object of the financing game is to get your sources in and out as you need them. You don't have to live with them the rest of your life. They lend you money; you pay them back. They invest in your business; you pay them back with a healthy return and then buy their investment back.

What if you don't want a partner?

Say you have had bad luck with a partner in the past or had bad luck with a factor or receivables lender or an equipment finance company. Don't generalize from one bad experience. Forget the past. You must be open to all the new ideas available to solve your financial problems.

You have financial objectives, and sometimes you must compromise to achieve those objectives. Don't harp on your own experiences or those of someone else. All financial sources, debt or equity, will be your partners. Don't just think that equity financing creates partners. If a bank has lent you money, it is as much a partner as a private investor. Don't kid yourself. If money is on the line, legal agreements mean very little. For example, the fact that Donald Trump's banks dictated what his monthly income would be proves that debt sources are just as much your partner as equity sources.

National concept

The authors of this book invite you to join them in supporting new ideas that will help small businesses in this country. Turn to the national issues facing all entrepreneurs and join us in supporting the following ideas:

1. *Establish a cabinet-level post for small business.* Nobody really talks for small business at the national level of government, and it is about time that *somebody* did. The SBA should be the voice *for* small business, but it turns out to be the voice *for* the government about small business. You need someone out there in the trenches every day, fighting for and helping small business in every way possible.

The SBA lending program was supposed to be the answer for small business financing problems. It turns out that its loan guarantee program is mostly collateralized with real estate. Why do you need an entire federal agency to make business loans based on real estate? It doesn't take a genius to know how to make a real estate loan. This country needs a creative agency with a real spokesperson for the entrepreneurs of this country.

2. *Defer taxes on start-up companies for five years.* Give the little guy a *real, measurable break.* Support entrepreneurism and reduce the

number of failures in the first 5 years of business — now a depressing 80%.

3. *Offset taxes for firms that create new jobs.* The government wants companies to hire more people. Let it put its money where its mouth is. The entrepreneur has to spend every day figuring out how to get rid of people because of all the taxes necessary to keep an employee. Reducing your taxes when you hire someone is long overdue.

4. *Establish a national small business training program to bring together industry, government, and education.* America needs powerful and coordinated programs to assist small business in this country.

5. *Revamp the SBA's national mentor program, Score, into an entre*preneur corps to include all ages of entrepreneurs, not just retirees. Let all types of successful, experienced entrepreneurs connect with new, inexperienced entrepreneurs.

6. *Establish training programs for workers about to be laid off to channel those resources to help small businesses.*

7. *Allow small business owners to advertise for investors and partners without having to go through an expensive registration process.* The SEC's laws and the states' blue sky laws had good intentions, but now they are preventing many legitimate small business owners from raising capital due to the complexity and cost of all the regulations.

Wake up, entrepreneurs!

When is the government going to wake up to the fact that *small business is America's big business*? This is the age of the entrepreneur, and political institutions must support that movement. Presidential candidates do not discuss any small business issues while campaigning. That has to change!

This country must wake up to the fact that small business is the backbone of the economy. The media must stop focusing on the Fortune 500 and start focusing on small businesses.

Finally, the entrepreneurs of this country have to wake up and be heard in the media, in Congress, in the community. You can't pretend there is no world outside your business anymore. The world *is* your business.

No government institution is addressing the issues facing small businesses today. No one is asking the tough questions to learn how to solve the problems of today's entrepreneur.

What is good for General Motors is *not* necessarily good for the United States. What is good for the entrepreneurs of this country *is* good for the United States! Tell your elected representatives to get off their duffs and start helping.

A final thought

Yes, guerrillas, there *is* a way to finance your business. Don't think for one moment that there is a lack of capital out there. It is not a lack of capital that stops most people. It is the information on how to *get* that capital. You now have that information.

Business can be tough and fun at the same time. Running your own business keeps you alive and is one of the great challenges in life. It is one of the most creative aspects of our society today. Go to it! And use the persistence and wisdom of a guerrilla as you do.

Index

Accounts receivable. *See* Receivables financing
Acquisitions, 161
Advance payments. *See* Prepayment strategies
Adventure capital. *See* Venture capitalism, non-traditional/informal
Advertising: agencies, 224; classified, 104, 105, 184–94, 215, 230, 233, 238; cooperative, 236; on property, 229
Agricultural financing, 135–38. *See also* Equipment, specialized
Agriculture Department, 135, 137–38
Aid for International Development (AID), 129
Air pollution control loans, 122
Amortization, 94, 107, 108, 313
Angels. *See* Venture capitalism, nontraditional/informal, angels
Annual reports, 316
Anticipation concept, 226
Appraisals, 58, 262; drive-through, 265; of leases, 20–21; real estate, 103, 264–65
Asset(s): appraisal of, 262; balance sheet, 17; -based financing, 7–8, 12, 15, 40, 71, 209, 326; business, 17; as collateral, 38, 219, 262; credit value of, 29; defined, 13, 14, 15; fixed, 116; intangible, 7, 9, 12, 17, 21, 23, 35, 36, 38, 50–51, 56, 149; liquidity, 15, 17, 58; market-ing value of, 15, 16–17, 58; net value of, 30–31; personal, 17, 27–28, 29, 56–57, 58; sale of, 233; /source matching, 9, 11, 13, 33, 36, 40–41, 61–62, 63; tangible, 9, 12, 16, 17–18, 24, 30, 32, 36, 51, 56; true net value of, 8, 11; unorthodox tangible, 38; valuation and analysis of, 8, 11, 12, 14. *See also specific types of property*
AT&T, 16

Back orders. *See* Purchase orders/back orders
Bad credit. *See* Credit, poor
Balance sheets, 17–19, 21, 23, 29; leasing fi-nancing and, 79, 81; sample, 33–34
Balloon payments, 107–8

Bank financing: 2, 4, 44, 141–43, 209; collateral requirements, 44, 58, 141, 142, 143, 147–48; for equipment, 88, 140, 141; for inventory, 140–41; long-term, 141; qualification require-ments, 142–43, 144; for real estate, 99–100, 101–2, 108, 140, 141; for receivables, 9, 71, 74, 76, 140; SBA loans, 120; short-term, 6, 140; types of, 140; unsecured, 62; for working capital, 140
Bankruptcy, 30, 75, 161. *See also* Defaults and foreclosures
Banks and banking: aggressive, 36, 48, 60, 139, 143, 144, 145–46; conservative, 139–40; de-posits, 144, 147; deregulation, 147; interest rates, 145; investment, 56, 179, 212, 238–47; money supply and, 146; risk and, 139–40, 144; venture capital subsidiaries, 151
Barter financing, 212–13, 231
Blechman, Bruce Jan, 4, 5, 179
Blind pools, 244
Blue sky laws, 208, 334
Bonds, 16, 27, 29, 144; as collateral, 57; indus-trial development, 116; surety, 121; tax-exempt, 113; umbrella, 116–17; zero coupon, 240
Boutique investment banking, 179
Brokerage firms and brokers, 57, 180; business, 184, 192, 197–98, 319; commercial mortgage, 49–50; commissions, 221; mortgage 93, 98, 101–2, 103, 104; securities, 105
Business development corporations (BDCs), 118–19
Business plans (general discussion), 169, 193, 267; adventure capital and, 178; complete, 249, 250; components of, 270–83; defined, 167, 251; financial figures in, 254–55; guide-lines for, 167–68, 251–54, 268–70, 283–84; 285–86; legal aspects of, 282, 284; mailing strategies, 169–70, 193, 273; as marketing tool, 252, 253; projections in, 194. *See also* Concept paper; Executive summary; Market-ing, plans; Presentation

Buy and sell arrangements, 55, 199

Calling of loans, 147, 314–15
Capital: internal, 235–36; leases, 80–81; leverage, 123; overseas, 243; private; 56, 61; working, 42, 60, 121, 315. *See also* Venture capitalism *listings*
Capital Institute, 4, 44, 179, 344
Cars and light trucks. *See* Rolling stock
Cash and cash equivalents, 17, 23, 28. *See also* Noncash solutions
Cash flow, 24, 37–38, 39–40, 53, 224; bank financing and, 141; break-even point, 255, 260; defined, 254; as down payment, 221–22; inventory and, 225; projections, 260–61, 313; in real estate financing, 95, 96, 99; in receivable financing, 75; venture capitalism and, 149
Cash management systems, 235–36
Certificates of deposit (CDs), 15, 17, 56–57
Charity, 232
Classified advertising. *See* Advertising, classified
Clean Air Act, 122
Closed-end leases, 80–81
Coal Mine Health and Occupational Safety acts, 122
Coca-Cola, 22, 51
Collateral, 37–38, 39–40, 110; for agricultural loans, 137; for bank loans, 44, 58, 141, 142, 143, 147–48; for debt financing, 51, 314; insufficient, 142; intangible, 52; in lieu of notification, 68, 73; liquidation of, 71; purchase of, 243; for SBA loans, 123–24; secondary, 140; third-party, 243. *See also specific types of property*
Collectibles: as asset, 27, 29; as collateral, 58–59, 123, 264
Collection services and costs, 67, 69–70, 73, 75, 230
Commerce Department loans, 127, 128–29, 132, 133, 134
Commercial mortgage brokers, 49–50
Commissions of brokers, 221
Commitment letters, 214, 324
Commodity Credit Corporation, 129
Competitor financing, 231–32
Computer(s): financing and leasing, 61, 82, 84, 88, 142; market, 158, 159
Concept paper, 273, 274; defined, 167; mailing strategies, 169–70
Concession sales, 213–14
Consignment merchandise, 231
Construction financing, 91, 108–9, 121, 265. *See also* Real estate financing, commerical and industrial
Consultants for bank loans, 147–48
Consumer protection loans, 122

Contracts: as asset, 8, 13, 18, 23, 28, 38; financing of, 43–44, 213; research, 246; terms of, 11
Copyright(s), 21, 155, 234; as asset, 22, 28, 38; financing, 50–51, protection, 277; sale of, 221
Corporate strategic alliances, 37, 39, 51, 245, 246; financing and, 61; for research and development, 53; success formulas and, 54; working capital and, 60
Corporations as source of capital, 173
Coupons, 229–30
Credit: 7, 142; as asset, 17; cash flow implications of, 64–66; enhancement, 243; other people's, use of, 213; of owners, 263; poor, 12, 13, 30, 71, 142, 147–48; pyramid, 218; sales, 64; services, 67; terms, 64, 65; of seller, 222; trade, 223–25
Credit cards, 218
Credit unions, 100, 217–18
Cross-default clauses, 316
Customer financing, 225–26
Customer lists, 221

Debt financing, 39, 51; negotiations, 310–17, 324; sources, 287, 293, 332
Debt service ratio, 95
Debt-to-equity ratio, 123, 315
Defaults and foreclosures, 314–15; cross-default clauses, 316; on real estate loans, 47, 48, 91, 92, 95, 97, 103. *See also* Bankruptcy
Deposits on orders, 230
Development companies and agencies, 113, 114–15, 121, 128
Dialing for dollars. *See* Telephone solicitation (dialing for dollars)
Direct loans and financial incentives, 115, 116
Direct response financing, 234
Direct response/preselling, 229
Disadvantaged persons. *See* Minority and disadvantaged funding programs
Disaster loans, 121
Disclaimers in business plains, 284–85
Discounted notes and mortgages, 238
Disney, Walt, 24
Displaced business loans, 121
Drive-through appraisals, 265
Due diligence process, 56, 176, 324
Dun & Bradstreet, 266

Economic dislocation loans, 122
Economic injury loans, 121–22
Economic opportunity loans, 121
Egg Products Inspection Act, 122
Emergency energy shortage loans, 122
Employees as asset, 13, 14. *See also* Management, as asset
Employee stock option plans (ESOPs), 246–47

Employment agreements, 55
Energy Department loans, 127
Energy loans, 121, 122, 127
Enterprise zones, 117
Environmental responsibility, 93
Equipment: as asset, 13, 14, 19–20, 23, 28, 61, 78, 79, 265; as collateral, 78; general, 84, 89; insurance, 88; leased, 13, 19–20, 46–47, 78–81, 83, 87; office, 86; purchase of, 80, 88; rental of, 80, 231; repairs, maintenance, and upgrading, 80, 81, 83–84, 88; resale value of, 82–83, 265; rolling stock, 20, 84, 85–86, 89, 220; salability of, 15–16, 82; sale and lease-back agreements for, 238; specialized, 84–85, 86, 121; types, 82; used and obsolete, 20, 47, 78, 79–80, 81, 82, 83
Equipment financing, 3, 6, 46, 61, 78–79, 332; advantages and disadvantages, 79–80; bank, 88, 140, 141; interest rates and, 310–11; risks of, 46–47; SBA loans, 121; soft costs in, 79; sources, 47, 84, 86, 88. *See also* Leases; Leasing financing
Equity and equity financing, 6, 39, 104, 105, 106, 160; debt-to-equity ratio, 123, 315; financing plans and, 265; investment programs, 117; negotiations, 318–23, 324; sharing, 215–16; sweat, 166, 320–21; sources, 287–88, 293, 332; unsecured, 35
Escrow financing, 222
Executive summary, 271, 272–73; defined, 167; mailing strategies, 169–70, 273
Exit strategies, 164, 209, 239, 242, 283
Expansion financing, 4, 11, 115, 117, 212
Export financing, 129
Export-Import Bank, 127
Export/import loans, 127
Export revolving line of credit (ERLC), 122
Exports, 76

Facilities management, 233
Factoring, 6, 70; advantages, 71; cost vs. benefit, 69–70; in receivables financing, 64, 68, 72–73; with recourse, 67–68; reserve accounts, 72–73
Factors, 36, 44, 60; credit and collection services provided by, 67, 73; customer evaluation by, 77; defined, 9, 66; notification arrangements and, 68; receivable financing by, 45, 66, 74; selection of, 70, 75. *See also* Receivable financing
Farm Credit Administration, 135, 136, 138
Farm Credit Program, 135, 136
Farmers Home Administration (FHA), 135, 137
Finance companies, 48, 86, 100; receivable financing by, 74, 76

Financial covenants, 315–16
Financial leases, 80–81
Financial ratios, 146–47
Financial Research Associates, 266
Financial restrictions on payments, 215–16, 317
Financial statements, 237–38
Financing: asset-based, 40, 71, 209; bridge, 103, 160; cost of, 330; fixed-asset, 116; fixed-rate, 79; holistic, 7, long-term, 109, 136, 137; mezzanine, 154, 160, 162; off-balance sheet, 79, 81; secured, 35, 38; seller, 106; short-term, 6, 103, 136, 137, 140; spot, 76; staged, 216, 217; steps, 8–11; techniques, 9–10, 11, 32, 57, 105–6, 211–12, 326–27; third-party, 14–15; time frame for, 329–30; up-front, 234; unsecured, 33, 35, 38, 61, 62, 217, 238–39, 287–88. *See also specific types and sources of financing*
Financing consultants and planners, 179–80
Financing plans, 249, 250–51, 252, 267; components of, 256–65; guidelines, 265–66
Finding Private Venture Capital for Your Firm (Gaston), 203
First-in, first-out inventory valuation (FIFO), 19
Floor planning, 76
Forced sale auction value. *See* Value, market (auction)
Ford Motor Company, 174
Foreclosures. *See* Defaults and foreclosures
Foreign investment in real estate, 101
Formulas, 9, 14, 55; as asset, 22
Franchises, 223, 228, 262
Free advice, 234–35
Future assets. *See* Contracts, as assets; Purchase orders/back orders; Work-in-progress

Gaston, Robert J., 203, 205
Genentech, 23
Goodwill, 7, 22, 23
Government funding programs, 3, 37, 110–12, 332; collateral for, 59; federal level, 119–34; local level, 113–15, 134; for management, 61; for incubators, 215; for patents, 51; private organizations and, 111; for real estate, 6, 49, 92; for research and development, 53, 61, 128, 130–31; for services, 61; sources, 60, 114–15, 119, 133–34; state level, 115–19, 134, 166; success formulas and, 54; venture capital enterprises, 151, 165–66; working capital and, 60
Government Printing Office Bookstores and Distribution Centers, 133
Grants, 117, 130
Guerrilla financing. *See* Financing, techniques
Guerrilla Marketing (Levinson), 5, 275

Guerrilla Marketing Attack (Levinson), 5
Guerrilla Marketing Newsletter, 233
Guerrilla Marketing Weapons (Levinson), 5

Handicapped assistance loans, 121, 132
Hard Money, 103–4, 238
Health and safety loans, 122
Hill, Napoleon, 247
Housing and Urban Development Department loans, 128

IBM, 24
Import protection loans, 128
Incentives, 55, 56; tax, 115, 117
Incubators, 115, 118, 119, 215
Industrial development agencies and financing, 113, 114, 116
Industrial development bonds (IDBs), 116
Initial public offering (IPO), 160, 244
Insurance: companies, 100, 173; on equipment, 88; key man, 55; valuation, 59
Interest rates, 106, 108, 109, 123; bank, 145; debt financing and, 310–12; fixed vs. variable, 312; sliding, 311
Intermediaries. *See* Venture capitalism, nontraditional/informal, intermediaries (advisers)
Interns and graduate students, 235, 237
Inventions, 227. *See also* Patents
Inventory, 16–17, 62, 230, 231; as asset, 19, 23, 28, 35; cash flow and, 225; as collateral, 76; flooring, 226–27; sale of, 220, 233–34; purchase of, 225; valuation, 19
Inventory financing, 45, 76; bank, 140–41; interest rates and, 310–11; risks, 45–46; sources, 46; term of loans, 141
Investment banking, 56, 179, 212, 238–47
Investor magazine, 184, 198–99, 201

Jet Skis, 214
Jobs, Steven P., 174
Joint ventures, 245–46
Just-in-time inventory purchasing, 225

Kentucky Fried Chicken, 22, 50
Keogh plans, 27
Key man insurance, 55
Kiam, Victor, 220–21
Kleenex, 22
Know-how, 155
Kroc, Ray, 254

Labor Surplus Set-Asides, 132
Land Bank Cooperative Associations, 136, 138
Land contributions, 106
Landlord financing, 101

Last sale commitment, 242–43
Leasehold improvement(s), 8, 19–20, 23, 28, 49, 232; as asset, 38; financing, 82, 95, 265; risks, 48; sources, 48
Leases: appraisal of, 20–21; as asset and collateral, 23, 28, 38, 262; buy-out terms, 84; checklist, 87–88; equipment, 13, 19–20, 46–47, 78–81, 83, 87; financial, 80–81; in financial plans, 265; land, 106, long-term, 47; market value of, 20; option to buy clauses, 109; purchase of, 222; space, 214–15; terms of, 87–88; types of, 80–81
Leasing companies, 37, 46, 48, 60, 76, 88–89
Leasing financing, 47, 48, 78, 82, 84–86, 87. *See also* Equipment, leased
Letters of credit, 76
Letters of intent, 214, 324
Leveraged buyouts (LBOs), 160–61, 220–21
Levinson, Jay Conrad, 4–5
Liabilities, 12; analysis, 14; assumption of, 221; current, 30; defined, 12, 13; in equipment financing, 78, 79; in financing plans, 262–63; intangible, 30, 32; long–term, 30; tangible, 32; in valuation formulas, 11, 12, 326. *See also* Liens
Licensing agreements, 227–28, 246
Liens, 14, 29, 30, 149; as collateral, 38; in valuation formulas, 8, 12, 30
Life insurance companies, 100
Liquidation value, 27–28. *See also* Value, market (auction)
Liquidity events, 164
Loan brokers. *See* brokerage firms and brokers
Loan companies, 100
Loan guarantee programs, 116. *See also* Small Business Administration (SBA), Loan Guarantee Program
Loan packages, 249, 250. *See also* Financing, plans
Loan-to-value (LTV) ratio, 108

Mailing lists, 195, 240
Maintenance contracts, 83–84
Management, 7, 8; as asset, 13, 25–27, 29, 38, 149; in business plans, 251, 269, 273, 281; companies, 233; in financing plans, 255, 263, 265, 278; incentives, 55; teams, 251, 278, 322, 328; valuation of, 25–27; venture capitalism and, 54–55, 56, 61, 156–57, 163
Maritime Administration loans, 128
Marketing: agreements, 246; costs, 65; multilevel, 233; plans, 250, 275–77
Mastermind concept, 247
Maturity period of loans, 106, 107, 108, 123, 312–13

McDonald's, 24, 254
Merchant banks, 179
Mergers, 244, 247
Minimalist entrepreneurs, 231
Minority and disadvantaged funding programs:
    federal, 126–27, 132, 133; state, 117, 121
Minority Business Development Agency, 126–27
Minority Business Set-Asides, 133
Minority enterprise small business investment
    companies (MESBICs), 151, 165, 166
Money finders, 180
Money market funds, 25
Mortgage(s), 30–31, 141; brokers, 93, 98, 101–
    2, 103, 104; discounted, 238; HUD, 128; par-
    ticipating, 105–6. *See also* Real estate
Movie credits, 237
Multilevel/party plan marketing, 233
Multiloan concept, 218

Negotiation of terms, 10–11, 266, 308, 309,
    325, 327; in debt financing, 310–17, 324; in
    equity financing, 318–23, 324; legal counsels
    and, 309–10; techniques used in, 315
Net operating income (NOI), 95
Net value. *See* Value, net
Networking, 196
Net worth, 31; increased, 63; personal, 142, 143;
    secured, 31–32, 33, 62
Net worth-to-debt ratio, 141
Newsletters, 233
NeXT, 174
Noncash solutions, 10, 11, 39, 60, 210; guaran-
    tee vs. cash investment, 209–10
Nondisclosure agreements, 284
Nordstrom department store, 24
Notes receivable, 19
Notification arrangements, 68, 73, 75

Obsolescence of assets, 15. *See also* Equipment,
    used and obsolete
Occupational Health and Safety Act, 122
Off-balance sheet financing, 79, 81
Office of Minority Business Development, 133
Office of Small and Disadvantaged Business
    Utilization (OSDBU), 126
Office of Small Business Policy, 208
Offshore capital, 243
Open-end leases, 80–81
Operations financing, 4, 11
Option financing, 222
Overseas capital, 243
Overseas company promotion loans, 127
Overseas licensing, 227–28
Overseas Private Investment Corporation, 128

Participating revenue certificates, 238–39
Partnerism, 3, 55–56, 245, 326, 330–32
Partnership(s), 222–23, 333; active, 187–88,
    197, 201, 206–7; agreements, 199–200, 242;
    criteria for, 199; financing strategies, 51; gen-
    eral, 187, 241; group, 201–2; limited, 27, 57,
    105, 187, 240, 241–42; master limited, 242;
    passive, 207–8; private, 105; registration of,
    241; research and development, 242; tenant,
    215; in venture capitalism, 162; working, 206
Patents, 9, 14, 155, 165, 234; as asset, 17, 21,
    22, 23, 28, 38, 52, 149; financing of, 50–51;
    protection, 277; sale of, 220, 221
Pawnbrokerage, 59, 237
Payroll financing, 61–62
Penny stock market, 245
Pension funds and plans, 27, 101, 173, 221
Per inquiry sales, 236
Perot, H. Ross, 174
Personal property as asset, 17, 27–28, 29, 56–
    57, 58–59
Piggyback strategies, 233
Pollution control loans, 121
Pool loans, 122
Preferential procurement programs, 132
Prepayment penalties, 316
Prepayment strategies, 226, 229, 230, 233
Pre-receivables, 18, 43–44
Preselling techniques, 229–30
Presentation, 33; mailing strategies, 289–90;
    management incentives in, 55; marketing ap-
    proach to, 10; oral, 2, 10, 11, 14, 147, 248,
    288–89, 296–305, 327; post-interview proce-
    dure, 306–7; rejection evaluation, 307–8,
    329; in venture capital proposals, 167–68,
    169; written, 2, 10, 11, 14, 147, 248–49,
    288–89, 327. *See also* Business plans; Concept
    paper; Executive summary; Financing plans;
    Marketing, plans
Private placements, 240
Private venture investors, 104–5. *See also* Ven-
    ture capitalism, nontraditional/informal
Production Credit Associations, 136
Product-preferred stock, 239–40
Products and services: in business plans, 253–54,
    270, 274–75; as collateral, 52, 61, 76; contract
    loans for, 121; delivery dates, 65; distributor li-
    censing, 227–28; durable vs. perishable, 16,
    45–46; federal procurement programs, 132;
    lead time, 155; vs. management, 55; proprie-
    tary, 155; sales units, 261; stages of growth,
    159–61; as substitute for cash investment,
    209–10; test marketing of, 216–17; venture
    capitalism and, 155, 158, 163. *See also* Mar-
    keting, plans

Profit: bank financing and, 141, 142; defined, 23–24; projected net, 24–25, 27, 53; retained earnings, 141, 142; risk, 53; venture capitalism and, 149, 157, 161, 163
Profit-to-sales ratio, 260
Project development, 91. *See also* Real estate *listings*
Projected earnings, 7, 8
Property. *See* Real estate
Proposals. *See* Presentation
Publications, federal, 133
Purchase of existing businesses, 4, 11, 212, 214, 219–38
Purchase orders/back orders, 13, 17, 18, 23, 28, 235; as asset, 38; financing of, 43–44

Q & A: *Small Business and the SEC*, 208
Quick sale value. *See* Value, market (auction)

Ratios, 266, 315; debt service, 95; debt-to-equity, 123, 315; financial, 146–47; loan-to-value, 108; net worth-to-debt, 141; profit-to-sales, 260
Raw land. *See* Real estate financing, raw land
Raw materials, 19
Real estate: appraisal, 103, 264–65; as asset, 21, 23, 28, 94; as collateral, 75, 100, 109, 124, 262, 333; construction and maintenance, 91, 108–9, 121; government funding for, 6, 49, 92; liquidity of, 16; management, 91; market, 102; market value of, 21, 91, 95, 99, 100, 103
Real estate financing, agricultural. *See* Agricultural financing
Real estate financing, commercial and industrial, 3, 6, 37, 49–50, 61, 62, 90–91, 93–94, 332; brokers used in, 93, 98, 101–2, 103, 104; building types and, 49, 61, 92, 94, 96–98; cash flow considerations, 95, 96; classified advertising for, 104; for development, 121, 128; difficulty of, 92–93; down payments, 95; environmental considerations, 93; equity sharing arrangements, 215–16; foreclosures and defaults, 47, 48, 91, 92, 95, 97, 103; forms, 6, 92; interest rates, 310–11; office and industrial condos, 94–95; raw land, 50, 97; refinancing, 96, 108, 109; risks, 47, 49, 50, 92, 100, 103, 105, 106; SBA loans, 121; sources, 48, 49–50, 60, 91, 93, 98–105; tax considerations, 94; terminology, 106–7; terms, 107–8, 124
Real estate financing, residential, 49, 92, 93, 96, 98, 99, 101; loan-to-value ratio, 108
Receivable(s): as asset, 9, 18–19, 23, 28, 35, 47, 64, 71, 74, 75, 76; as collateral, 44, 71, 74, 75, 76; defined, 18, 64; foreign, 76
Receivable financing, 3, 16, 33, 35, 65–66, 332; advantages and disadvantages, 74, 75; assump-

tion of loans, 221; collection services and costs, 67, 69–70, 75; concept of, 74; cost of, 74, 75; defined, 66; vs. factoring, 72–73; interest rates, 310; qualifications for, 43–44; risks, 43, 44–45; sources, 9, 44, 45, 60, 64, 66, 77; spot, 76; term of loans, 141. *See also* Factoring; Factors
Receivable lenders, 44, 45, 64, 66, 70, 71; cost of, 72; credit and collection services provided by, 73; customer evaluation by, 77; notification arrangements and, 68, 73; reserve accounts of, 72–73; selection of, 75; sources, 74. *See also* Factors
Recourse, 67–68, 73
References, 264
Refinancing arrangements, 96, 108, 109
Regulation D offerings, 240
Remington Electric Shavers, 220–21
Rental of equipment, 80, 231
Replacement/substitution, 232
Research and development, 23, 28; as asset, 38; business plans and, 281–82; contracts, 246; federal grants for, 53, 61, 128, 130–31; financing, 51–53, 159, 161; partnerships, 242
Return on investment, 24–25, 53; in equipment leasing, 79; fixed, 29; in venture capitalism, 155, 156, 177
Return policies, 75
Revenue-sharing notes, 238–39
Reverse mergers, 244
Robert Morris Associates, 266
Rolling stock (cars and light trucks), 20, 84, 85–86, 89, 220
Royalties, 227, 228

Salability of assets, 15–16, 19, 82. *See also* Value, market (auction)
Sale and leaseback arrangements, 83, 106, 220, 234, 238
Sales strategies, 277
Savings and loan associations, 99, 100
Schools and clinics, 236–37
Secured net worth, 31–32, 33, 62
Securities, 27, 29; brokers, 105; as collateral, 56–57; laws, 207–8, 243
Securities and Exchange Act, 240
Securities and Exchange Commission, 208, 240, 244; laws, 334
Security deposit programs, 116
Seed financing. *See* Start-up (seed) financing
Seller carryback, 95
Seller financing/earnout, 219
Seminars, 233
Services. *See* Products and services
Sharks, financial, 165

Shells, 244
Shoestring economies, 230–31
Shows and showrooms, 232
Simultaneous selloff, 234
Small and Minority Business Advocacy (SMBA), 133
Small Business Administration (SBA), 1, 95, 113, 119, 120, 133, 333, 334; advantages and disadvantages of financing through, 123–24; Certificate of Competency program, 132; direct loan program, 121–23; Loan Guarantee Program, 100, 110, 120–21; Procurement Automated Source System (PASS), 132; sources, 125; venture capitalism and, 165
Small Business Innovation Research Program (SBIR), 128, 130–31; Set-Asides, 132
Small business investment companies (SBICs), 151, 165, 166
Small Business Set-Aside Program, 132
Sources of financing, 143, 329; asset matching, 9, 11, 13, 33, 36, 40–41, 61–62, 63; debt, 287, 293; equity, 287–88, 293, 332; identification of, 2, 3, 4, 9, 11, 326–27; nontraditional, 39; qualifications of, 6, 42; secured, 9, 35, 36–37, 38, 39–40, 54, 60; size of loans, 4; traditional, 39, 40; unsecured, 9, 35, 37, 38, 39, 54, 60. *See also specific sources and types of financing*
Spinoffs, 244
Spot financing, 76
Start-up (seed) financing, 2, 4, 11, 94, 117; business plans and, 251; founder's equity determination in, 320–21; market testing for, 216–17; stages of, 217–18; tax strategies for, 333–34; types of, 212–16; venture capitalism and, 151, 153, 154, 162, 175–76, 322
State funding. *See* Government funding programs, state level
Stock(s), 16, 27, 29; as collateral, 57; exchanges and market, 244–45; product-preferred, 239–40; venture capitalism and, 164
Strategic alliances. *See* Corporate strategic alliances
Strategic arms economic injury loans, 122
Subcontracting, 231
Subleasing, 228–29
Subordination of loans, 315
Success formula, 22; as asset, 23–25, 29, 33, 38, 53, 54, 149; management and, 26; projected earnings and, 53–54, 63; risks, 53–54; sources of financing and, 54
Surety bond guarantees, 121
Syndications, 105

Target programs, state, 117. *See also* Government funding programs, state level

Tax incentives, 115, 117
Tax returns, 255, 259, 263
Technical assistance, 115, 118
Technology transfer, 245, 246
Telephone solicitation (dialing for dollars), 184, 194–97, 248; presentations and, 289, 290–96
Terms. *See* Negotiation of terms
Term sheet, 324
Third party: assets, 17, 27–28; collateral, 243; financing, 14–15; guarantees, 243
Thrift institutions, 100, 218
Tight money, 146–47
Timesharing, 228
Trade credit, 223–25
Trademarks, 9, 14, 234; as asset, 22, 23, 28, 38; financing of, 50–51; sale of, 220, 221
Trade secrets, 155
Training programs, 334
Treasury bills, 15, 144
Trucks, vans, trailers. *See* Equipment, specialized
True net asset value, 8, 11, 12, 30, 31; formula for determination of, 31–32, 35, 36, 62–63; low or minus, 32–33
True net profit, 24
Turnaround situations, 161

Umbrella bonds, 116–17
Undercapitalization, 2
USA Today, 187
U.S. Treasury bills, 15, 144
Usury laws, 239

Valuation, 12, 24, 59
Value: of assets, 15, 16, 17, 21, 319; defined, 7, 12, 31; future, 15, 18; lendable, 29, 30, 31; market (auction), 15–16, 20, 27–28, 29, 59, 265, 319–20; net, 30–31; residual, 88
Vendor financing, 84, 86
Vendor leasing companies, 89
Venture capital clubs, 180
Venture capital firms and subsidiaries, 151, 161, 165
Venture capitalism, 6, 35, 149–50, 332; collateral and, 161; corporate, 245; equipment financing and, 61, 87; equity, 117; formal, 56; investment stages, 159–61; leasing companies and, 46; management and, 54–55, 56, 61, 156–57, 163; patent, trademark and copyright, 51; private, 9; profit motivation in, 149, 157, 161, 163; real estate financing and, 103; research and development, 53, 61; risks, 149; for services, 61; sources, 37, 61, 149, 150; start-ups and, 151, 153, 154, 162; success formula and, 54; working capital and, 60. *See also* Equity financing

Venture capitalism, nontraditional/informal, 3, 56, 87, 149–50, 170, 175–76; angels, 152, 174–75, 176–77, 181–84, 188, 191, 207–8, 217, 237, 239, 242, 243; business brokers and, 184, 192, 197–98; client characteristics, 158; decisionmaking, 176–77, 178; exit strategies, 209; guarantee vs. cash investment, 209–10; guidelines, 200–201; intermediaries (advisers), 152, 174, 175, 179, 184, 207; investment statistics and scenarios, 150, 153, 172, 175, 205; investment stages, 159–61; investor contact strategies, 207–8; investor profiles, 202–6; "last person in" technique, 202; negotiations, 193–94, 200; risks, 172, 173; start-ups and, 175–76; techniques, 171; telephone strategies, 184, 194–97

Venture capitalism, traditional/professional, 87, 162–63, 166, 169–70, 172–73; advantages, 164; client and product profiles, 154–55, 158–59, 163; concept of, 153; exit strategies, 164; government-sponsored, 151, 165–66; investment stages, 159–61; investment statistics, 149–50, 151, 154–55; management qualifications and, 54–55, 156–57, 163, 164; negotia-

tions, 193; partnerships and, 162; presentation requirements, 167; return on investment, 155; risk strategies, 173; sales projections, 153, 155; sources, 167, 168–69, 173; start-ups and, 322

Venture Capital Network, 180–81

Venture leasing companies, 84, 87

Veteran assistance loans, 123

Wall Street Journal, 185, 187, 191

Warehouse financing, 76

Water pollution control loans, 122

Wetzel, William, 180

Wholesale Meat Act, 122

Wholesale Poultry Act, 122

Women-owned businesses, 132, 133

Working capital, 42, 60, 121, 315

Working financiers. *See* Partnership(s), active

Work-in-progress, 13, 18, 23, 28; financing of, 43–44

Xerox, 86

Zero coupon bonds, 240